New Perspectives in Urban Change and Conflict

New Perspectives in Urban Change and Conflict

Edited by
Michael Harloe

HEINEMANN EDUCATIONAL BOOKS

Heinemann Educational Books Ltd
22 Bedford Square, London WC1B 3HH

LONDON EDINBURGH MELBOURNE AUCKLAND
HONG KONG SINGAPORE KUALA LUMPUR NEW DELHI
IBADAN NAIROBI JOHANNESBURG
EXETER (NH) KINGSTON PORT OF SPAIN

ISBN 0 435 82404 X

Typeset by Pearl Island Typesetters (Hong Kong) Ltd and
printed in Great Britain by Biddles Ltd, Guildford, Surrey

Contents

The Contributors

Brian Elliott, Department of Sociology, *University of Edinburgh*

Rob Flynn, Department of Sociological and Political Studies, *University of Salford*

Michael Harloe, Department of Sociology, *University of Essex*

Robert Kraushaar, School of Architecture and Urban Planning, *University of California, Los Angeles*

John Lambert, Department of Social Administration, *University College, Cardiff*

David McCrone, Department of Sociology, *University of Edinburgh*

Robert Miles, Department of Sociology, *University of Glasgow*

Robert Moore, Department of Sociology, *University of Aberdeen*

Howard Newby, Department of Sociology, *University of Essex*

Annie Phizacklea, Social Science Research Council, Ethnic Relations Unit, *University of Aston*

Gareth Rees, Department of Town Planning, *University of Wales Institute of Science and Technology*

Bryan R. Roberts, Department of Sociology, *University of Manchester*

Peter Saunders, School of Cultural and Community Studies, *University of Sussex*

Dan Shapiro, Department of Sociology, *University of Lancaster*

Ignasi Terrades, formerly Department of Sociology, *University of Manchester*

Introduction
New Perspectives in
Urban and Regional Research:
progress and problems
Michael Harloe

Origins of the new approach

This book contains, in revised form, eleven of the papers presented to
the Urban Change and Conflict Conference, organised by the Centre
for Environmental Studies and held at Nottingham University in
January 1979. This conference was the third in a series – the first was
held in 1975 – set up to encourage the emergence of new approaches
to the understanding of urban and regional development by present-
ing some of the best of the new work now being done in the field
to a critical forum and, in the process, by helping to establish an
informal network of researchers. Some measure of the degree to
which this has been successful is indicated by the fact that the third
conference was heavily oversubscribed: it attracted significant
international as well as national attention despite its main focus
being, as always, on British topics. Moreover, there has been a
continuing and heavy demand for the published proceedings of
the earlier conferences: hence the decision to issue the present
volume in a more widely available format.

The origins of the Urban Change and Conflict Conferences
can be traced back to the late 1960s and early 1970s and were
outlined in the introduction to the first set of conference proceedings
(Harloe, 1975). Throughout the 1960s the 'urban question' had
been an increasingly pressing consideration for most advanced
capitalist economies. The form which the problems took varied
from country to country; for example, in the US they had their
most dramatic manifestation in the explosive situations in the black
ghettoes of the larger and older cities, whereas in Britain concern
was perhaps more diffuse and more closely linked to the effects of
the growth of state involvement in urban affairs, especially in matters

of housing and urban planning. Moreover, despite the persistence of the urban referent in much that was spoken and written, there was also a concern with regional problems, for example, in Italy where the social tensions caused by a situation of continued poverty of the South alongside the domination of the North were mounting.

In response to such problems there had been a substantial growth in research, much of it sponsored by governments. Parallel with this development there was in the universities a growth of radical social theory and of a radical critique of society. Here the most significant development was the re-emergence of Marxism as a serious approach to the study of society. But, it must be stressed, this was only the leading trend, for Marxism had and still has no monopoly in this field, as the contents of this book will demonstrate.

On the whole though very few of the new theoretical developments occurring in the universities had filtered through into the rather enclosed world of urban research. In Britain it is true an important start had been made in altering this picture by the publication, in 1967, of Rex and Moore's highly critical study of housing and the role of the local authority in Sparkbrook, Birmingham, and by the attention that Pahl (1970) had paid to the role of the 'urban gatekeepers' or 'managers' in controlling access to scarce urban goods and services. But, important though these were (and the essentially Weberian influence that they reflected has continued to be significant), they seemed, in some respects, to be unsatisfactory to many of those embarking on the examination of urban problems for the first time from perspectives that had been formed in the radical political and intellectual climate of the university in the 1960s.

The need, it was felt, was to relate the theoretical understanding of advanced capitalist societies as social formations, divided by class, based on exploitation and driven by the search for capital accumulation, to the everyday realities of urban life and its problems. And this theme, above all else, became the central focus of the attempts that have been made throughout the 1970s to arrive at a more adequate understanding of urban and regional problems – a theme which, as will be seen, is clearly evident in all the contributions to this collection.

Those who have carried out this research have come from a variety of disciplinary backgrounds and have worked in a variety of contexts. Thus there is no single school or body of researchers. For example, much of the best work by economists has been done under the auspices of the Conference of Socialist Economists; geographers – heavily influenced at the start by the pioneering work of Harvey – have tended to publish much of their work in the radical geography journal, *Antipode*; and perhaps the most impressive achievement of all was the output of a group of people working for government rather than in the universities – in the Community Development Projects. But the successive Urban Change and Conflict Conferences have provided an important forum for sociologists, while also drawing on the contributions of those mentioned above. Internationally the Conferences have gained from their links with the Research Committee on the Sociology of Urban and Regional Development of the International Sociological Association and its journal, the *International Journal of Urban and Regional Research*. This committee was founded in 1970 by an international group of researchers, which included Ray Pahl, Manuel Castells, Enzo Mingione and Ivan Szelenyi, who had come together out of precisely the same dissatisfaction with the current state of urban sociology which led to the holding of the first Urban Change and Conflict Conference, a meeting to which Pahl, Mingione and Castells made key contributions.

This dissatisfaction and the need for new departures were expressed in a position paper presented to the first session of the first Conference (Harloe, 1975, pp. 9–14). As the international group had done sometime earlier, it criticised existing urban sociology for being only marginal to the broader developments then occurring within sociology, for being elitist and technocratic, for being positivistic and, finally, for failing to challenge existing political institutions and the dominant social order. But it was equally critical of the diffuse and largely untheorised 'radical' critique of existing urban policies then emerging from the growth of community protest, regarding it as a form of 'academic populism' with severely limited analytical power. Instead the position paper suggested that there were three interlocking themes that were central to the urban structure and therefore to urban sociology. These were the development of capital, the social control of the labour force and organised opposition to these two factors.

Significantly, the opening speaker at the discussion of the position paper which followed its presentation was Manuel Castells. For it was his work in particular which first tackled the problem of reconstructing urban sociology along the lines which the position paper had advocated – notably in his book *The Urban Question* (1977a), some aspects of which were beginning to be known to a British audience through the publication of Pickvance's collection of the new Marxist urban sociology then emerging in France and through the references made to it by Pahl and others in direct contact with such work (Pickvance, 1976b; Pahl, 1975). It would be an exaggeration to say that Castells's approach monopolised the development of the 'new' urban sociology in Britain in the mid-1970s: for as already noted there continued to be a significant development of work within a Weberian perspective by, for example, Pahl, Elliott and McCrone, who were influenced themselves by the challenge of the new Marxist work as well as the gradual penetration of other writers such as Lojkine (see, for example, Pickvance, 1976b). Nevertheless, the citations to his work, as well as the attention paid to a critical examination of it indicate that Castells's writings were of central importance.

What were the special contributions made by this body of work? The first one has already been mentioned: its stress on the link between capitalist development and urban patterns and policies. Beyond this, Castells provided a penetrating and so far largely unchallenged critique of earlier urban sociology as ideology and, controversially, a reformulation of the theory based on an Althusserian reading of Marx. Today, ten years or so after his earliest writings appeared, it is clear to all (including Castells himself) that this reformulation was fatally flawed at a number of points.[1] But its importance lay in its influencing the reorientation of a field of study and the setting of an agenda for theory and research, an agenda which emerged as often as the product of a rejection of Castells's approach as of its adoption and which is still effective today, as the contributions to this book help to make clear.

It is perhaps an oversimplification, but nevertheless significant, to suggest that each of the three Urban Change and Conflict Conferences held so far have marked the emergence of three successive stages in the development of the new work. The first Conference, as already noted, marked the start of an effort to break away from an old and inadequate approach and, in reconstructing the study of urban development and policy, to assimilate the new insights of

Castells and others, insights which themselves arose out of the growth in Marxist theory. But the criticism of these new ideas began very soon after their assimilation. There were two main grounds to this critique. The first was a largely theoretical one derived from the broader debates then occurring about social theory and especially of course about Althusserian 'structuralism'. The second derived from a more specifically British context and, interestingly, from a factor which it appeared was both a strength and a weakness of earlier work, its stress on an adequate empirical base, on the under-standing of what was actually occurring on the ground as well as, though to a lesser degree perhaps, an historical sensitivity to the variations by time and place in the form and detail of urban development.[2]

By the time of the third Conference, the contents of which are represented by this book, this rather negative but essential phase of reacting to the first wave of work was largely over. Now, increasingly, research and theory is seeking to build on what has been achieved so far and move from a rather simplistic, sketchy and preliminary model of the real world to modes of understanding that more ade-quately grasp such a reality. The papers included in this volume serve to underline this conclusion and some detailed ways in which this is so are noted below. But it will be useful to structure this discussion by referring back to some of the major features of Castells's model and the criticisms of it. In doing this it is not the intention to provide a full account; this has been done extensively elsewhere. Nor, as already mentioned, was Castells's work the only important influence in the 1970s. Finally, it will be clear from reading the papers that their authors have been influenced by a wide variety of sources; in few cases is their work any longer an explicit response to Castells and in some cases, especially where the work deals with matters wholly beyond his early perspective, the influence is minimal. But a brief account and critique of Castells is nevertheless a useful way to consider some of the central themes and problems of current urban and regional research as represented by the papers in this collection.

The work of Castells
The first point is that Castells adopted the Althusserian approach which led him to a radical separation of theory and empirical

material. His main concern was with the elaboration of an urban structure, a largely formalistic model of the urban system in advanced capitalist societies. This was then applied to the analysis of urban struggles in a way which recalled Castells's own characterisation of earlier urban sociology as inadequate because it imposed sets of predetermined categories on the data. As a result, much of the early work inspired by this approach lacked a sensitivity to the variations attributable to individual circumstances, to differing national or local situations, and was, in this sense, rather ahistorical.

Secondly, there was an attempt to redefine the 'urban' in terms of the sphere of consumption and therefore questions relating to issues of production were referred to the separate study of regional phenomena. But this radical disjunction broke down in practice, for neither 'urban' nor 'regional' patterns or policies could be successfully analysed within such narrow constraints. Moreover the connection in practice between the uneven development of capitalist space in cities and regions was too evident to be swept aside for the benefit of any neatly self contained theory.

Thirdly, and perhaps most importantly, the conception of urban politics which was proposed suffered from severe defects, for the subject matter of this study was limited to, on the one hand, urban planning and, on the other hand, urban social movements, i.e. organised forms of protest centred on urban issues which achieved significant modifications in the urban structure. Yet in reality the field of urban policy encompassed far more than urban planning, and urban social movements, far from being the central focus of class struggle, were at best a rather minor phenomenon in many countries.

This limited conception of urban politics was linked to a set of supposedly common changes in the spatial development of advanced capitalism and the role of the state. Briefly, these involved the increasing concentration of the workforce in urban units and the increasing provision by the state of the means of collective consumption in order to guarantee the adequate reproduction of the labour force required by capital. Thus, to repeat Castells's striking phrase 'the state becomes through its arrangement of space, the real manager of everyday life' (1977b, p. 64). And, as state involvement grew inexorably, so did an urban politics based on struggles concerning the nature and terms of its intervention. But the failure to pay adequate attention to the empirical realities of urban development and to its variations, noted above, was evident in this chain of reasoning, as was pointed out by many critics. For example, it was by no means universally true that advanced capitalist development resulted in an ever greater spatial concentration of the labour force, nor was it necessarily the case that there was an inexorable growth of state provided collective consumption (a term which in itself came in for a good deal of criticism) and, by means of increased politicisation, a growth in conflict. Indeed much of the empirical material concerning state intervention tended to suggest that it often defused conflict, fragmented the bases for class action and, in general, acted to 'manage' urban and regional tensions and problems, albeit often only at a price in terms of creating new difficulties and usually in ways that failed to tackle fundamental causes. Nor was the link between the growth of state intervention and the growth of the collective mode of consumption at all clear. In reality state intervention often supported and even fostered a return to privatised modes of consumption; this is the case, for example, in housing where, throughout Western Europe and the US, owner occupation now dominates the housing market and socialised housing is in retreat.[3] In passing it should be noted that, just as urban politics was confined to a narrow and unsatisfactory definition, there was too in Castells's work a failure to examine the central role played by ideology in maintaining the dominant social order – as evident in the field of urban and regional policy as elsewhere – a significance going far beyond the limits of the ideologies of urban life and urbanism discussed in *The Urban Question*.

To summarise, Castells's work (and, for that matter, the work of his main Marxist critic in France, Lojkine[4]) failed to take adequate account of the historical variations in urban and regional development, often and mistakenly drawing general conclusions from the rather specific French experience. The study of class struggle was confined to the rather peripheral activities of urban social movements. State intervention was analysed in ways that, in practice at least, stressed its functionality for monopoly capital and, in the case of Castells alone, limited the scope of study to questions of the consumption of urban goods and services and, within this, to questions of collective consumption.

As already mentioned, the critical response to this body of work had the positive effect of helping to establish the agenda for subsequent research. We can now identify some of the main aspects of this agenda, themes which will be highlighted in the next section of this introduction. The first aspect has been mentioned a number of times already – the need for careful empirically based studies of the variations of historic experience; in this context the use of the comparative method is obviously of importance. Second, there is the need to avoid falling into the trap of a purely instrumental view of state action and, in this connection, the need to understand not just the outcomes of state action but the means by which they are achieved – the 'how' as well as the 'why'. The third aspect is analyses that combine a consideration of urban and regional developments within a common framework, embracing considerations of consumption and production and of differing modes of these two factors. The fourth aspect involves the need to appreciate that class conflict is pervasive and indeed constitutive of the policies and patterns of development being studied, rather than being confined to a special and limited subset of such struggles. This aspect also includes the need to examine such conflict in all its diverse forms in a systematic way (all too often class struggle is treated as a sort of 'black box', an added element which is appended to a structural analysis of a logic of capitalist development, not analysable except in a *post hoc* manner, a feature which has obviously limited the extent to which the new work could achieve its stated aim of informing and furthering contemporary political and economic struggles round urban and regional issues).

With these conclusions in mind, we now turn to consider the individual contributions to this collection. One final caveat is necessary: the purpose of the next section is not to give a rounded summary and critique of the subsequent chapters but merely to indicate some of the ways in which the overlapping concerns of the authors are contributing to the development of a distinctive body of urban and regional research, much of which is concerned with the types of issues outlined in the preceding paragraph.

The contributions
The first feature to note is that all of the contributors base their conclusions on careful empirical work which is concerned with

understanding both the more general and the more specific features of the phenomena being studied. This is true even of the most wholly 'theoretical' paper in the collection, that by Saunders (Chapter 1), for it draws heavily on the results of a study of community power in Croydon which he has described in his recent book on urban politics (Saunders, 1979a). And by acknowledging the varieties of experience found in practice, we are forced to recognise that earlier simplistic explanations must yield to more complex and varied accounts of the ways in which capitalist development structures urban and regional patterns and policies.

Saunders's paper addresses itself to some of the issues concerning urban politics referred to above, providing a critical account of the three main approaches to this topic so far proposed: elitist–liberal theories, managerialist theories and Marxist theories. Four different descriptions of how power is exerted appear to be incorporated in these theories: pluralist, instrumentalist, structuralist and mana-gerialist (bureaucratic) relations. But none of these approaches is adequate. Instrumentalist and managerialist theories can only explain occasions when ruling class or bureaucratic imperatives do not appear to determine the outcome of issues by positing an un-analysed and untheorised margin of 'autonomy'; pluralist and structuralist explanations may be reduced to mere tautologies.

In discussing the problems raised by these explanations, Saunders refers to the importance of the need to understand not just what the state does to sustain the dominant order, but how it tends to act in ways that achieve this end. In tackling this problem he turns, as others have, to the writings of Claus Offe on the workings of the state and in particular to a conception of the state in relation to urban policy which considers the role of the state in managing production, and hence capital accumulation, as well as consumption, and hence the reproduction of the labour force.

Saunders concludes that the state tends to act as an allocator which responds to pressures when operating in the sphere of consump-tion, and that such activities are mainly, though not exclusively, the preserve of local government. In such a situation pluralist explanations can go a long way towards providing an adequate explanation of local power structures. On the other hand, instru-mentalist explanations are powerful tools for understanding state action when it is directly concerned with production, action which mainly, though again not exclusively, is reserved by the national government. These conclusions have serious consequences for any theory of the centrality of urban social movements because the pluralistic nature of consumption based struggles effectively prevents the emergence of the type of radically effective action which these movements were held to promise.

So Saunders's paper contributes to the development of theories of urban politics and of the role of the state, including the question of how, as well as why, its policies take the form that they do. A notable feature of his work is that it draws on earlier theories of of urban politics when these appear to be of value to his description of the observed realities of power. Opinions will vary about whether this attempt is ultimately successful, the point being rather that, after a period in which much of the new urban and regional research felt it necessary, in rejecting earlier theories, to ignore aspects of them that might be of continuing value, many of those now working in the field recognise that this rejection may, at times, have been too sweeping and dogmatic.

Flynn's paper (Chapter 2) is concerned with many of the same themes that run through Saunders's contribution. In particular he too turns to the work of Offe to aid his study of the processes of policy formation and of the internal operations of the state; he too stresses the need to understand the *how*, as well as the *why*, of state action. His paper is based on a detailed study of professional town planners engaged in formulating and gaining agreement to a plan. He too finds some value in earlier studies, in this case studies of the sociology of organisations. At the centre of the planners' advocacy of their plan was the establishment of a consensus about the issues to hand – a set of 'shared norms and commitments among decision-makers, which diminish the chances of fundamental disagreement, which provide the means for reconciling disputes, and which are part of a 'culture' within which administrative decisions are made'. In essence Flynn is stressing the importance of an understanding of the ideologies which underpin and legitimate a state intervention. He goes on to provide a detailed examination of the techniques by which such a consensus was established, techniques which involved the selective application of persuasion, bargaining and coercion according to the relative strengths of the parties involved and selective appeals to the flexibility and the commitment embodied in a plan which had as its main aim the fostering of suitable conditions for enhanced capital accumulation.

Elliott and McCrone's paper (Chapter 3) moves us closer to a consideration of the nature and varieties of class divisions and consciousness in the urban sphere. It is notable too for its acceptance of the location of urban problems and processes within a broader political economy and for its claim that the Weberian analysis of the history and politics of the city still has much of value to offer. In particular, they suggest that the Weberian concept of domination – the legitimised power of a ruling group or groups – is helpful in the analysis of urban politics and class structure. In passing it should be mentioned that this concept seems close to the Gramscian conception of hegemony which recent French research, especially that carried out by Lojkine, Bleitrach and Chenu on local power, has adopted.[5] Elliott and McCrone then point out that an examination of the historical development of cities demonstrates the importance to ruling groups of maintaining the control and support of the urban populations. At times when their domination is threatened such groups make concessions which, while sustaining such domination, also tend, in the longer run, to weaken it and to strengthen the power of rising classes or strata. A brief examination of these factors at play in nineteenth century British cities illustrates this contention.

In looking at Britain in 1980, however, they suggest that in the last twenty years or so a new group has emerged, a group characterised by its possession of technical and professional skills and expertise, many of whom are employed by the state. This group is in conflict with the traditional bourgeoisie – that is to say, the traditional holders of urban power – and with the working class. This new division obscures and cuts across older established patterns of class division. A similar fragmentation is also visible within the working class: in addition to the persistence of the traditional division between the more skilled and organised workforce and the rest, an important division based on race, the effects of which have been most visible in the inner cities, has newly emerged.

Thus Elliott and McCrone, like Saunders, and in contrast to Castells, are indicating that many urban conflicts concerned with consumption issues both cut across and serve to fragment the class structure. In this sense the chances of urban conflicts reinforcing more traditional class based struggles seem poor. They also suggest that a focus on the urban managers is still essential, as these are the local allocators of the goods and services around the provision of which many of the new forms of urban conflict arise. For it is the urban managers, drawn from the newly emergent group mentioned earlier, who are exercising increasing domination at the urban level and who are the targets for much of the new protest activity which is taking place outside older class based institutions such as the Labour party and the trade unions on the left and the Conservative party on the right.

The importance of race as a new factor dividing the working class, stressed by Elliott and McCrone, provides the subject matter of the next paper by Miles and Phizacklea (Chapter 4). In this they report on the findings of a survey of working class explanations for the social and economic decline of an area of inner London. Their work adds to our understanding of the complexity of class structure and consciousness and therefore of the difficulties that undermine any very simplistic association of these two factors, for they found that workers tended to advance what from any rational viewpoint were confused and conflicting reasons for the decline. In short, there was a mixture of reasoning which recognised, to a degree, that changing strategies of capital accumulation were responsible for decline but which also associated the influx of blacks to the area with this result. Interestingly, even some active members of the labour movement seemed to share this split consciousness, despite the Labour party's local campaign against racism. Again, the prospect for the emergence of a unified base for class struggle around urban issues seems remote.

This last issue is more directly addressed in the paper by Kraushaar (Chapter 5) which examines the problems faced by local Community Development Projects which tried to organise such struggles in the deprived urban environments in which they were located. The CDP experience is of great interest because it was the most coherent and determined attempt for many years in Britain, by the Left at least, to develop fragmented community struggles into a wider movement for change. It is a study of the ways in which the state 'manages' social conflict and how it acts to preclude collective action at community level.

An important feature of this management, as others have also noted (for example, Lambert, Paris and Blackaby, 1978), is the ease with which the state succeeds in defining social problems as individual rather than collective ones and then proceeds to impose individualised systems of provision to deal with such problems. In explaining why the various efforts of the CDP which are discussed in the paper were unsuccessful, Kraushaar points out that forms of collective action, if any, are determined by the everyday experiences of those who participate in them and that this everyday experience is heavily influenced by the state (a remark which recalls Castells's comment that the state becomes the manager of everyday life). To understand this process further, Kraushaar follows Saunders and Flynn in seeking to grasp how the state operates, and he too turns to Offe's work for the insights which it provides in this context. Offe describes the increasing extent to which the state is involved in productive functions and, as a result, becomes increasingly an arena of struggle ('providing the rudimentary model of organisation of social life that is liberated from the commodity form without being able to live up to the promise implicit in that model', 1975, p. 256). One way of dealing with growing conflict is to try to de-politicise the issues by turning them from issues of collective concern to the working class into individual and technical–administrative problems (the latter tendency was also noted in Flynn's paper, and is a more generally-used technique for managing conflict). A further basis for fragmentation is one that has already been extensively referred to in connection with the earlier papers, namely divisions within the working class based on distinctive consumer interests: it is in this sense that, for example, the notion of housing classes has some empirical validity. Finally, there is the cooption of protest organisations that begin to have some effect; again this has been regularly noted by other writers who have examined the strengths and weaknesses of community groups.

Faced with such difficulties the CDP activists have gradually evolved a strategy which they hope will, in the longer run at least, enable new and effective political organisation to occur in older and deprived working class communities. Three interesting points are made. The first is that there is now very little hope that the more organised aspects of the labour movement, the Labour party nationally and the union leadership, will be anything other than supporters of the dominant order; rather the new community organisations have to build links with similar grass roots organisations in the productive sphere (such as trades councils and shop stewards committees). Second, the 1960s was an era of expansion in which distinctive types of community groups arose to resist the locally disruptive effect of the growth of state activity and/or to get a larger share of the benefits of such activity, but the 1970s have been an era of retrenchment, in which the need is to defend gains already made; this requires new forms of organisation which have been slow to emerge. Here one might add that the situation to which Kraushaar refers in this latter comment has become even more evident and pressing in the short space of time since his paper was written with the election of a Government which is strongly opposed to many of the developments in social welfare and the social wage of the last thirty or so years. The third point, and this echoes conclusions in the Elliott/McCrone and Miles/Phizacklea papers, is that while the decline of allegiance to the traditional political system, opens up opportunities for new struggles for socialist goals, at the same time it opens up the possibility of new right-wing initiatives, especially when they are linked to a racialist appeal. Such a conclusion is far from the optimistic hope, as expressed in the early work on urban social movements, that they might become the basis for a working class based alliance of class fractions, active in opposition to the urban effects of the growth of monopoly capital.

Rees and Lambert's (Chapter 6) paper opens with a specific and critical reference to the 'metropolitan provincialism' of earlier work and the scant regard which it paid to class consciousness as expressed in local variations of political tradition and of historical experience. Their paper deals with the development of state policies towards the 'peripheral' region of South Wales and of the influence of nationalism in this area. Their study of the ways in which the nationalist ideology has been exploited by the state in order to underpin a regionalist consensus, which in turn has legitimated the development of the area in the interests of capital and to the detriment of many of its inhabitants, bears comparison with Flynn's paper, which described the development of a legitimating consensus in connection with a structure plan which had a similar economic aim. Once again then the themes include those of state management and the deployment of legitimating ideologies in the context of capitalist accumulation. The paper contains other familiar elements too, including the role played by the traditional organisations of the working class in supporting restructuring, and the divisive effects of what has occurred on this class, which is being split into 'a relatively affluent stratum, able to capitalise on the new employment opportunities which have become available, and an increasingly marginalised and impoverished stratum, unable to "make out" in changed economic circumstances'.

Moore's paper (Chapter 7) is explicitly addressed to the need to consider urban issues in the context of regional development and, more broadly, in the context of the global and uneven development of large-scale capital. He is concerned with the effect of the development of offshore oil on the small town of Peterhead on the northeast coast of Scotland. Developments here raise theoretical problems concerning notions of industrialisation and development. Moore points out that our image of these processes is rooted in a stereotype of the English industrial revolution involving the concentration of the rural population in rapidly growing towns: it was essentially this kind of image which also underlay the analysis of the urban effects of the growth of large-scale capital outlined by Castells and others. Yet in Peterhead capitalist *development* is taking place in ways that do not also involve such effects. Moore suggests that a greater understanding of what is happening in this town and its region may be gained if we draw on theories of dependent development, although it is also important to go beyond an analysis that deals with the nature and causes of inequalities at a regional level to consider the unequal and class based distribution of costs and benefits within each region.

As elsewhere, the role played by the state was central to what occurred in Peterhead, and the paper contains a detailed analysis of the ways in which regional policy, whose ostensible aim was to counter high unemployment, gave most help to capital-intensive industries and very little to existing local firms or to the new service industries, the latter being the best potential source of increased employment. Yet, Moore notes, care must also be taken to avoid slipping into a purely instrumental conception of the state's role, various examples are given of conflicts among state agencies and among levels of government which have had significant consequences for the town. Finally, the paper contains a further interesting description of the effects of development on the class structure, in this case it introduced into the economy and politics of the town a group of 'new' capitalists (the multinational oil and related firms) to stand alongside the older, local concerns.

Shapiro's paper (Chapter 8) continues the consideration of the effect of the development of North Sea oil, addressing itself to the question of industrial relations. Once again the concern is to avoid an overgeneralised and oversimplified model of reality, for, as he shows, the rules and institutions of class conflict that have been developed in an urban context are often quite ineffective when they are translated to the remote locations in which developments such as those concerned with North Sea oil occur. The focus is on the 'dependent' industrial relations of oil, that is the ways in which particular forms of exploitation of the labour force characterise this industry. Such forms involve various means of coercion and constraint which, far from being some sort of feudal hangover, as has often been suggested, are a normal form taken by capitalist exploitation in circumstances in which workers do not have access to effective means of resisting their imposition. As Shapiro notes, the remote locations in which the oil industry operates is only one such possibility, for example it might be fruitful to consider the situation of marginal inner city labour forces in this manner too. The main body of the paper deals with a number of labour disputes, all of which ended with defeat for the strikers. In the course of these disputes the companies made use of the fact that the labour force only had very limited access to resources with which to carry on their struggle and by the support that they were given by the trade union leadership and then the Labour government within an ideological framework which identified the employers' goals with notions of an overriding national interest and which suggested that employment in the oil industry was a privilege for those locals involved (a claim not at all borne out by the poor conditions and very low rates of pay endured by such workers).

Most of the papers discussed so far have stressed the variety of regional and local experiences of capitalist development. In Chapter 8 Terrades adopts the comparative method to illustrate differences among national urban politics. His concern is to compare the role of the state in contemporary urban–industrial development in Spain (with particular reference to Catalonia – the most industrialised Spanish region) with that in Britain. According to Terrades such development in Spain has taken a quite distinctive path, largely as a result of the central state's indifference or even hostility to industrialisation. In order to fully understand this comparative work is necessary.

The critique of earlier work is quite explicit. As Terrades writes, 'Most interpretations of urban–industrial systems in terms of capitalist development have a tendency to posit a common theoretical level based on a wide variety of contexts. . . . Thus, for example, in the model presented by Castells the logic of urban–industrial development is reduced to the logic of a theory of capital; that is, the criteria used to analyse urban–industrial questions consists exclusively of basic elements of the capitalist mode of production. . . . But the dynamic, historical characteristic of capitalist development is precisely its differential character: the fact that the capitalist world arises from differential costs and rents and differentials in the integrations between economic activities and their political conditions.' He suggests that market structure and its political integration vary greatly and hence are the key points to consider when comparing social formations.

The paper concentrates on the significance, in this context, of the forms adopted by urban planning and of the participation of local populations, local economic interests and regional interests in it. There are two ways in which the central state can relate to local populations with respect to the coordination of economic and administrative activities. In Britain this process has been marked by the centralisation of economic control involving, at first, intervention on a rather fragmented basis and, later, more comprehensive planning. Conceptions of the state as acting in such a manner have of course been advanced in other papers, already discussed. But there is an alternative pattern, where the central state fails to perform this role, which involves privatisation – the appropriation of state concerns by those directly involved in economic activities (i.e. private initiatives). An alternative exists which stands between privatisation and centralisation; this consists of 'regionalisms or nationalisms within the orbit of the central state'.

Terrades then provides a detailed analysis of the historical isolation of the Spanish state from the dynamic productive forces of the country with the failure to achieve effective planned action supportive of capital accumulation and the consequent growth of privatised initiatives and of movements for national or regional autonomy.[6] Particularly in Catalonia the result has been a failure of the state to provide sufficient urban goods and services and to implement effective urban planning and the imposition of a heavy financial burden on the Catalan bourgeoisie which has sought to provide such matters in order to facilitate capital accumulation.

But with the end of the Francoist period and the institution of a parliamentary democracy, Spain is now trying to adopt the more familiar path followed by British industrial development which was rapidly integrated into the political system and which enjoyed the benefits of state support from an early stage. The problem is that these changes are being attempted at a time when economic growth has disappeared, yet in Britain and elsewhere growth was the essential precondition for the 'welfare state' to be developed without damaging the confidence of private investment.

Roberts's paper (Chapter 10) also considers the Spanish example: he compares nineteenth century Manchester with contemporary Barcelona and Lima. His concern is to examine the migration patterns that accompany urbanisation and to explore the significance of these patterns for urban and industrial organisation. He suggests that distinctive patterns of industrialisation have occurred in the three countries that he considers because of their differing structural positions within capitalist development. The growth of Manchester took place in a country at the centre of the international economy, whereas Barcelona is located in a semi-peripheral economy where there has been some development of national capital and of an internal market but only to a limited and patchy degree, with much dependence on foreign capital. In contrast Lima is located in a peripheral economy with a weakly developed internal market and with a high degree of dependency.

In Manchester the circumstances noted above led to the creation of a settled urban working class with a distinctive culture and consciousness, whereas in Barcelona migration did not lead to residential stabilisation, and in Lima there has been a high degree of pendular migration and a continuing exchange between the city and rural areas. The paper also considers the wide range of local conditions which can affect the pattern of state intervention, a theme which also runs through Terrades's paper.

Roberts concludes that the residentially stabilised and segmented working class which arose in Manchester resulted in a situation where the relationship between the state and the urban population has not been as conflicting as for example those occurring in Spain or France. In Barcelona the development of smaller scale, less stable industries (in comparison with Manchester) as well as developments in the agrarian structure have resulted in a continuous process of inter and intra city mobility and the failure of an internally stratified and residentially stable urban working class to emerge. Because of the precarious situation of these urban populations and the failure of the state to provide effectively urban goods and services (as noted by Terrades), class struggle in the urban milieu of Barcelona has been sharper than that which occurred in Manchester. Here we do find the existence of urban social movements somewhat akin to those described by Castells, although, as Roberts notes, they are weakened by their lack of a stable base in a settled, industrial population.

Finally he discusses the case of Lima. In Peru large-scale production tends to be capital-intensive and in foreign hands and smaller scale production is more marginal to the dominant economy and less remunerative than in Barcelona. As a result, as already stated, there is a good deal of pendular migration between urban and rural areas. There is a large floating labour force in the cities still closely tied to the countryside and making rather few demands on welfare and other state services; the contrast to the situations in Manchester and Barcelona is clear. In recent years the central state has intervened more thoroughly than hitherto; nevertheless, Roberts concludes, the net result of its activities has been to leave the pre-existing situation largely intact.

In conclusion, stress is again laid on the need to understand the range of variations in the modes of industrialisation and of their effects on urban class structure and development, but in analysing this variation there are certain key factors which are of importance – structural position within the world economy, the social characteristics and mobility of labour and the labour process. Clearly, Roberts's paper offers important insights into the analytical approach which will be necessary if the movement away from a simple and universalistic model of urban and regional development towards a more realistic assessment of the range and variety of the historic experience of these features is to be followed by new and more satisfactory syntheses, rather than a relapse into atheoretical historicism.

The final paper in this collection, by Newby (Chapter 11), is concerned with the effect of urbanisation on the rural class structure. The impact of capitalism on the countryside has been an important theme in many studies of development in the third world, but far less attention has been paid to it in the British context. This is hardly surprising, given the very high proportion, even as long ago as the turn of the century, of the British population living in cities. Nevertheless the omission is serious, as the agricultural industry is a leading sector of the economy; moreover it is one which has been extensively restructured since World War II. Rather more attention has, it is true, been paid to the out-migration of those who are dependent on urban labour markets to homes in the country (for example, Pahl, 1965), but Newby's work, which considers the interlinked effect of both these events on the rural class structure, has broken new ground.

His paper considers the situation in East Anglia, where much of the most capital-intensive and prosperous British agriculture is located. Traditionally, this society was marked by a deep divide between local landowners and farmers, controlling both the local economic and political systems, and farm labourers and other related workers who remained, unlike their counterparts in the cities, largely powerless. But this rigid and hierarchical class structure has been disturbed by the arrival of the newcomers from the cities, people who are overwhelmingly professional and managerial by occupation – a new 'middle class' inserted into the dichotomous class structure.

The changes that have occurred can be considered both in ideological and in more material terms. At the former level there has often been a reduction in the social distance between farmers and workers, both finding a common identity in the face of the disruptive influence and alien life-styles of the newcomers. One of the main effects of this change has been to reduce the extent to which there is antagonism between farm workers and their employers because of poor wages and conditions of pay, although this diversionary effect has often very little basis in improved material conditions.

But in other respects, as Newby shows, rural life is characterised, as before, by the relative economic and political weakness of the farm worker in the face now of an alliance between the newcomers and the farmers. He then examines the changing economic position of the agricultural industry and the role that the state has played in bringing this about. Since World War II successive governments have supported and subsidised the production of cheap food and the capital intensification of agriculture to a remarkable degree. In fact this economic aim has dominated agricultural policy and precluded any serious attention being paid to its social consequences. The main beneficiaries of this process have been the larger farmers and those who consume the food that they produce, the urban populations, whereas other groups in the countryside, such as small farmers and farm workers, have been relatively disadvantaged. Moreover the net effect of the recent growth in controversy about agricultural subsidies, which has arisen since Britain joined the European Community, may simply be to benefit the larger producers still further.

The domination of these farming interests may be seen in the forms that rural planning and housing policies have taken: the desire to maintain a low-wage labour force and to dominate land use has ensured that housing and alternative employment opportunities in the countryside have been greatly restricted, despite the fact that, in many areas, there has been an increasing pressure on the housing stock from the ex-urban newcomers and an increasing need to generate alternative sources of employment, as demand for an agricultural labour force has declined in line with increased capital investment. One effect of these restrictions has been to reduce the chances of those joining the labour market for the first time being able to stay in the countryside, with all the accompanying negative effects that this has on the social and economic framework of such areas.

The newcomers have, on the whole, tended to support the conservationist stance of professional town planning in the countryside and in this they have come into conflict with farmers, pursuing the aim of ever more efficient production. But a closer analysis shows that, despite the existence of some conflicts between the farmers and the newcomers (the basis, in part, for the new fellowship between farmers and farm workers noted above), in a number of important ways the newcomers have formed an alliance with the farmers which enables the latter to maintain much of their traditional dominance. Thus, for example, the newcomers share the farmers' aversion to the further expansion of housing and employment in the countryside, albeit for different reasons. More generally, as large ratepayers they have supported the limitation of the development of local social and other services by the conservative, farming dominated councils. Newby concludes that, whereas at the level of ideology the rural divide is between farmers and farm workers on the one hand and the newcomers on the other, 'at the level of access to material resources and the distribution of life chances the polarisation occurs between an affluent majority (comprised of both newcomers *and* local farmers and landowners) and a poorer and *relatively* deprived minority. The nature of these cleavages draws the resentment of the deprived minority towards the newcomers.' Here again then, as in some of the earlier papers, we see how the interaction of ideology and material circumstances must be traced if we are to make sense of class structure and consciousness, whether in the town or in the countryside.

Conclusion – some prospects for theory, politics and research

The purpose of this final brief section is not to summarise what can be learnt from the papers which follow, for that would be to usurp a responsibility which more properly belongs to the individual reader. But some reference to the situation and prospects that they reveal may nevertheless be appropriate.

The first point concerns the state of development of the new theoretical approaches to the sociology of urban and regional development. What we see in these papers is a much clearer understanding of the variety of national, regional and local experiences of capitalist development and hence the need for the adoption of a far less simplistic set of assumptions and theories about such development than was current until recently. In particular much of the work is now concentrating on uncovering the varying patterns of class structure and consciousness in cities and regions, on examining the varied form which capitalist economic development takes, together with its spatial consequences, and on examining the varying modes of state intervention and management. In short the ideological, political and economic aspects of urban and regional development are being studied in far more elaborate detail and the necessity for historical sensitivity and the value of the comparative method is coming to be more deeply appreciated.

Clearly, at one level, there needs to be a further growth in the number and range of detailed case studies such as those reported on in this book. One particular omission merits special notice. It is the lack of research concerned with the nature and changing role of women in urban society, especially striking in a body of work much concerned with the reproduction of the labour force.[7] But there could be a danger that in the process of a proliferation of case studies the more ambitious aims of the earlier work, especially the attempt to forge some more general concepts and theories about the relationship between capitalist development and patterns of life in towns and regions, will be forgotten. This is not to suggest that the aim should be some 'general theory' as first attempted by Castells, for in many respects this was a hopeless and misleading endeavour. Rather, what are required are analyses that show a detailed grasp of individually and historically varied situations, but then use these to fashion more general and globally applicable, theoretical tools. Of all the papers in this collection, Roberts's contribution (Chapter 10) is the one which perhaps follows such a strategy most clearly.

The political message which emerges from these papers is, on the whole, a depressing one. Certainly it is far less optimistic than the one which was presented in the early writings of Castells and others, who saw in the growth of urban conflict the basis for radical social change towards a socialist society.[8] There are two reasons for the failure of these hopes. The first is that the early theorists simply failed to carry out any very penetrating examination of the actual state of the class structure and of class interests and consciousness in cities and regions. They tended to be greatly overinfluenced by a few highly selected examples in which the possibility of radical political action was manifest; for example, the Allende period in Chile, the 'hot summer' of 1969 in Italy and above all, of course, the events of May 1968 in Paris. If more attention had been paid to the more normal circumstances in which the working class found itself, the political message might have been a good deal less optimistic. (As an aside it is worth noting that, if this had occurred, urban and regional research might have been much the poorer, as it was precisely the potential visualised from new and effective working class organisation and struggle which persuaded many, such as Castells, to work in this field.)

The second reason why the political message arising from the type of work reported on in this collection is less optimistic than that emerging a few years ago is because the times too have changed. As Kraushaar noted (Chapter 5), the 1960s and early 1970s was a time when the capitalist economies were still expanding, and when struggles were over the terms on which the growth in state activity then occurring took place. Today the situation is very different; most of the major capitalist economies are undergoing a period of sustained crisis, unemployment is high and the labour movement is on the defensive. Programmes that distributed benefits to sections of the working class are being cut back or abolished. In Britain, although this development was already obvious during the tenure of the last Labour government, the process has been greatly intensified and extended by the present Government. Increasingly, the fight is not to extend urban and regional policies but to defend and resist the erosion of what remains. In short, the vision of progressive radical social change which, more than anything else, inspired the dissatisfaction with older theories and research at the end of the 1960s, has been replaced by the vision of social reaction.

Moreover, on the evidence of these papers, resistance to such changes may not be very effective. Here a key issue, and one that urgently requires discussion at greater length, is the position of the organisations which have traditionally supported and extended redistributive policies. Several of the contributors to this book highlight situations in which the Labour party (or, rather, Labour governments) and trade union leaderships have acted, in the interests of advanced capital, to defuse or oppose community groups and others. At other times there has simply been an indifference to the demands being made. Kraushaar's paper discusses some of the alternatives open in such a situation, but it would perhaps not be unfair to suggest that his account does not promise very encouraging prospects for the success of the strategies on which he reports.

Finally, the question of the future prospects for the production of the type of research contained in this collection must be mentioned. As noted in the first section of this introduction, the upsurge of urban research which occurred in the 1960s and early 1970s was largely funded by the state. An examination of the reasons why, as a part of this research effort, work that was highly critical of the state's role and policies was supported would be fascinating; suffice to say here that it happened. More specifically, of course, the three Urban Change and Conflict Conferences were sponsored by the Centre for Environmental Studies (as a very minor part of its whole programme of work, which was allied to no single theoretical or political viewpoint), and much of the research presented at these Conferences was the product of quite substantial research programmes funded through the universities or through institutions such as the CES and the Centre for Urban and Regional Studies at Birmingham.

Today the era of large-scale support for urban and regional research and of tolerance for, or even interest in, its findings is almost over. Heavy cuts have been made in the funds available through academic sources for research and post-graduate training and the pressures to fund what is familiar and relatively non-controversial are easy to appreciate. Under the last Labour government the relatively liberal research funding of the earlier years was cut back, and, under the somewhat spurious claim that greater efficiency and value for money was being sought, new and expensive research bureaucracies were installed, and the subject matter and progress of projects more closely monitored and controlled.[9] More active control was exerted over publication too, and it became increasingly difficult for researchers to step beyond a narrowly technocratic role to adopt a more critical stance and to advocate change.[10]

But, again, the advent of a radical Conservative government, philosophically opposed to whole areas of policy which had been more or less accepted by all previous postwar governments, has heralded even more pessimistic prospects for the continuance of critical urban and regional research on anything other than a modest scale. Indeed, with the virtual ending of research funding from government in topics such as housing and planning, the attack has grown from a mere attempt to control and sanitise the output of a relatively small section of the research community to an attempt to withdraw government from research altogether. The arguments being used to support such an endeavour are not of a very high quality, nor are they likely in the long run to be sustainable but their effects are very clearly felt.[11] One particular effect might appropriately be mentioned here. The Centre for Environmental Studies itself was an early victim of this withdrawal of state support for research. As a result, at the time of writing, the future of the Urban

Change and Conflict conferences is in doubt, although the network of researchers and the development of the approach which they have so materially helped to foster is likely to continue, even if in a more constrained manner than in the past.

1 Community Power, Urban Managerialism and the 'Local State'*
Peter Saunders

Both the periodisation of history and the categorisation of different bodies of thought are hazardous undertakings. Nevertheless, it is useful to begin this paper by identifying three relatively distinct developments in the analysis of urban politics in advanced capitalist societies since World War II, each of which has tended to be associated with a different time period, a distinct theoretical tradition, and, indeed, different parts of the globe.

The first of these developments, which was confined mainly to North American social and political science during the 1950s and early 1960s, was the concern with community power research. This approach, which was oriented towards the documentation of local power structures in a wide range of US towns and cities, gave rise to the now well-known protracted dispute between those who claimed to have discovered monolithic–pyramidal power structures dominated by local business elites and those who countered such claims with reports of relatively open, dispersed and pluralistic power structures (for a summary of this vast literature, see Rose, 1967 and Bell and Newby, 1971). In this way, community power research re-opened a much longer tradition of political debate and argument between elitist and liberal interpretations of representative democracy.

*This chapter has been through several drafts, and it owes much to comments and criticisms made on earlier versions given at staff–student seminars at Sussex University, Kent University and Birmingham Polytechnic, as well as at the 1978. Institute of Local Government Studies conference on central–local relations and the 1979 CES conference at Nottingham. In addition, Jenny Backwell, Alan Cawson and Michael Filby have been particularly influential in the development of the arguments presented here, though the usual disclaimers obviously apply.

Very little community power research was ever attempted in Britain. Instead, from the late 1960s onwards, a research perspective developed which largely took for granted the question of where local power resided (the organisation and structure of the UK local government system appeared to rule out any effective centres of power other than the town hall), and therefore addressed itself to the rather different question of how that power was used. Increasingly, British urban research focused upon the actions of strategically-placed individuals, such as local authority housing managers, planners and the like, in an attempt to explain how inequalities of access to crucial urban resources (notably housing) were generated and perpetuated through the allocative decisions of urban 'gatekeepers'. This approach, which was made explicit by Pahl (1975) with his concept of 'urban managerialism', was derived in large part from the Weberian tradition of political sociology with its emphasis on the state as the centre of legitimate domination, and on the purposive actions of individuals as the primary focus of sociological analysis.

It was precisely these core theoretical and methodological postulates, however, which were increasingly challenged through the 1970s by the development of Marxist urban analysis. The application of Marxist political economy to the study of urban politics had its origins in continental Europe, and notably in France where the events on the streets of Paris in 1968 fused with the newly-emergent structuralist philosophy of Louis Althusser to stimulate a radical theoretical departure involving a fundamental epistemological critique of previous perspectives. Urban politics now became conceptualised in terms of the class struggle between the agents of capital and the popular forces, and this in turn led to a theoretical concern, on the one hand, with the role of the state in the urban system in maintaining the conditions for capital accumulation, and, on the other, with the significance of urban political struggles in uniting various anti-capitalist interests in the fight for a socialist alternative. Although this new theoretical initiative originated in Europe, it was soon taken up with some vigour (though not always with an equivalent degree of theoretical sophistication) in Britain and the United States, and by the late 1970s it had become an established alternative to what it disparagingly dismissed as 'bourgeois theory' in urban studies.

So it is that today we are confronted with three different traditions in the study of urban politics which among them have given rise to four competing theories: pluralism, which stresses the represent- ativeness of state institutions; instrumentalism, which stresses the domination of the state by particular elite or class interests; mana- gerialism, which stresses the political autonomy of those in key positions within the state; and what may, perhaps somewhat mis- leadingly, be termed structuralism, which stresses the necessary structural relationship between the state and dominant economic class interests in a capitalist society.

The central theme of this paper is that, taken on their own, each of these theoretical approaches to urban politics is inadequate. In part this is because of the logical, methodological and epistemo- logical weaknesses which represent internal problems within each perspective ('internal' in the sense that they refer to the theories themselves rather than to their application in particular contexts). More importantly, however, this inadequacy derives from what I consider to be a misguided attempt to develop all-embracing unitary theories. In other words, I suggest in this paper that any attempt to formulate a coherent explanation of the role of the state in the urban system should take as its starting point a fundamental division in state functions between what O'Connor (1973) terms 'social investment' and 'social consumption'; and that, because these functions are increasingly determined through different political processes operating at different levels of government with different political consequences, different theoretical approaches are appropriate to each. The essential dualism which characterises the form and function of the capitalist state cannot in my view be subsumed under a single and undifferentiated theory.

Four theories of urban politics

The four theories identified above may be differentiated on two principal criteria. First, a distinction is to be drawn between those theories that posit a necessary class bias in the function of the state and those that do not. Secondly, there is a distinction between those theories that seek to explain policy outputs in terms of external pressures exerted upon the state, and those that explain such outputs in terms of an analysis of the state itself. While the first of these criteria therefore refers to the question of *function*, the second refers to the question of *cause*, and as Gough (1975) has argued, these represent two analytically separate questions. The relation of the four theories to these two criteria is set out in the following typology.

Four theories of the capitalist state

		Policy functions	
		Necessary class-correspondence	No necessary class-correspondence
Policy causes	External	INSTRUMENTALISM	PLURALISM
	Internal	STRUCTURALISM	MANAGERIALISM

I have discussed these four theoretical approaches in some detail elsewhere (Saunders, 1979a, Chapter 4), so my discussion here will be brief. Basically I shall argue that two of these theories fail to resolve the crucial question of the autonomy, or lack of autonomy, of the state, while the other two fail to provide any criteria of empirical adequacy. It is only through some combination of different approaches, relating to different aspects of the state's role, that these problems of theory and methodology can be overcome.

The problem of autonomy: instrumentalism and managerialism
We have cited as an example of an instrumentalist approach the various elite studies of community power in which American urban governments were deemed to be passive tools in the control of business elites operating behind the scenes. In retrospect, many of these studies appear methodologically crude, e.g. in their reliance on the reputational technique for studying power, and theoretically naive, e.g. in their explicit or implicit endorsement of notions of business conspiracies, but the instrumentalist approach which they exemplify, i.e. a view of the state as necessarily biased mainly because of the power exerted over it by dominant economic interests, has since been developed in rather more sophisticated forms. Of particular significance here is the work of Miliband (1969; 1977).

For Miliband, three factors operate to ensure that, in a capitalist society, the state safeguards and promotes the interests of dominant economic classes nationally and locally. First, the various agencies of the state are invariably controlled by members of these classes, and any new recruits from other class backgrounds are socialised into ruling class culture before they reach key positions. Secondly, the capitalist class as a whole constitutes the single most powerful political interest in society and therefore achieves considerable influence over state policies by exerting pressure from outside. Thirdly, because the state is ultimately dependent for its revenue on continuing capital accumulation in the private sector, its primary function must always be to support the interests of capital.

There are three problems with Miliband's analysis which have a particular significance for the argument to be developed in this paper. First, although he recognises that different economic 'elites' may sometimes diverge in their interests, he nevertheless suggests that they share fundamental interests in common as a class, and that they act accordingly. This appears problematic, especially in relation to the division between the so-called 'monopoly' and 'competitive' sectors of capital. Lojkine (1977), for example, has shown how urban redevelopment may favour large national capitals at the expense of smaller local ones, and I have documented one such case in my research on Croydon (Saunders, 1979a, Chapter 8). Secondly, Miliband, in common with many other writers, suggests that local government in Britain is merely one branch of the state apparatus, and he thereby implies a degree of unity and coherence which is highly questionable. As we shall see later, there is a tension between the central and local levels of the state which reflects a degree of local autonomy which is necessary if the state is to function at all.

The third and most fundamental problem with Miliband's position, however, concerns the relation he traces between the state and the dominant classes. He is uneasy with a view of the state as simply the instrument of dominant economic interests, and in his later work he introduces the concept of the 'relative autonomy' of the state. In order to avoid confusion with Poulantzas's use of this concept, which is discussed below, it is important to emphasise that for Miliband, the concept of relative autonomy refers only to the argument that while those who control the state apparatus are tightly constrained by external economic and political forces, they are not entirely determined by them. To some extent, in other words, the use of state power is discretionary.

The problem, however, is that Miliband fails to theorise the scope of this discretion. He provides no criteria for assessing where the structural constraints end and political power begins, and as a result his work displays an inconsistent variability between determinism (where the state is seen as merely an instrument and thus as entirely passive) and voluntarism (where the actions of state personnel are seen as crucial factors explaining state policies). For example, in his review of the failings of the 1964–70 Labour government, Miliband claims that, 'What happened . . . was above all due to the ideological dispositions which the men who ran the government brought to their tasks' (1972, p. 360), yet this wholly voluntaristic analysis simply cannot be reconciled with the assertion in his next book that, 'The question is not one of purpose or attitude but of structural constraints' (1977, p. 93).

This failure to theorise the degree to which the state may operate autonomously of dominant classes appears to be a characteristic of most instrumentalist theories. Lojkine (1977), for example, sees the state as an instrument of monopoly capital but, recognising that this may not always be the case, then proceeds to explain its relative autonomy from this class by arguing that it may favour other classes where it anticipates possible political troubles or where control over certain state agencies is wrested from the hands of the bourgeoisie (as in Communist party victories in municipal elections in France). Yet the first of these arguments rests on an assumption of ruling class foresight which is historically highly dubious, while the second would appear more consistent with a pluralist than a Marxist analysis in that it leaves little justification for suggesting that the state is inherently class biased. What is clear from the work of both Miliband and Lojkine, therefore, is that a theoretical commitment to an instrumentalist view of the state breaks down at the point where it becomes necessary to explain the apparent autonomy enjoyed by the state in certain contexts.

The managerialist approach, in contrast, suffers precisely the opposite problem. This is true of both its application to the analysis of urban politics (the urban managerialism thesis) and its wider applications (the Weberian tradition of political analysis in which state policies are explained in terms of the motives and values of politically-powerful individuals, the most recent example of which is the discussion of corporatism by Winkler, 1976).

In its original version (Pahl, 1975, Chapter 10), the urban managerialism thesis suggested that the distribution of key urban resources such as housing was a function of the values and goals held by the various managers of the urban system (a category which included not only local state employees, but also councillors, estate agents, building society managers and so on). While Pahl recognised that these managers operated within a context of ecological constraints, he nevertheless identified them as the 'independent variables' of any analysis. This position suffered from two weaknesses, however. First, it was by no means clear how managers were to be defined and how their relative power was to be assessed; indeed, as Norman (1975) pointed out, the identification of urban managers was largely descriptive rather than analytical. Secondly, this approach seriously under-emphasised the importance of the market and of central government in constraining the actions of urban managers.

These problems led Pahl to reformulate his analysis (1975, Chapter 13). In his second version, he maintains that while it is still important to study the values and aims of those who control the allocation of resources, any analysis must be grounded in a specific theory of the economic and political environment in which the state operates. In this way, he limited his identification of urban managers to state officials at the local level and argued that they perform crucial functions in mediating between the central state and the local population on the one hand, and between the private sector and the welfare sector on the other. Urban managers therefore remain significant as allocators of scarce resources, but their control over the availability of these resources is negligible. From being the independent variables, they have become the intervening variables of any analysis.

It will be apparent that, in developing this second version of the managerialism thesis, Pahl encounters the same difficulty as that which confronts Miliband and Lojkine in determining the limits on state autonomy. While he identifies the nature of the constraints on urban managers – namely, ecological forces, the dependency on the private sector and central–local relations – he fails to theorise the situations in which these constraints may become paramount and to distinguish these from those situations in which managers may enjoy discretion in the use of their power. We may also note in passing that the same problem attaches to Winkler's work on corporatism which ends up in a hopeless confusion as a result of his attempt to reconcile a recognition that the state is dependent upon the private sector with the argument that it is increasingly directing the economy in accordance with principles which reject profit maximisation and market competition (see Panitch, 1978). In short, both instrumentalist and managerialist approaches founder on the problem of state autonomy in relation to the private sector.

The problem of tautology: pluralism and structuralism

Pluralist theories of politics have been applied both in the analysis of community power structures (for example, Dahl, 1961), and in more wide-ranging works on liberal representative democracy (for example, Schumpeter 1954, Dahl 1956, Birch 1964, Parsons 1967). What all these studies share in common is a view of the state as essentially neutral in its functions and autonomous of any particular class interests. Indeed, the very notion of 'class politics' appears problematic from this perspective because the fundamental assertion is that different alliances of social groupings are formed in relation to different political issues such that political mobilisation constantly crosses class lines; hence Dahl's concept of 'minorities rule'. The overall neutrality of the state is guaranteed by the electoral process, that is, by periodic competition for popular support among different political elites, and is grounded in a basic value consensus which results in the occurrence of relatively minor political conflicts within a context of widespread consent about the legitimacy of the political system itself. Despite the existence of political inequalities, which are recognised to a greater or lesser extent by all of these writers, the state therefore retains its overall neutrality because no administration can afford to favour one group against others for fear of the electoral consequences. The state thus functions as a political marketplace in which the weight of effective demand, i.e. the intensity with which people's demands come to be expressed, determines the supply of enforceable policies.

This perspective has been widely reviewed and criticised, and there is little need to rehearse all the arguments again here. The key point to note is that the concept of 'effective demand', when applied to the analysis of politics, is highly problematic (see Mac-Pherson, 1973; Lukes, 1977). This is because the political preferences which people articulate are seen as synonymous with their real interests. As Dahl puts it, people's interests correspond to what they say they want, 'even though from the point of view of observers [their] belief is false or ethically wrong' (1961; p. 52n). Yet by drawing such an equation between preferences and real interests, pluralist theory fails to confront the crucial question of ideology and therefore rules out *a priori* the possibility that people may be prevented from recognising their true interests with respect to any specific political issue.

The consequence of this is that pluralist theory becomes self-confirming whenever it comes to be applied. The basic premise regarding the responsiveness of the state to different interests is rarely challenged by empirical research because inaction, which is the characteristic response of most people to most political issues, is taken as indicative of consent. The widespread consensus in the western democracies (which Dahl correctly identifies as an essential precondition of stable forms of political domination) is thus taken as given in the pluralist approach while the factors which create and sustain it remain unquestioned. It then becomes possible to begin a text on the British political system with the words, 'Everyone knows that the British constitution provides for a system of representative and responsible government' (Birch, 1964, p. 13), secure in the knowledge that the theory itself denies the possibility of empirical challenge.

This failure by pluralist theory to specify the counterfactual conditions by means of which its fundamental assertions could be subjected to empirical analysis is echoed in more recent structuralist approaches. Deriving principally from the work of Poulantzas (1973), the structuralist approach begins by theorising the capitalist mode of production in terms of three 'levels' – economic, political and ideological relations. Each of these three levels is in a relationship of 'relative autonomy' with the other, although one of them (in capitalism, the economic) is dominant. In other words, the orthodox Marxist base–superstructure metaphor is replaced in structuralist theories by a view of economics, politics and ideology as mutually influencing aspects of a total mode of production in which the economic relation between wage labour and capital is nevertheless dominant.

To each of these levels of the capitalist mode of production there corresponds a level of practices. For example, at the economic level, individuals enter into a set of objective and determinate relations, either as agents of capital or as agents of labour, and thereby realise these relations as individual capitalists or as individual workers. Each level of practices, like each level of objective relations to which they correspond, is relatively autonomous, so that, for example, political struggles cannot simply be reduced analytically to economic class categories. The implications of all this for a theory of the capitalist state are that the individuals who administer the various organs of the state apparatus are merely agents inserted into a structure of objective relations, that the state is itself relatively autonomous of any particular economic class interests, and that any explanation of state policies must recognise that, far from being an active subject, the state is a 'condensation' of political class forces which gives expression to the balance of the class struggle at any one time. In this way Poulantzas and those who have attempted to apply these ideas to an analysis of urban politics, such as Castells (1977a), develop the argument that the objective and structurally-determined function of the state is to support the long-term interests of the capitalist class under the hegemony of the monopoly capital fraction (since the economic level of the mode of production is dominant in relation to the political level) while at the same time remaining relatively autonomous from any particular section of that class (because the relation between economics and politics is not totally determinant).

One question, which is immediately raised by all this, is that if the causes of state policies lie in the historically-specific balance of political class forces, how does this *necessarily* lead to the long-term function of such policies in maintaining a system of capitalist social relations? Gold and his co-authors express the point succinctly when they observe that Poulantzas fails to 'explain the social mechanisms which actually generate a class policy that is compatible with the needs of the system' (1976, p. 36). It is in response to this problem that Castells tacitly introduces notions of human agency into his work, referring for example to the 'aims' and 'intentions' of the state (1977a, pp. 263 and 432); however, this clearly contradicts his argument that state personnel are merely bearers of objective structures and that the state itself is not a thing but a condensation of class relations. Objective structures do not have aims, nor do class relations have intentions. Human agency is thus smuggled into the analysis in order to resolve the problem of teleology, but it remains totally untheorised.

A second problem is that the concept of relative autonomy appears logically contradictory. As Hirst (1977) and Hindess (1978) argue, politics are either the direct reflection of economic class categories (as instrumentalists try to argue) or they are not. Poulantzas fudges the issue and attempts to reconcile a Marxist insistence on the primacy of the economy with the recognition that the state may stand aloof from the interests of capital by suggesting that, although political institutions do not correspond directly to economic class categories, they do in some way 'represent' them, and that, although practices are merely a reflection of objective structural relations, they are not directly determined by them. The conclusion reached by Hindess and Hirst is that apart from its necessary role in maintaining the conditions of existence for the economy to operate, the relationship between the state and the economy is one of 'necessary non-correspondence' (an argument which appears to lend some credence to pluralist and managerialist theories). However, as we shall see, Hindess and Hirst make the same mistake as the other theorists discussed in this paper of assuming that the problem of the capitalist state has to be addressed through unitary theories.

While the problems of teleology and logical inconsistency alone appear sufficient to make us doubt the usefulness of structuralist approaches, there remains a third problem which these theories share with the pluralist perspective. The problem, paradoxically, is that structuralist theories claim to be able to account for anything the state does: reforms on behalf of the working class are explained in terms of relative *autonomy*, while policies in support of capitalist interests are explained by the fact that this autonomy is only *relative*! But nowhere in this neat formulation is there any identification of possible counterfactualities against which the retrospective explanations of state activity could be assessed. The theory is tautologous, and while Pickvance (1976a, p. 204) is surely justified in suggesting that 'the role of authorities in initiating changes is an empirical question', there is nothing in structuralist theory that would enable such a question to be put. In other words, whether we collect evidence of the state acting in the interests of capital or against the interests of capital, the result is always the same: the theory stands.

There is, it should be noted, a spurious counterfactuality implicit in the structuralist approach, and this is revealed in the suggestion by Castells that, 'Not every conceivable intervention is possible because it must take place within the limits of the capitalist mode of production, otherwise the system would be shaken rather than regulated.' (1976, p. 166). In other words, the state cannot legislate capitalism out of existence. But even this broad counterfactual claim is empirically inoperable. For example, Castells maintains that the state cannot change capitalist ownership relations but does not specify how such a change could be identified (public ownership of industry evidently does not qualify). Similarly, he suggests that the state cannot intervene directly to control capital accumulation, but he gives no indication of what such intervention would look like. The conclusion suggests itself that whatever the state does in relation to the economy, the theory will never be falsified; not because it is correct, but because it is tautologous and immune to empirical test.

A note on the empirical testing of theories

It may well be contended at this point in the argument that my critique of pluralist and structuralist approaches betrays a naive and untenable methodological position as regards the relation between theory and empirical research. As I have attempted to consider some of the epistemological issues raised by this question elsewhere (Saunders, 1979b), my comments will be very brief.

Following the widespread flight from positivism in recent years, the social sciences have been suffering from considerable anxieties regarding the scientific validity of the 'knowledge' they produce. Most contemporary methodologists appear to agree that inductivism and what Kolakowski (1972) terms the positivist postulate of phenomenalism are no longer tenable because knowledge cannot be the direct and unmediated product of pure experience. There is general agreement, in other words, that theory plays an important role in the determination of 'facts'; that what we 'see' is in some sense theory dependent. This, however, raises the question of how theories can ever be tested against empirical research findings.

This problem is clearly revealed in Popper's methodology. Popper (1959) argues, on the one hand, that the impossibility of an experientially based knowledge means that knowledge is generated deductively and, on the other, that the criterion of scientific adequacy lies in the rigorous attempt to falsify theories by resort to empirical evidence. But these two stipulations appear logically incompatible. As Hindess asks, 'If all observation is to some extent theoretical, then how is it possible to maintain that all knowledge is reducible to observation and that theory is to be tested against the "facts" of observation?' (1977, p. 18).

This dilemma has tended to provoke one of two responses. The first is a retreat into cognitive relativism and ultimately into the absurdities of a Winchian social science in which the lack of a neutral observation language justifies the claim that knowledge is only valid within specific forms of life and that different claims to knowledge cannot therefore be compared or evaluated against each other. The problems with such a position have been exposed on many occasions, and we need only note here that the claim that observation is theory dependent does not necessarily imply that different theories or paradigms will differ in their criteria of observation. In other words, theory dependency does not mean that different theories cannot agree on any common body of facts. To cite just one example, consensus and conflict theorists may disagree over the reasons for social order, but this itself suggests that they can agree on the sort of evidence which indicates the existence of social order.

The second response, which is more pertinent to our present concerns, is to reject the fact–theory division altogether. Althusser (1969), for example, follows Marx's arguments in the introduction to the *Grundrisse*, and suggests that the reality of the material world has to be reconstructed in thought through a process of theoretical production which is analogous to the process of material production in society. Thus, scientific knowledge is the product of the application of a particular set of theoretical tools to certain pre-scientific raw materials of thought. While the real world can never be directly known, it is progressively reconstructed in theoretical practice by breaking down appearances into their constitutive elements and determinations which then enable the complexity of the real world to be explained. It is important to recognise that this epistemology is radically anti-subjectivist (in that knowledge is the product of the application of a determinate theoretical system and is in no way dependent upon the subjectivity of the individual theorist who is merely the agent of this process) and anti-empiricist (in that the real world is never directly known and is never directly present in theoretical practice). It is also important to note that for Althusser, scientific knowledge, the product of theoretical practice, cannot be tested in any conventional sense against reality. The only 'test' conceived by Althusser lies in the application of scientific knowledge to political practice, in its efficacy in guiding the actions of the Marxist parties, i.e. in the dialectic of praxis.

It is basically this epistemology which lies behind the structuralist theories of the state discussed earlier (more recent work by both Poulantzas and Castells has tended to reject some aspects of Althusser's work but has generally failed to develop any alternative epistemological justification for the scientific status of its theoretical assertions). It is, however, an epistemology which is fundamentally flawed in that it is grounded in the claim that Marxist theory provides the only valid basis for theoretical practice, yet this claim is not, and cannot be, justified. Many Marxists have themselves recognised this. Thompson (1978, p. 208) asks why the truth of Marx's method has to be taken at face value, while Walton and Gamble point out, 'We might well ask, "Why is Althusser's science not itself an ideology?" ... Althusser's attempt at avoiding relativism is a pseudo-solution because his idea of science gives us no clear criteria for choosing between theories at the conceptual level.' (1972, p. 125).

Nor have more recent attempts to found a consistent Marxist epistemology proved any more convincing. Sayer (1979), for example, argues that science involves the discovery of necessary laws, but that these laws cannot be subjected to empirical falsification because they are only realised under certain contingent conditions. Just as, say, the chemical laws of combustion are not falsified when gunpowder fails to explode when ignited (because, for example, it may be damp), so too Marxist laws such as the tendential law of the falling rate of profit are not falsified when they are not actually realised (for example, because of the mobilisation of counter-tendencies). Where this analogy breaks down (as Sayer himself recognises) is that Marxist theories provide no means for controlling contingent conditions (or, in the terms used earlier, no criteria of counter-factuality). It there were no way of predicting the conditions under which gunpowder would explode, nor for recognising empirically the situations under which these conditions pertained, then chemists would be rightly sceptical about the laws of combustion. Faced with this problem, Sayer justifies the claims of Marxist theory by resort to logical deduction, but this is only likely to prove convincing to those who are predisposed to accept the premises on which it is based.

My insistence in this chapter on the importance of counterfactuality as a criterion of theoretical adequacy does not, therefore, rely on any naive falsificationist methodology. Quite simply, it refers only to the necessity for any theory to support the possibility of disconfirming instances and to stipulate the criteria by means of which such instances may be identified in empirical research. Theories should not be merely self-confirming tautologies. They should be open to empirical test in accordance with conditions laid down within the theories themselves. As we shall see, this criterion of theoretical adequacy can be met in respect of theories of the state when different explanations are advanced for different aspects of the state's role.

Towards a dualistic perspective

In an influential paper, Offe (1975a) has distinguished between the allocative role of the capitalist state (in which the conditions for capital accumulation are maintained in a purely authoritative way – for example, through compulsory education, regulation of the money supply, land-use planning, etc. – and its productive role (in which the state takes responsibility for producing necessary resources such as housing, transportation, energy supplies and so on). According to his argument, the former role has traditionally been accomplished by virtue of the state responding to pressures exerted upon it by powerful interests in society, but the productive role cannot be discharged in this way because what is necessary for future capital accumulation – for example, housing to aid the reproduction of labour-power – will not necessarily coincide with what the most powerful interests deem to be important at any one time. In its productive interventions, therefore, the state must develop its own criteria for action, and in this it encounters a severe problem of rationality.

Offe outlines three possible strategies by means of which the state can develop its own policies, but argues that all three are inadequate in resolving the rationality problem. The first is to rely on the growth of the state bureaucracy, but Offe claims that this would be ineffective since bureaucracies may be efficient in administering policies but are ill-suited to initiating them. The second is to attempt to increase state planning of the economy, but this option is frustrated by the inability of the state to plan effectively in a situation where investment is still controlled mainly by the private sector (the British experience of economic planning since the early 1960s would appear to bear this out). The third possibility is to encourage participation in state policy-making, but this is likely to be counter-productive in that it opens up the state to non-capitalist interests whose demands are largely inconsistent with the overall need to support capital accumulation.

Offe's analysis is in many respects convincing, but it is worth considering the third strategy – what he terms the 'participatory mode' – in rather more detail. The point here is that, as Offe (1974) has himself recognised in another paper, the state can operate selectively with regard to the participation of different types of interests, including some while excluding others in the policy-making process. Of particular significance here is the structural organisation of the state apparatus, for as Offe observes, 'One can only have power over something which according to its own structure allows power to be exercised upon it and responds to it.' (1974, p. 35). This question of structural organisation leads us to consider two related issues; the mode by which different types of interests are represented within the state, and the different levels of the state at which these interests tend to operate.

The question of the mode of interest mediation has recently been examined by Jessop (1978). While rejecting Winkler's argument that a new type of corporate state, qualitatively different from the capitalist form, is developing in Britain, Jessop does nevertheless recognise that the state appears to be discharging its traditional function of supporting capital accumulation in a new way. He suggests that representatives of large capitals and of organised labour are increasingly being drawn directly into the policy-making process, and that a new 'corporate sector' of politics is developing as a result. This enables the state to mould its economic policies more effectively to the needs of the large companies while at the same time regulating economic class struggles by co-opting the trade union leadership.

It follows from this analysis that the state now tends to exhibit

a dual form. On the one hand, the traditional institutions of representative democracy function as a forum for non-incorporated interests –
for example, small business, welfare state clients, consumers, etc. –
while at the same time aiding the legitimation of state policies;
on the other, the newly emergent corporate sector, which is exclusive
to the representatives of the functional interests of big capital and
organised labour, functions to enable the state to develop supportive
policies in relation to the private sector. However, Jessop also notes
that there is a 'contradictory unity' between these two modes of
interest mediation, since popular pressures exerted through the
competitive democratic sector will tend to challenge the policy
commitments that emerge from the corporate sector. He suggests
that such tensions are most effectively managed by a social democratic party, for it is in the best position to integrate popular and capitalist demands into a single programme of 'national unity', but
this part of his argument appears less than convincing in the light of
the 1978/79 'winter of discontent' and the subsequent electoral
defeat of the Labour government.

More effective as a means of managing this contradictory unity
between the corporate and competitive sectors is a second structural
division; namely, that between different levels of the state apparatus.
Jessop notes that corporate modes of interest representation can be
found at all levels of the state, including local government, and
evidence such as that discussed by Flynn in his account of the
development of a county structure plan in Chapter 2 clearly bears
this out. Nevertheless, it is clear that the corporate mode of representation is more characteristic of the national level, for example, the
National Economic Development Council (NEDC) and the rapidly
expanding regional level, for example bodies such as the regional
development boards, than of county and district levels of government.
In other words, not only are crucial economic policies increasingly
determined outside the competitive democratic sector of politics,
but they are also increasingly removed from local control (the
growth of the regional level is particularly significant because of
the total lack of representative elected bodies at this level). The
reason for this is that local government appears most susceptible to
popular (non-capitalist) political pressures as the well-known
example of Clay Cross illustrates only too well. As Friedland and
his co-authors suggest,

The electoral-representative arrangements which underpin municipal governments make them vulnerable to popular discontent ... local governments are often important loci for popular political participation because they are structurally accessible, the point of daily contact between citizen and state. The relative visibility of local government policies and the relative accessibility of local government agencies make them a more susceptible target of political opposition than other levels of the state.

(1977, pp. 449 and 451)

This insight enables us to draw together a number of points. First, it situates Pahl's second urban managerialism thesis in a broader theoretical context, for it explains why local representatives of the state find themselves in the position of attempting to mediate among the cross-cutting pressures of central government, the private sector and the local population. Urban managers straddle the divisions between the corporate and competitive sectors, the central and local levels, and economic and social policies. Secondly, it reinforces the argument made earlier in this paper that local government cannot be conceptualised merely as one branch of the central state apparatus, for we now see that the so-called 'local state' has its own specificity. Not only is it increasingly the site of competitive, as opposed to corporate, political processes, but it is also the locus of what O'Connor (1973) terms 'social consumption', as opposed to 'social investment', policies. In other words, while social investment, which involves the socialisation of elements of constant capital investment by the state in order to reduce the costs of the private sector, is typically the responsibility of national or regional state agencies in the corporate sector, social consumption, which involves the provision of collective support for the working population in the form of housing, social services and so on, is now the prime responsibility of local government operating in the competitive sector. The tension between corporate and competitive politics and between central and local government can thus be seen as a manifestation of the more fundamental tension between the state's need to support capital accumulation through social investment policies and its need to accommodate popular demands through social consumption provisions.

Thirdly, recent changes in the structural organisation of the

British state can be explained in terms of the need to resolve these tensions. The growth of regional levels of administration which have increasingly taken over responsibility for social investment functions such as transport planning and water provisions from local authorities can now be seen in terms of the need to insulate these crucial economic functions from popular control. Similarly, the increasing importance of land-use planning in facilitating the spatial restructuring of capital may be seen as one factor behind the division of planning functions among regional, county and local levels of government. And the reorganisation of local government itself in 1974 can also be interpreted as an attempt to dilute working-class control over the more significant aspects of state activity (see Dearlove, 1979). In other words, there is evidence of a growing rationalisation of state functions in which different types of policies are located at different levels involving different degrees of accessibility for different types of political interests. To quote Friedland et al.,

> Urban governments are organised in ways which allow them to absorb political discontent through political participation which is limited to agencies and issues which do not impinge upon economic growth . . . . The devices by which [this] is accomplished include locating potentially contradictory functions in different agencies; structuring these agencies so that access to economically important decisions is difficult while access to integrative ones is relatively easy; and locating these different functions at different levels of government.

> (1977, pp. 453 and 457)

The dualism of the state thus consists in the (ideal–typical) division between a corporate sector located at national and regional levels of government and producing social investment policies designed to support capital accumulation in the 'monopoly' sector of the economy, and a competitive sector located principally at the the local level of government and producing social consumption policies in response to popular pressures but within an overall context of political and economic constraint. The relevance of all this for the four theories discussed in the first part of this paper is that the dualism of the state must be reflected in a dualism of theory. In particular, it is necessary to break down the problematic concept of 'relative autonomy', for although structuralist theories appear to offer a fairly accurate *description* of what the state does overall (that is to say, in emphasising that its commitment to securing the conditions for capital accumulation does not rule out the possibility of policies in support of non-capitalist classes), we saw that they fail to offer any adequate *explanation* of how these results are achieved. The analysis offered here suggests that the apparent relative autonomy of the state is the product of two discrete processes which have to be theorised differently. More specifically, the reason why the state appears to act in the long-term interests of capital while also responding to the political demands of other classes is that social investment policies are developed in close consultation with capitalist interests within corporate state agencies, while social consumption policies are relatively responsive to popular pressures within representative state agencies. The interests of capital prevail in the long run because social investment takes priority over social consumption, because of the dependence of the state on future capital accumulation, and this is reflected in the subordination of local to central government.

Breaking the problem down in this way, we see that pluralist theories may be pertinent to an analysis of social consumption policies at the local level where the state is relatively open to popular demands. It should be emphasised, of course, that local government is not entirely open and that some groups in the population may still be excluded from any effective participation, so that any application of a pluralist approach to the analysis of local political issues must be cognizant of the possibility of 'non-decision-making' in its various forms, and must therefore use a concept of interests that is analytically separate from the concept of subjective preference (see Saunders, 1979a, Chapter 1). Indeed, it may be that in some towns, including some of those reported in the community power literature, one particular section of the population may succeed in virtually monopolising access to the agencies of local government, in which case an instrumentalist perspective may prove more appropriate than a pluralist one. What all this amounts to is that the long-running debate between pluralist and instrumentalist interpretations of local politics remains relevant to an analysis of one aspect of the state's role at one level of its organisation.

Neither of these perspectives appears particularly relevant to the analysis of social investment policies at regional and national levels of government, however, for here we have seen that the state is relatively insulated from popular demands – thereby rendering pluralist approaches untenable – but is also obliged to address itself to the maintenance of capital accumulation by distancing itself from any one sectional interest – thereby refuting an instrumentalist approach. While both Weberian theory, in its emphasis on the state as a locus of political power in its own right, and Marxist theory, in its emphasis on the dependence of the state on the private sector, have something to offer in the analysis of this level of state activity, it is clear that neither has provided a wholly adequate explanatory framework. The development of Weberian theory through Winkler's work on corporatism is flawed in respect of its emphasis on state autonomy, while the development of Marxist theory by Poulantzas and others fails to take account of the state as an active agent in the political process. Arguably the most fruitful approach to these problems is provided by writers such as Habermas and Offe whose analyses reveal something of a cross-fertilisation between these two traditions.

The significance of the urban managerialist approach in all this is that local authority officers stand at the intersection of central and local government and of investment and consumption policies. They are subject to the conflicting pressures between a central state committed to supporting private sector profitability and a local population pressing for resources which, if provided, would constitute a drain on profits. In this situation, urban managers appear to have little significance for an analysis of the causes of state policies, but they have a crucial significance for an analysis of how the tensions among these policies are mediated. As Lambert et al. (1978) suggest, what is important about urban managers is the style in which they perform their tasks of allocating resources among different local groups, for this is likely to affect the response or non-response on the part of these groups to state policies. The study of urban managers therefore remains an important part of any analysis of local political struggles.

Conclusions

I suggested earlier that the four theories of urban politics discussed in this paper were individually inadequate either because of their failure to theorise the problem of state autonomy or because of their inability to support counterfactual statements. Both of these problems can to some extent be overcome through the development of a dualistic perspective which recognises the theoretical specificity of the different levels (central/local), functions (investment/consumption) and modes of representation (corporate/competitive) of the state. The problem of relative autonomy is resolved by demonstrating that some policies reflect the dependence of the state on the private sector while others reflect its openness to popular pressures, while the problem of specifying counterfactual conditions is similarly resolved by explaining these different policies by means of different theories, thereby specifying the limits on the applicability of any one theory.

The implications of such a dualistic perspective for the study of urban politics are threefold. First, it undermines any conceptualisation of local government as 'local state' (cf Cockburn, 1977) in so far as this term implies a similarity among analyses of different levels of the state apparatus. The state is internally fragmented and local government has its own specific functions and mode of operation.

Secondly, it poses a challenge to those who argue that urban protests may bring about an alliance among different non-capitalist classes which can be integrated into the socialist movement. This is because urban politics have their own specificity: urban struggles involve the mobilisation of interest groups around specific issues of consumption involving local government. It is no accident that, in Britain at least, such struggles have been geographically fragmented (different areas competing with each other for resources), strategically limited (different groups focusing on different single issues) and politically isolated from the wider labour movement, for urban politics are essentially localised and issue-specific. Classes are not constituted through, or represented in, urban political movements, for each issue of consumption affects a different social base which cannot be defined in class terms. It is for this reason, for example, that I have argued elsewhere (Saunders, 1979a, Chapter 2) that conventional Marxist analyses of housing tenure divisions as mere ideological distortions of underlying class cleavages must be rejected, for housing tenure may provide as important a material base for political action in relation to urban politics as does the division of labour for political action in relation to wage struggles.

Attempts to integrate urban protest movements – which are not class-based – into the labour movement – which is – therefore fail to recognise the specificity of urban political alignments.

Thirdly and finally, the argument outlined here serves to redirect our attention to some almost forgotten areas of urban political analysis. In particular, it suggests that the study of urban politics cannot afford to neglect the issues raised in the community power debate of the 1950s and 1960s, nor to dismiss as irrelevant the work conducted in Britain on urban managers. The study of community power remains central to any attempt to explain the causes of local authority consumption policies, just as the study of urban managers remains crucial in situating such an explanation in the wider economic and political context. It is a cause for some regret, therefore, that in British urban studies, the former has attracted very little serious attention while the latter has been widely rejected.

2 Managing Consensus: strategies and rationales in policy-making
Rob Flynn

Introduction

As a result of the debate about urban managerialism (Pahl, 1975; Harloe, 1975) and the burgeoning interest in Marxist theories of the state (Lindberg et al., 1975; Holloway and Picciotto, 1978), there is fundamental disagreement about the best mode of analysis of state intervention in capitalist urban development. Arguments continue about how to evaluate the determinants and outcomes of state action, but increasingly attention is being focused on the processes of policy formation and the internal operations of the state (Offe, 1974; 1975a). However, the amount of empirical research on these processes is very limited, not least because of the theoretical and methodological problems involved (Saunders, 1979a).

The purpose of this paper, therefore, is to present some evidence about the bureaucratic context of policy-making in local government, based on a study of professional planners engaged in formulating strategic planning policy. The aim is to illustrate the process through which council officers devised policies, mobilised support and secured their acceptance at a series of bureaucratic and political levels. It is argued that the core of this policy-making was concerned not just with a particular set of substantive planning objectives but also with a number of assumptions about their implementation. More specifically it is suggested that planners create a consensus about substantive policies *and* about decision rules and the scope for flexibility in dealing with conflicting demands arising from such policies. Indeed, it is this capacity to interpret or translate the rules or principles of policy (allied to the active gatekeeper or broker role of planners in mediating among the bureaucracy, politicians, private sector, etc.) which constitutes the basis of professional planners' power in local authorities.

Planners try to create, and then manage, a consensus about policy among themselves and their councillors, with other local authorities, industrialists and a range of other interest groups. Consensus here refers to shared norms and commitments among decision-makers, which diminish the chances of fundamental disagreement, which provide means for reconciling disputes, and which are part of a 'culture' within which administrative decisions can be made. It is also assumed here that consensus-management is a continuous activity, and that it comprises the 'infrastructure' (Heller, 1977) of policy-making in local government planning. Further, it is suggested that the professional officers play a crucial role in establishing these norms, and that they adopt specific strategies and rationales to secure agreement among different groups.

The empirical material on which this paper is based is drawn from a recent intensive case-study of a county planning department as it prepared a structure plan (Flynn, 1979). The local authority involved was a large shire county council, controlled politically by the Conservative party. The structure plan process, despite major criticisms of its inherent lack of direct influence over public and private bodies etc. (Drake et al., 1975), represented an explicit and formal mechanism requiring extensive inter-organisational bargaining, and thus formed a suitable vehicle for examining planners' perceptions and actions in the face of different constraints. This paper therefore illustrates some of the strategies and rationales used by structure planners as they prepared, negotiated and guided policies through their own department, council committees, district council planners, and as they tried to create and maintain a pragmatic consensus at each level.

Intra-departmental policy-making: commitment and conformity

Studies in the sociology of organisations have alerted us to the significance of internal differentiation within organisations and the effects of this and bureaucratic hierarchy on the distribution of power among groups (Crozier, 1964; Downs, 1967; Blau, 1973; Pettigrew, 1973). However, these common features of organisations are often neglected in approaches to urban policy which are mainly concerned with 'structural' causes and outcomes. It is arguable that the heterogeneity and fragmentation of local government itself places limits on the inferences we might wish to make about the purposes and consequences of state actions (Flynn, 1978). More importantly, it is especially necessary to consider the relevance of intra-organisational aspects of policy-making if we are to arrive at a comprehensive understanding of state intervention. Clearly within local authorities, as in all organisations, there are problems of securing commitment to, and conformity with, certain policies, and these may be significant in explaining not only the emergence of policy but also its subsequent implementation.

In the case of the structure plan studied, it was apparent that within the planning department there was a persistent problem of securing officers' commitment to some proposals, and a problem of obtaining consent for (or enforcing compliance with) these proposals. The department involved was large, staffed by a high proportion of professional planners, and was divided into different functional or specialist sections responsible for various aspects of county planning matters. It was also organised on a hierarchical basis with an elaborate chain of command which allocated different responsibilities (and thus discretion) to officers in order of ranked seniority. In preparing the structure plan it was deemed necessary to coordinate the work of different sections under the supervision of one senior officer who convened a steering group of other senior planners. This group decided on the division of labour for structure plan work, evaluated draft reports, and acted as an editorial board preparing policy statements for councillors' and other official agencies' consideration.

The regular meetings of the steering group offered different sections an arena for debating the merits and defects of proposed policies. Meetings were often lengthy and dominated by arguments about goals, methods and substantive policies as they affected areas of the county. At two important stages–the presentation of initial broad choices to councillors and drafting the official consultative version of the structure plan 'written statement'–there were fairly major disagreements between planning officers. A number of issues recurred in the meetings, but among the most important were firstly criticisms of the economic emphasis, or 'growth bias' of reports and an associated *laissez-faire* stance towards district councils; and secondly criticisms of the lack of 'effective' internal consultation in drafting reports. Thus there was a dispute inside the planning department not just about the contents but about the methods of making planning policy. Debates about the fundamental philosophy of the plan revolved around opposed professional perceptions of what the main problems were in the county, and these reflected the functional cleavage between local and strategic planners.

In overcoming internal friction about policies the main device employed was that of bureaucratic seniority (coercion) and a stress on the flexibility of the proposed plan itself (persuasion). Steering group members were reminded by senior officers that preliminary documents were intended merely to stimulate discussion by county councillors and other local authorities, so were not to be regarded as final or comprehensive. Once the planning committee had endorsed the 'strategic principles', critical planners were warned that there was no longer any room for debate and that there was an imperative need to avoid delay. Thus it was evident that if commitment were not forthcoming, compliance could be enforced.

There was a general awareness among the officers of their conflicting perspectives, and, indeed, their difficulty in reaching full agreement on policies was candidly admitted to district council planners (but not, significantly, to county councillors). Planners' attempts to 'strike a balance' were eventually resolved by interventions by the chief planner which led to a reduction in the role of the structure plan steering group, and the establishment of a small, informal group of officers who finally wrote the 'consultative' version of the plan. This smaller group also took on the task of assessing the importance of objections to the plan after public participation and official consultations, and then produced a revised document for final council approval.

Relationships among different sections of the planning department did, therefore, influence the expression as well as the substantive content of policies. Obtaining agreement on reports was an exercise in diplomacy or bargaining, and eventually bureaucratic power. Recognising that differences of professional opinion were likely to persist, the most senior officers attempted to achieve common adherence to some (tacit) understandings between colleagues about the meaning or interpretation of policies (a stress on 'flexibility' for example, thus deferring matters for further discussion). While there was among senior officers a pragmatic acceptance of the need for internal negotiation and debate, nevertheless the essentials of the structure plan were effectively protected from challenge. Intra-departmental policy-making thus proceeded on the basis of forming a consensus through commitment (persuasion and bargaining) *and* conformity (coercion). This, of course, was only one element in the structure plan process, and other departments, county committees, district councils, etc. also had to be incorporated. This required slightly different tactics and sanctions. For the purposes of this discussion we are restricted to examining only two of these other groups – the county politicians and the district council planners.

Persuasive rationales: presentation of policies to councillors

For planning officers, the planning committee was the primary hurdle to overcome in obtaining approval for structure plan reports. The business of getting councillors' authorisation for technical studies, acceptance of officers' reports, and the explicit endorsement of key planning principles, was problematic. Much depended on the presentation of issues in committee and a sensitivity to the political preferences of the majority group (derived formally from briefing meetings between chief officers, committee chairmen and the council leader). It is important therefore to consider some of the rationales employed by officers in their discussions with councillors in committee.

In the case of the structure plan, problems not normally encountered in routine committee business were apparent: the planning officers had to guide councillors through a protracted series of stages of policy-making and familiarise them with 'strategic' considerations rather than routine or 'detailed' development control decisions. Not only was the exercise a time-consuming statutory procedure complicated by a range of central government directives, but it was also a process requiring numerous technical studies, extensive official consultations with public and private sector agencies, and of course involved formal participation by the public. Planners were therefore faced with the problem of evolving politically acceptable proposals that could be technically justified *and* with mediating between their own councillors and the host of external bodies and interest groups.

At the early stages of the structure plan, planners emphasised that reports put before committees were essentially research or survey material, and entailed no firm commitment by the county council. When major alternative policies were subsequently suggested to the councillors, it was stressed that the documents were only vehicles for discussion, to be used as briefs for future meetings with district councils. Senior officers frequently pointed out in committee that the papers were neither final nor comprehensive, but posed questions for debate by council members. However, when the committee was eventually asked to decide between two alternative planning strategies, chief officers advised councillors that the choice of one option effectively excluded policies entailed in the other option. In addition, officers underlined the extent to which the county council was constrained in its choices, and argued that if the most 'realistic' option was adopted (a strategy geared to 'wealth-creation' and employment growth) then inevitably other objectives would have to be forgone.

When the planning committee actually considered the first draft of the structure plan written statement, three dominant ideas ran through the officers' introduction to the report. Firstly, it was pointed out that councillors had seen most of the material previously because they had been continuously informed about the survey results. Secondly members were reminded that the plan was a statutory requirement which necessitated complex negotiations with outside bodies. Finally planners insisted that the hallmark of the plan was its intrinsic flexibility, and the fact that it established 'broad principles' to guide future planning decisions throughout the county. The net effect of these prefatory remarks was to pre-empt fundamental criticism by the politicians, and yet at the same time reassure councillors that policies were not rigidly fixed.

At the joint policy and resources and planning committee meeting which ratified the final document, officers again stressed the flexibility of the structure plan and its capacity for reacting quickly to changed circumstances. Councillors' anxieties about lack of precision or detail in the plan were allayed by frequent references to the need to set out 'broad guidelines' or 'starting points' for policy. Once more, however, officers argued that the scope for amendments to the report was limited because of prior discussions with external groups. Indeed the council leader himself observed that as the plan represented the outcome of lengthy detailed discussions and hard-won compromises between the county and many other organisations, the policies expressed in the document could not be radically altered.

The main feature of officers' presentations of structure plan policy to councillors seemed, therefore, to be a constant emphasis on two basic rationales or maxims. One was the insistence that policies were not finite but 'contingent', and so could not irrevocably commit councillors. Implicit in this rationale was the assumption that in *interpreting* the degree to which policies could or should be changed, and in *explicating* the policies' meanings, the officers' advice was essential, because their professional expertise lay in monitoring environmental changes *and* in their role as gatekeepers or brokers between the county council and other agencies. The second theme or rationale comprised a recognition of 'constraint' as both the justification for 'realistic' policies and as a limitation imposed by the need for compromise with other organisations. Paradoxically, perhaps, flexibility and constraint were invoked by planners to legitimate the content of policy and the reasons for its emergence and application. It was taken for granted that the ability to translate these principles of policy into specific decisions lay very largely within the officers' professional domain.

Co-option: incorporating district planners

Reorganisation of local government divided planning functions between county and district councils. This change meant that the county council was faced with a number of independent planning authorities with their own departments and committees, and their own local priorities. From the outset of structure plan work, county planners regarded it as essential that district council planners should be involved in the preparation of the county plan, and therefore officers' working groups were established on an area basis. These joint working groups considered draft reports prepared by county planners, debated proposed policies as they might affect different areas, and discussed general matters of liaison between the two tiers of planning. Regular meetings were attended by senior officers from the county and districts, and there was a mutual recognition that the groups performed a useful function. From the county planners' perspective, district involvement was necessary because, it was hoped, it would prevent inter-authority disagreements not just over the structure plan but over other planning issues.

Draft proposals were thus tested out by county planners on their district colleagues at meetings of the joint working groups. District officers frequently questioned and criticised county reports, and elaborate debates about goals and methodology were common. In the discussions which ensued, a number of recurrent themes emerged in the county planners' justifications for policy, which are important to consider.

Realism

Criticisms of the assumptions and implications of county policies were often rebutted on the grounds of the plan's inherent 'realism'. Thus for example, some districts' accusations that the economic philosophy was a *laissez-faire* one, favouring non-planning, were rejected by county planners because, they argued, the scope for positive intervention was minimal, and this implied an acceptance of reality. One variant of this theme was county planners' assertions that it was unrealistic to have a plan concentrating growth on only a few areas because it was geographically and economically difficult and politically unacceptable. Another variant amounted to a professional doctrine, which stressed that in a context of uncertainty (economic stagnation, public expenditure reductions) it was prudent to admit the limitations of planning in making forecasts or influencing events: planners had, therefore, to come to terms with reality.

Equity

The dominant aim of the structure plan was to encourage economic growth throughout the county, but while some districts clamoured for 'growth', others resisted it. As a consequence there were conflicting demands for an accentuation of the growth policy in some areas and a rejection of it by other authorities. However, county planners adamantly refused to modify the structure plan's fundamental goal of 'maximising the economic potential' of the county. This was justified not only in terms of its realism but also because it was vital for securing public sector resource allocation, and was in the interest of the county as a whole. It was argued that the proposed plan was designed to promote the general welfare of all areas, and county planners insisted that they had tried to be fair to all districts.

Partnership

There were, nevertheless, many cases where compromises were

made in redrafting policies considered objectionable by district planners. One usual means of reducing district anxieties was for county officers to emphasise that the interpretation of particular policies, and the practicalities of implementation, were matters which could be dealt with in future collaboration. In meetings where sustained and detailed criticisms arose, county planners often agreed that further discussions would improve understanding, and that working together would resolve any difficulties. Moreover, county planners became increasingly concerned with the necessity for close working relationships and mutual understanding between the county and districts once the structure plan was adopted. County officers actively sought a *modus operandi* with district colleagues which was to be based on the norm of professional partnership. Thus while county planners accepted that they had no right to determine the precise content of district local plans, they insisted on their role in 'setting the parameters' and advising on matters of strategic importance. Discussions about an appropriate division of labour were consequently dominated by county officers' repeated emphasis on the desirability of partnership and professional inter-dependence.

Contingency

Throughout the negotiations with district planners (*and* inside county hall) the principle of 'contingency' (or 'flexibility') was invoked as a special characteristic of the structure plan. Briefly, what this principle entailed was a capacity to modify policy rapidly as external circumstances changed. One implication of this contingent approach was that it was not always necessary to have rigid, well-defined policies but rather built-in flexibility to accommodate future changes. Such a rationale was often used to forestall district planners' complaints and criticisms: proposals which were not of major significance, but which prompted district objections, were held over for further consideration 'in the light of future developments'. Thus for example, opposition to county guidelines on maximum permitted residential development was countered by reference to contingent planning's ability to alter the guidelines as and when it became necessary. This virtue of elasticity in policy is, of course, related to those other themes already identified—realism and partnership – and also to another rationale, that of specificity or precision.

Specificity

A concern with the phrasing of policies preoccupied district and county planners alike. The dilemma was that the specificity or ambiguity of policy statements was itself a source of controversy. For different officers, and at different times, policies were said to be too explicit or too vague, too detailed or too general, depending on their interest in the substance or intended effects of those policies. One common observation by district *and* county planners was that the proposals were imprecise and gave too much scope for different interpretations. On the other hand, the alternative was also problematic because exactitude implied restrictive or limited interpretations, pre-empting discretion. Several district planners argued forcibly for 'room to manoeuvre' and pleaded for statements of policy which permitted councils to deal with specific problems *ad hoc*, on their merits. The degree of precision or ambiguity involved in the expression of policies was thus a continuing focus for debate and negotiation between officers. The dilemmas over phrasing were variously resolved by reference to one or more of the other rationales identified, and by assessing the extent to which *councillors'* perceptions and attitudes needed to dominate. Planners at both levels were acutely aware of the sensitivity of certain issues to their respective councillors, and they therefore tried to adopt a vocabulary and style compatible with their politicians' views.

Constraint

As with their own councillors, county planners responded to some district planners' objections in terms of constraints, that is, they explained the necessity of policy in terms of constraint, in association with other rationales. Organisational and procedural constraints were regularly mentioned by county planners in an attempt to minimise delays caused by consultations. Determined to keep to schedule, structure planners imposed timetabling deadlines on most agencies consulted, thus reducing the time available for discussion and effectively restricting the scope for bargaining.

Two other factors were also referred to by county officers as reasons why certain amendments or suggestions were unacceptable, or why some policies were not open for negotiation. Firstly there were 'internal' constraints such as the political demands and values of county councillors, intra-departmental officer support for particular proposals, and other departments' insistence on some policy (e.g. transport). Here the point was that internal arguments had already occurred, and some decisions reached at county hall were virtually non-negotiable. Secondly there was an appeal to 'external' constraints as justifications for policy. In this case, statutory requirements, ministerial directives, regional planning policy, and so on were regarded as placing severe limits on the county's discretion. In addition, the county's limited role *vis-à-vis* other public agencies (quite apart from the private sector of the economy) restricted the structure plan's scope still further. These external constraints, together with procedural exigencies and internal political and professional demands, were said to have established the terms of reference within which negotiation had to take place.

In an effort to minimise conflict, pre-empt major objections, and to obtain consensus, county planners attempted to co-opt or incorporate district planners into the structure planning process. In negotiations, several norms, or principles, or rationales – realism, equity, partnership, contingency, specificity, and constraint – were used to explain and defend policies, and to support county rejection (or acceptance) of district planners' objections. Similar rationales were evident in structure planners' dealings with their own professional colleagues in county hall and with county councillors. The county planners' appeals to such axioms or principles, in each case, can be regarded as simultaneously a means for engineering consent and a device for maintaining their role as the principal interpreters of policy.

Conclusions

Evidence drawn from one case-study, based upon research into a particular kind of planning, obviously cannot be used to sustain large-scale generalisations. However, it is argued that the empirical material discussed here does offer fruitful insights into the complex process of policy-making. Theoretically, 'why' questions seem to have taken precedence over 'how' questions in recent explanations of the state's role in urban policy. This paper has sought to demonstrate that the *way* in which policy is created and managed, especially by state professionals or bureaucrats, is itself very important if we wish to understand in detail the dynamics of policy-making in planning.

The structure planners studied appeared to be creating a 'culture' within which bureaucratic and political values were operationalised. Both inside and outside county hall, the officers used various strategies and rationales. Whether such strategies and rationales were employed consciously or not, their effect was to establish a pragmatic consensus which reflects two dimensions of policy. Firstly it translated explicit political prescriptions(and tacit assumptions) into 'technical' policies. And secondly, it supplied the norms through which intra- and inter-organisational conflicts (both political and bureaucratic) could be managed.

The 'strategies' identified can be described generally as problem-solving, persuasion, bargaining and coercion (Scharpf, Reissert and Schnabel, 1978). Such analytical distinctions are not mutually exclusive in practice, and while elements of each may be observed in planners' relationships with different groups, some categories appear more important than others. Thus, for example, although structure planners' dealings with other county planners moved between problem-solving (technical agreement on certain goals), persuasion (appeal to common norms), and bargaining (adjustment of demands), coercion through bureaucratic power was the ultimate sanction to secure conformity. However, in relating to councillors, planners adopted a problem-solving approach combined with persuasion, and this was backed up by an implicit acknowledgement of the officers' professional expertise in giving technically neutral advice. Problem-solving and persuasion were similarly intermixed in the county officers' relationships with district planners: such bargaining as occurred was supported by references to the structure plan's statutory superiority over local plans, and by an appeal to a common professional identity between officers.

The use of such strategies to achieve compliance also involved a number of 'rationales' to legitimate policy, and these rationales varied according to the nature of the audience. While the strategies described are common to most organisations, the question of how far the rationales identified are context dependent (that is, reflecting a particular set of political values peculiar to the case-study and to structure planning) requires further analysis. Offe (1975) has suggested that, at a macroscopic level, when state policy is oriented to 'consumption' functions, the role of the state is responsive or market-reinforcing, and the primary 'logic' of policy formation is 'consensus' (accommodating different demands). He also notes that it is possible for a consensus policy mode to operate in conjunction with 'bureaucratic' and 'technical–rational' logics, but with contradictory effects. When applied to the structure plan process described here, Offe's approach seems plausible and relevant. However, the way in which such logics are connected with actual behaviour by different groups and organisations (particularly state bureaucrats) remains to be demonstrated. Nevertheless, in this case-study, both the strategies and the rationales of the planners can be interpreted as maintaining the professional officers' role as mediators between different interests and organisations, and reinforcing their role as the principal interpreters of policy.

3   Power and Protest in the City
Brian Elliott and *David McCrone*

Introduction

During the 1970s it has become widely recognised that our studies
of urban problems, processes and issues must be located within the
broader analysis of 'political economy'. It has become increasingly
plain that most of the traditional themes – the concern with spatial
arrangements, with territorial inequalities and the structures of
power – cannot be treated as exclusively 'urban' but must be related
to wider societal processes. In order to grasp what is going on in the
city, it is necessary to look outside it, at what is happening in the
total social structure, in the economy at large and in the polity. This
paper is an attempt to develop this approach by drawing upon the
kind of historical and political analysis which Weber (1958) developed in his essay on the city. His work encourages us to look at
structural conflicts in a broad, historical perspective and his writings
about power and domination have – in our view – much to offer
in the rounding out of a 'political economy' approach.

Some of the best and most sociological material on the city is
currently being produced not by sociologists but by historians. In
some of this one finds very detailed description and analysis of
transformations of social structure and of the complex struggles for
power which these generated. Reviewing a number of recent articles
in urban history in his introduction to *Towns in Societies*, Abrams
invites us to think about cities within the framework of a power
struggle. He suggests that

> considerable progress might be made in understanding the social
> nature and historical function of towns if we took to considering
> them in relation to a large context which, following Weber, we
> might call the complex of domination. By a complex of domination
> I understand an ongoing and at least loosely integrated struggle
> to constitute and elaborate power.
>
> (1978, p. 31)

When Weber wrote of domination, he defined it in ways which stressed its sustained and internalised character. Thus domination referred to:

> The situation in which the manifested will (command) of the ruler or rulers is meant to influence the conduct of one or more others (the ruled) and actually does influence it in such a way that their conduct, to a socially relevant degree, occurs as if the ruled had made the content of the command the maxim of their conduct for its very own sake.
>
> (1968, p. 946)

Domination then, involves legitimacy; power need not. To talk of a 'complex of domination' implies that there exists a number of competing groups vying with each other for supremacy, trying to turn 'power' into 'domination'. At any given moment the diverse groups will have available to them different resources, different means for exercising power. Thus, a declining class or status group may hold formal political power but find that its economic and social base is being eroded, that is 'domination' is being challenged as new social aggregates commanding new resources deny and seek to undermine the legitimacy of its commands. A rising class or status group struggles to develop and consolidate its economic power by extending its cultural influence, using this subversively, to aid it in the quest for political office and for the political supremacy with which it can establish the widest and most secure authority. Thus, the efforts to acquire and sustain 'domination' involve cultural as well as economic forms of appropriation.

If we think in historically concrete terms about cities it is not difficult to recognise the clashes of interest, the struggles between classes and status groups that have been played out within them and the importance to ruling groups of control or support of the urban populations. The conflicts in the cities then are to be seen as part of a larger drama – some broad societal transformation that finds expression there. Continuously developing social structures produce constantly shifting constellations of interest and periodically the tensions generated are too great to be contained by those mechanisms which have been established to channel or suppress conflict. Extensive political unrest, popular agitation and forms of defiant behaviour mark periods of rapid or profound societal transformation. Often, in order to relieve the pressure of discontent the ruling groups make concessions to the rising classes or strata but generally these serve not only to weaken their control over their subordinates but they even give heart to the latter and fuel their ambitions.

Some of these processes can be clearly seen in the political history of British towns in the years since the Industrial Revolution. Periodic outbursts of urban unrest accompanied the development of the economic and social structures of industrial capitalism and loose associations – 'parties' in Weber's sense – were formed by bourgeois, petit bourgeois and proletarian to give expression to their interests and to their struggle for power and domination.

In the early nineteenth century, the major confrontation was between the new industrial bourgeoisie and the aristocrats, gentry and established merchants who ran the old urban centres or who controlled those small communities which expanded so rapidly. Wresting political control meant, for the industrial capitalists, extension and consolidation of their economic power in a locality. Often the search for political dominance led to *usurpation*, with packed vestries and rigged ballots being the means of winning control over at least some of the fragmented institutions by means of which the towns were governed. The *legitimacy* of the quest for political office and for domination was based on business expertise and evident success. It was this which made them 'fit and proper persons' to run municipal corporations.

But as industrial capitalism grew, the locus of economic and political life shifted more and more towards the centre. Gradually, the larger industrialists withdrew or were squeezed out from local politics leaving the stage to a host of petit bourgeois elements who sought control of the cities and thereby some influence on local taxes and on the local markets in which they traded. A good many studies show that throughout the Victorian period – and, indeed, well into the twentieth century in some cases – political conflict in the cities consisted mainly of struggles among factions of the bourgeoisie, rather than struggles between bourgeois and proletarian (Briggs, 1968; Hennock, 1973; Fraser, 1976; Elliott et al., 1978).

For the working class it was in the factories and workshops that the first battles had to be fought, for these were the institutions which most immediately shaped *their* lives. Only when their unions were firmly established and when some of the worst excesses of exploitation were alleviated could they direct their attention to the sphere of institutional politics. When they did so the cities were once again important arenas. Little by little, since the 1930s the Labour party has become a real force in local politics. In a few places it has even established political supremacy and sometimes systems of patronage which have reminded at least one writer of 'Tammany Hall' (Bulmer, 1977). But such superiority is rare. Almost everywhere any dominance achieved by Labour has been precarious. Typically it has been opposed by anti-socialist alliances of diverse elements – some strictly bourgeois – others drawn from the proliferating white collar, technical or professional sectors of the occupational structure.

The histories of our cities reveal the unfolding of several broad phases of economic development. Merchant capitalism giving way to industrial capitalism, industrial capital being challenged in recent years by finance capital. They reveal too the struggles of the various social groups caught up in these major structural changes, groups whose identities are given by their place in these systems of economic and social relationships: industrialists posed against merchants, manual workers against factory owners, financiers and property tycoons against workers and small businessmen. Of course, they reveal stabilities and persistence as well as dramatic changes. In cases such as those so well documented by the Benwell Community Development Project (CDP) team (1979) some local economic elites show themselves adept at changing their course, switching their investments to ride the tide of profit. In the Newcastle area at least, we cannot ignore the continuities. Families that exercised great power economically and politically two hundred years ago continue to do so today.

But our concern here *is* with change – and some of the ways in which new social groups created by the economic processes of the last twenty years or so have sought power and domination in the city. The cities of the West have certainly been noisy places in recent years. They have witnessed a good many popular demonstrations, riots, protests and diverse forms of defiant behaviour. Such a spate of agitation must surely indicate some profound discontents and possibly some important structural shifts. Looking back over the years since the Industrial Revolution it is easy to see that many struggles in the cities were shaped by the underlying structures of class relationships. Groups were defined in large part by the positions of their members in the system of production. The policies they pursued and the interests they defended reflected their locations in the market.

Today, in all Western economies there is a new group, a stratum with no satisfactory name, distinguished by its possession of technical skills and expertise. It consists of those whose 'capacity for income' rests on their knowledge and on their specialised education. To some writers it is unquestionably 'a new class' (Harrington, 1979; Kirkpatrick, 1979); to others, simply a new stratum (Bell, 1973; 1979). There are serious problems in calling this a new class for the recent technological, economic and educational developments of which it is a product have created a multitude of locations in public and private enterprises; such a multitude that it is hard to identify a single material base for the whole group. We would prefer then to think of it as a new stratum, a stratum which is neither 'bourgeois' nor 'proletarian', a stratum which is currently, and often at the level of the city, engaged in a quest to extend its power at the expense of the bourgeois elements – both large and small – and less certainly, at the expense of the working class. It is engaged in a struggle against both these 'traditional' elements and against dissidents from its own ranks, as we shall see. As with other social aggregates seeking power and domination its members strive for forms of economic influence, for political expression and cultural dominance.

The 'demoralising' of capitalist society

What effect has this numerous stratum had on the patterns of social conflict in Western societies? Has it rendered obsolete or supplanted older specifically *class* conflicts? Our answer would be 'No'. Class conflicts remain absolutely fundamental in capitalist societies, but the growth of this stratum has weakened some of the ideological defences of traditional bourgeois elements, for the new group contains many who are highly critical of capitalism. To steal a phrase from Kirkpatrick (1979) this new intelligentsia has been engaged in the 'demoralising' of contemporary capitalist society. That is to say, it has been making explicit, as well as criticising, the beliefs and loyalties that hold such a society together. In literature and drama no less than in social and political writings the exploitative nature of much capitalist activity both in the UK and abroad has been laid bare. (Even a Tory prime minister admitted that there was an 'unacceptable face' of capitalism.) The rational, questioning, sceptical attitudes which had much to do with the development of capitalism have flourished within it and turned upon that system itself. Bell (1979) argues that there has grown up an 'adversary culture' among the large stratum of highly educated men and women produced by our universities and colleges over the past twenty years. This is not to claim that they are offering any specifically leftist alternative: few among them do that. But the dissemination of their misgivings about capitalism nourishes an extensive disenchantment and licenses many forms of defiant behaviour. The values and institutions that sustained deference and docility have been challenged and broken by both structural and ideological developments in the last few years. Thus, we can observe that many 'who find themselves in subordinate positions, and notably those who work in factories, mines, offices, shops, schools, hospitals and so on, do what they can to mitigate, resist and transform the conditions of their subordination' (Miliband, 1978, p. 402). They are encouraged in this by members of the new 'service' stratum. The state of 'de-subordination' of which Miliband writes owes a good deal, in our view, to the growth of this new stratum. Inspiration or assistance, leadership and organisation of many forms of popular protest are undertaken by its members.

This rising stratum of salaried professionals, administrators, educators and technologists is beginning to assert itself. As yet it lacks clearly formulated, distinctive political orientations but we would agree with Goldthorpe's assessment that 'in terms of size, resources and stability of membership its potential as a socio-political force is considerable' (1978, p. 438).

The fragmentation of social conflict
It is not only the ideological unruliness of this new stratum that obscures, cross-cuts or weakens traditional class conflicts in the city; the fact is, the rise of such an aggregate is part of a broad pattern of structural changes. The middle class, for instance, has been profoundly affected first by secular changes in the occupational structure which have followed shifts in the economy, then by government actions which have favoured the expansion of public service work and the contraction of some parts of the market sector. The

overall effect has been to reduce the size of the traditional bourgeoisie and greatly to expand the professional, semi-professional and technically trained workforce, much of which is employed not by private enterprise but by public agencies.

The middle class is both bigger and more diverse than hitherto. It has become structurally diversified as technical knowledge and skill have played an ever greater part in determining the market capacities of various occupational groups and at the same time, processes of education and social mobility have done a great deal to undermine cultural unity. It is not just the 'post-industrial society' of writers such as Bell (1973) and Touraine (1971) who claim to see the emergence of important divisions and the growth of a new stratum. Work by Roberts et al. (1977), Bertaux (1977) and forthcoming publications by Goldthorpe and Offe and Berger all refer to this phenomenon. The social, economic and political interests of the new stratum are by no means coincident with those of traditional bourgeois groups.

At the same time, the working class has also become less unified. It is divided by levels of skill, levels of organisation and by sectors of employment. Those whose skills are most sought after, especially if they have become highly unionised, have been able to command markedly better pay and conditions than the unorganised. There remain very considerable differences in levels of material well-being and little evidence that overall changes in earning capacities have led to any significant upgrading of the relative position of the poorest groups in recent years. Status differences in the British working class remain important manifesting themselves in disputes about 'differentials' or in complaints about the movement of less 'respectable' families into 'desirable' public housing areas (Gill, 1977).

Most importantly though, in our opinion, the working class is divided by race. Since 1960 there has been created in Britain an underclass, a pool of imported cheap labour without which transport, the health services and parts of the textile industry would be difficult to operate. Increasingly the black population is being forced to defend its interests through separate associations and movements. The failure of the unions and the labour movement to defend the black workers is leading, as Rex (1979) has recently pointed out, to more comprehensive and more militant defensive organisations. The sense of rejection that blacks have come to feel as a result of their dealings with white trade unions and the suspicion with which the Labour party and leftist groups are viewed is very evident from the most cursory reading of the black press (Moore, 1975).

These fundamental structural divisions militate against the organisation of protest on class lines. If, as Castells (1978) has argued, urban conflicts are currently very much at the centre of political life in many Western countries, then it is important to notice how frequently the agitations cut across the traditional class divisions, how often the protesters, over say urban renewal or transport systems, are drawn from different positions in the system of production. It is important because it alerts us to the growing significance of an alternative basis for group allegiances and oppositions: consumption.

Consumption and social conflict

Of course, there is nothing very new about the idea that a group or an individual's position in a system of consumption may confer interests or help shape patterns of conflict, but today a number of writers of varying theoretical orientation are impressing upon us the relative 'independence' of positions in the systems of production and consumption. It seems no longer adequate to treat 'consumption' as essentially 'dependent' on location in the labour market and the rewards acquired there.

Rex and Moore's (1967) taxonomy of 'housing classes' is perhaps the best known scheme proposing that housing tenure be treated as exercising independent effect on life chances – and the debates about the idea need no repetition here. More recently, though, Saunders (1978) has argued in a much more convincing way that one of the factors dividing the working class is the ownership of private housing. In essence, his claim is that housing is a unique item of consumption because it has not only a consumption value, as a form of shelter, but most importantly, it is also a means of accumulation. Those who take out a mortgage to purchase a house receive tax concessions and thus money at a very low rate of interest and with steeply rising prices most owner occupiers stand to make considerable capital gains.

In a very recent article Dunleavy (1979) develops the idea of conflict arising from 'consumption sectors'. He tries to show how the declining association between occupational class and political alignment in Britain may be explained in terms of consumption interests suppressing or displacing more fundamental, less proximate 'class' interests. Most importantly he forces us to think about the position of groups and individuals with respect to state intervention in the provision of resources such as houses, roads, schools, etc. What really structures conflict and moulds political attitudes is the access to and perceptions of state subsidies. As state intervention in the processes of consumption grows, so different 'locations' with regard to important items such as houses or transport become the bases for political action. And specifically political action is appropriate because *collective* consumption is so evidently shaped by politicians and administrators.

So, as state intervention in the provision and allocation of collective goods increases, we should expect more political action to be organised around consumption issues, and this may well bring together some who, in class terms, are unlikely bedfellows. As the importance of consumption issues rises so the salience of class interests rooted in the production system recedes and support for those political parties that grew out of the long-established class divisions becomes less coherent and predictable. Moreover, recognition of *class* interests is impeded by the relatively rapid changes in the occupational structure and the apparent diversification of the two big blocs of 'middle class' and 'working class'. In these circumstances much conflict becomes 'de-institutionalised'; traditional agencies of representation – not just the political parties – are by-passed in the search for novel means of political expression. Inevitably this means that much of the action is sporadic, many of the associations ephemeral or schismatic. But the climate of doubt and criticism, the availability of ideologies stressing the need for participation and political innovation ensures easy regeneration of grass-roots political activity.

Protest: the local bases
But why should we argue that in assessing contemporary social conflict we need to look particularly at the city and the region rather than say the political or administrative processes in Westminster and Whitehall? Quite simply, it seems that it is through local agencies that national decisions about welfare provision, housing, transport,

education and medical services are implemented and often local politics leads to significant variations in those national policies. Thus, it is the local offices of state bureaucracies or the administrative and political institutions of local government which most obviously affect people, and it is to these institutions that they have some immediate access; it is in these that they see the prospect of bringing about change.

One way of interpreting the recent urban and regional discontent is to see much of it as a response to a kind of alienation. It is concerned with the conspicuous impotence of the citizenry *vis-à-vis* the legislators and administrators. A great deal of protest activity is directed to this problem; it attempts to establish or re-establish a measure of popular control, it tries to resist the threats to identity. Homes, neighbourhoods, schools, local places of entertainment have always contributed to an individual's sense of identity and security but to the extent that work for many people in a contemporary industrial society becomes less absorbing of energies and commitments, to the extent that position in the systems of consumption becomes more important, so they acquire greater significance.

For most people the network of social contacts, the groups and associations in which they participate, the places in which they meet and spend their leisure are mainly local; the boundaries of their social and cultural life are to a large extent given by their town and the district they live in. The resources on which they depend for the creation of their cultural life are therefore mainly local. Not surprisingly then, people fight to defend resources such as schools, shopping areas, pubs and places of recreation which are subject to manipulation and sometimes to destruction at the behest of public agencies.

Today many important confrontations occur away from the places of work. Groups of citizens now find themselves facing up to those who threaten them in their non-work lives and it is not the working class alone which is threatened. For while it is the poorer sectors of the population who are most dependent on public provision of housing or welfare payments and most subject to arbitrary and oppressive controls, the growth of state power impinges on the lives of all citizens. Thus, we find businessmen affected by planning decisions and by the development strategies of regional and urban authorities; we find middle class citizens taking to the streets, demonstrating inside and outside town halls and breaking up public inquiries. Schemes to destroy and rebuild old quarters of our cities may impinge on many diverse groups: ageing workers, students, small businessmen and others may have their homes and livelihoods threatened in the name of progress. And the threats come from faceless agencies whose executives are elusive, whose decisions are made with reference to esoteric and abstract criteria. What is most resented is the sense of being manipulated and of having so little capacity to respond.

At the very moment where non-work life has become more extensive for families and individuals, the capacity for political and bureaucratic manipulation of these elements has greatly increased. The protests are as much as anything about winning back a measure of freedom, security and identity through resisting arbitrary change of the environment – social as well as physical – in which people are set. These are the objects of the new struggles. Since 1970 in Britain we have seen rent strikes and squatting campaigns; innumerable community action groups consisting of residents and tenants' associations involved in direct, defiant confrontations with planners and politicians; groups formed to oppose transport plans, to protect the environment, to oppose or to urge industrial development, to contest educational changes and a host of other manifestations of discontent (Perman, 1972; Donnison, 1973; Leonard, 1975; O'Malley, 1975; Wates, 1976; Bell and Newby, 1977). All of this takes place in a society supposedly remarkable for its political stability (Verba, 1965; McKenzie and Silver, 1968; Rose, 1974).

Such a sudden increase in unconventional politics, such a surge of protest and defiance must surely signal some major structural changes as well as some evident inadequacies in the institutionalised means of representation and democratic control.

The threat of bureaucratic domination

The major change in our view is the rise of the new stratum of highly educated professionals and semi-professionals. Much of the protest in the city, and indeed broader protest too, is directed against them and understandably so. For this group exercises control over the burgeoning public property, the vast stock of funds and resources which is *collectively* consumed. The growth of state intervention, the growth of systems of collective consumption and the rise of this stratum go hand in hand. A great many of the jobs in education, public administration, the health and welfare services did not exist twenty years ago. They are the product of massive state intervention. This bureaucratised intelligentsia moderates the day-to-day flow of public goods and services and exercises the powers to license, inspect and regulate many forms of economic activity.

Of course, it may be objected, this power is limited and conditional. Ultimately the public bureaucrats are, like their counterparts in the corporations, subject to the will of others – in their case the will of the politicians. The elected representatives in the town halls determine the budgets and can hire or fire. If in practice dismissals are rather rare, that is probably because the mere threat of the sack is sufficient to bring a recalcitrant official back in line. Or, going beyond this, it is argued, because business interests, and particularly property industry interests, are so obviously well represented in the council chambers, we should see that the planners and managers of municipal affairs really dance to the tune of the finance capitalists and real estate developers. There is much truth in all of this and the case has been well argued by a number of authors (Counter Information Services, 1973; Lorimer, 1972; 1978; Ambrose and Colenutt, 1975). But it does not amount to a total denial of the power of the bureaucrats for it is quite obvious that the relationship between politicians and officials varies widely (Hill, 1972) and that 'bureaucracy-directed government' does occur. Nor can it be denied that bureaucrats have interests of their own which are by no means always congruent with those of politicians. If, at all levels, the ranks of the bureaucrats have grown, that is in some measure the result of their skill, their effectiveness in extending the scope of their various bureaux, adding research capabilities to their administrative tasks and generally proliferating the hierarchies of office. We are not talking here of some trivial processes of featherbedding individual careers; what is at stake is the growth and regeneration of a stratum. Bureaucrats in town halls and officials in welfare agencies and the health service have skilfully used the 'model' of the traditional professions to win for themselves a considerable autonomy, a capacity to sustain and recreate these occupational niches. If, bureaucrats are really very vulnerable to political authority then one should see considerable reductions in their ranks when local or national govern-

ments committed to 'rolling back the state' take charge. We know
of no very good evidence that this has happened, and even with the
election of a new 'radical' Tory government in Westminster we
doubt that it will happen.

What we are looking at is the possibility of bureaucratic usurpation
and domination. The stock of public resources is now so large,
the areas into which municipal and other public control now reaches
are so extensive, that we must surely concede the *possibility* of illegitimate extensions of power and authority, the considerable tempta-
tions to hoodwink councillors or unorganised publics.

The power of bureaucrats in local governments rests on several
things. First, and most obviously, on the capacity to shape the flow
of goods and services to determine, within limits, who shall benefit
from municipal largesses. Often, indeed, mostly, their discretionary
powers favour the dominant economic interests in an area. But the
pattern is not invariable, for there is nothing inevitable about this.
It is contingent upon the precise political and economic structure
in which they are embedded. Just as significantly, for our purposes,
routine disposition of resources puts these members of the 'service'
stratum in a position where, through a good deal of dickering with
the politicians they can utilise public funds to foster the growth
of positions to be filled by others like themselves. And, at this point
we should be careful not to confine ourselves to local government
officials, for alongside the regular bureaucracies there have emerged
a whole host of new 'authorities' – the so-called quangos – whose
actions and decisions are subject to extremely weak forms of account-
ability.

Secondly, the power of the new stratum, and especially of those
of its members in public agencies rests not on material, but on moral
force. Principally, bureaucratic power works through the rule of
law – ever refining and developing it, but bureaucratic influence
for its day-to-day operation also establishes moral conventions,
and it is these customary rules governing say, the queuing for scarce
resources or defining eligibility, which probably do most to facilitate
the illegitimate extension of bureaucratic power. The growth of
bureaucratic control has created the moral subjugation of large
parts of the population amounting in some areas to an abject dependency on those who manage public property. Such is the scale
of public resources that trends towards bureaucratic domination

affect not only the working class, but many 'middle class' people too. Today, bureaucrats, like priests, are arbiters of moral worth, only for them it is not knowledge of sacred tradition but 'expertise' which legitimates this function.

Like all groups seeking to consolidate or extend their power, the bureaucratised intelligentsia, is engaged in processes of cultural appropriation. Indeed, the manipulation of a society's system of symbols is something at which this stratum excels. It manipulates the cultural life of the working class when it plans the 'renewal' of old inner city districts, changing the physical environment in ways which inhibit old patterns of sociability, and controlling the admission of leisure and recreational resources in the 'renewed' environment according to its own criteria of desirability. And it has other means at its disposal. Through television, radio, newspapers and journals it can exercise considerable influence, much of it, of course, is supportive of bourgeois society, helping to shape audiences, tastes and needs in ways which facilitate commercial exploitation. But it is through these same channels that the messages critical of bourgeois cultural standards are conveyed, that the 'demoralising' of capitalism occurs. The cultural force of the new stratum is perhaps most evident when we consider how public bodies determine the content of education, give grants and subsidies to approved art forms and generally mould the cultural environment. Increasingly the canons of approval or disapprobation are established not by the bourgeoisie, but by a bureaucratised intelligentsia. Finally, one might argue that the tastes and values, the patterns of consumption – the life-styles – of this stratum become powerful visible models to be sought after and emulated. Thus, we can watch the insidious processes of cultural domination at work.

The rising stratum not only has economic and cultural resources at its command: it has also been gaining political strength. In debates and protests over many aspects of urban development it has often been alleged that the elected representatives were a poor match for the 'expert' officials in the municipal bureaucracies – that they lacked the appropriate background and training to allow them to scrutinise and criticise planning proposals effectively. One response to this situation has been for the major parties to try to reassert political mastery by matching the expertise of the officials. Thus, it looks as though more and more councillors are being drawn

from the ranks of the professionally qualified, and those with experience of 'professionalised protest' (Elliott et al. 1978) are most welcome
in either party. When we consider that the tendency to recruit
from this same stratum has also been a feature of national politics
(Johnson 1973) it begins to lend credence to the idea that traditional
groups – both bourgeois and proletarian – are being displaced by an
'ascending' group.

Attempts at incorporation

Many forms of popular protest are directed against the local politicians and the permanent officials in local government in ways
which indicate just how fundamentally 'consumption' interests
divide the population. Thus, we encounter a plethora of associations
representing the homeless or defending squatters' rights, a great
many 'community action' groups typically in the old working class
areas or in the new public housing estates, fighting for better provision
not just of housing but of transport, nurseries, play areas, shops
and recreation facilities. They experience first-hand the moral
authority of the municipal bureaucrats and often, the indifference of
politicians. Frequently they allege their interests are neglected while
other groups, for example the owner-occupiers, are favoured.

For their part, some owner-occupiers form themselves into
'parties' – ratepayers' associations – with the intention of restraining
the perceived 'profligacy' of the public officials and the 'subsidies'
given to council house tenants. We find privileged groups occupying
desirable suburban environments forming defence associations to
prevent the building of public housing in their territories (Young
and Kramer, 1978).

There are environmental groups protesting about industrial
pollution, the building of nuclear power stations or the disposal
of nuclear waste. There are 'conservation' groups urging programmes
of rehabilitation rather than new construction, groups lobbying
for or against new road construction, groups advocating the expansion of public transport systems and a host of others.

Efforts are constantly made to encapsulate these discontents in
the conventional framework of 'left' and 'right', to tie them to
underlying class divisions, to give them coherence and ideological
force. Thus local Labour parties from time to time attempt to harness
the enthusiasm of community action groups to their own political

purposes. Community action groups themselves have established a
network of communications to publicise problems, to advertise
successful methods of protest and to coordinate campaigns on
symbolically important issues. CDP workers in many parts of the
country have played an important role in widening political appre-
ciation of urban problems and encouraging a more refined and
radical critique.

Ratepayers' groups, proclaiming their non-partisanship, enter
the political arena directly, and in recent years there have been
attempts to deliver their support to more militant class based
organisations. At the height of the 1973–4 inflationary crisis, there
were threats of 'rates strikes' and one of the national leaders of the
ratepayers' groups approached General Walker and his Civil
Assistance organisation with the aim of making ratepayers' associations part of the envisaged network of 'apprehensive patriots'
available to ensure that essential services were maintained in the
event of a general strike.

New associations of bourgeois elements have appeared arguing
that there is a need to 're-educate' the middle class, that the problems
of the society are at root moral problems, that free enterprise is the
pre-condition for freedom. Groups such as the National Association
for Freedom (NAFF) and many of the petit bourgeois associations
such as the Association of Self-Employed People or the National
Federation of the Self-Employed specifically identify the growth of the
new bureaucratic stratum as a major source of the 'demoralisation' of
British society. Some such as NAFF (or 'The Freedom Association' as
it now calls itself) actively intervene in local authority affairs, urging
tax cuts and the breaking of closed-shop agreements. They see themselves confronting both labour and the bureaucratised professionals
in their attempts to 'remoralise' capitalism. Their reaction is one of
fear: the fear of the old enemy, labour, and the fear that a rising
stratum within the middle class has interests significantly different
from their own and is seeking to extend its power.

Overall, it seems unlikely that attempts by either 'right' or 'left'
will easily incorporate the new protests into the old framework of
class politics.

Conclusion

Despite the efforts of the traditional bourgeois and other elements the growth of public agencies, of state intervention, of forms of collectivism will surely continue, but the growth of collectivism, as Harrington points out (1979) could lead to markedly different situations.

> On the one extreme, there could be an authoritarian, or totalitarian collectivism run by a bureaucratic class; on the other, there could be a democratic communitarianism with considerable decentralisation and self-management.
>
> (1979, p. 25)

Popular protest and aggressive, innovative, disrespectful forms of political action are essential if the power of the new stratum is to be limited. And that is recognised most clearly perhaps by 'dissidents' from the ranks of the bureaucratised professionals, those planners, lawyers and educators who can so readily be found at the head of the parades, leading or advising the protestors.

If the cities today are 'noisy' places that is not to be regretted, not to be compared adversely to the consensus, the relative tranquility of some imagined time past. Rather it is to be welcomed, for that combination of political cynicism and political competence (Marsh, 1977) now so pervasive among the relatively young and highly educated is probably our best safeguard against the threats of bureaucratic domination and our best hope for some renewal of public life in our cities.

4 Racism and Capitalist Decline
Robert Miles and *Annie Phizacklea*

Introduction

In its White Paper, *Policy for the Inner Cities*, the Labour government suggests that the contemporary problem of the 'inner city' consists of a number of different dimensions: economic decline, physical decay, social disadvantage and ethnic minorities (1977c, pp. 2–5). We are told that ethnic minorities constitute an element of the 'inner city problem' because, like previous immigrants they have tended to settle in the inner areas of major conurbations: as a consequence they share with other residents the disadvantages of 'inner city life'. But if they share these disadvantages why distinguish them as 'ethnic minorities'? The reason must therefore lie in the subsequent reference to 'their special needs' which, we are told, are to be taken into account when planning and implementing 'inner city' policies, although what those needs actually are is not specified.[1] As an exercise in clarity of analysis, these paragraphs therefore leave much to be desired.

We believe that there is an unstated, but perhaps more important, reason why the presence of 'ethnic minorities' has been singled out for special attention, a reason which is cogently summed up by Sivanandan: 'the forced concentration of immigrants in the deprived and decaying areas of the big cities highlighted (and reinforced) existing social deprivation; racism defined them as its cause' (1976, p. 350). It goes on to point out that the Notting Hill 'riots' in 1958 indicated that racism was becoming socially counterproductive and had therefore to be 'managed'. Twenty years later the process continues: periodic outbreaks of conflict are met with periodic injections of money and schemes for the 'inner city'. But in the course of those twenty years the inner areas of our cities have continued to decline as a result of, as the White Paper admits, 'social and economic forces which could be reversed only with great difficulty or at unacceptable cost' (1977c, p. 5) and the white working class who remain have continued (with the support of certain politicians and racist parties) to blame the black people for that decline.

Thus we agree with Paris when he argues that 'race is a crucial issue at the heart of the government concern' about the "inner city"' (1978, p. 165) despite the fact that the Government was coy about saying so in the White Paper. But it is necessary to be clear about what it is that is specifically 'racial': we argue that it is not race but racism which is a crucial element of the 'inner city' crisis (Phizacklea and Miles, 1981). In the course of our research in the southern part of the old borough of Willesden we have attempted to gain a fuller understanding of the content, extent and the basis of working-class racism and the intention of this paper is both to reconsider and to expand our arguments on this subject (Phizacklea and Miles, 1979). We begin with a brief recapitulation of our basic position.

Working-class racism in the 'inner city'

Racism is a concept which refers to the ideological element in the social process of racial categorisation. This process involves the identification of a group in terms of some physical or biological feature and attributes other, negatively evaluated, physical and/or social characteristics in a deterministic manner to that group. Reference to these features can subsequently be made to justify the exclusion of the group from equal access to goods, services and rights.

We talk of working-class racism when those initiating and/or confirming the process of racial categorisation occupy a structurally determined position in production relations that excludes them from control over investment or the physical means of production. Such a position ensures that they do not control the labour power of others and that they must either sell their labour power for a wage or, if not directly involved in the wage labour relation, are dependent upon that sale (Wright, 1976; Gardiner, 1977; Poulantzas, 1978).

In the context of those 'inner city' areas which contain black residents, we believe that the racism of the white working class is best understood not simply in terms of the racial stereotypes inherent in British culture but also in relation to the socio-economic decline and competition for scarce resources which characterise such areas. By documenting both the objective economic and social decline of the old borough of Willesden in London, and the working-class perceptions of the problems of that area (and hence its decline) we have shown how the white working class 'can immediately identify the cause of their problems in the very presence of black people in the area . . . working-class racist beliefs . . . are therefore an attempt to understand and explain *immediate daily experience*, while the real reasons for both the socio-economic decline and New Commonwealth immigration are to be found in much more abstract and long standing social and economic processes' (1978, p. 118).

Our original analysis focused only upon the racism of the male, manual working class and did not consider the beliefs of the female working class. We rectify that omission here and show how their racism is equally grounded in the material realities of working-class life in the 'inner city'. Second, it can be argued that our original analysis failed to take account of what might be termed the *ideological context* of working-class racism. That is to say, we neglected to compare the extent to which our respondents attributed the material decline of the 'inner city' to the presence of black workers with the extent to which they believed other factors were responsible. We shall evaluate this criticism in relation to a further analysis of our data. Third, an understanding of the nature and extent of racism in the 'inner city' does not necessarily tell us very much about the nature and extent of social and political action that has black people as its specific object. We consider this issue, again in connection with further findings from our research in northwest London. But before taking up these points, we briefly consider the validity of the 'inner city' concept and the possibility of generalising our analysis based on data collected from a small area of London to other 'inner city' areas.

The 'inner city' concept

We believe that there are at least two reasons for arguing that the 'inner city' concept is misleading (Phizacklea and Miles, 1981). First, it implies a spatial location which is not always found in reality. For example, it is difficult to argue that the old borough of Willesden is part of London's 'inner city' in a geographical sense. Rather, it is a section of one of three concentric rings (Lomas, 1975, p. 5) and not part of an inner core. Second, much common usage of the concept implies the existence of some new phenomenon, urban decay. However, not only is urban decay not a new phenomenon but, moreover, the use of the concept should not be allowed to disguise its underlying dynamic, i.e. *capitalist* decline. The work of the Community Development Projects have clearly shown that 'The events which are shaking Britain's older towns and inner cities are the end product of a much wider process of economic change' (1977, p. 5).

We here use the 'inner city' concept as a shorthand way of identifying those urban areas which were once a centre of capitalist production but which are currently undergoing socio-economic decline as a consequence of a downward turn in the cycle of that mode of production. In the next section, we shall elucidate briefly the growth, maturity and decline of capitalist production in Willesden and then argue that the downward turn has provided a particular dynamic to working class racism in the area. It is relevant to note here that evidence from the Inner Area Studies suggests that similar ideas are articulated in other areas of capitalist decline, allowing us to conclude that our findings relating to Willesden have more general applicability (Birmingham Inner Area Study, 1974; 1977a; 1977b; Lambeth Inner Area Study, 1974; Department of the Environment, 1977a).

Willesden: a declining centre of capitalist production[2]
Until the early twentieth century, the old borough of Willesden was first an agricultural area and then, from the mid-nineteenth century, a pleasant dormitory suburb, which retained a rural character. Railway construction between central London and Willesden, and subsequently between London and the Midlands, was an important factor in both the development of the dormitory suburb and the later industrialisation of the area. The initial phase of industrialisation occurred between 1900 and 1910 with the establishment of light engineering, printing and foundaries at various sites in Willesden. But a substantial industrial development began after World War I with the establishment of many small manufacturing firms on what became the Park Royal industrial estate. By the mid-1930s, many of these firms had grown substantially and Willesden was dominated industrially by four major activities: car production, general and electrical engineering, chemical production and food and drink manufacture. These were all 'new' industries, and many developed to supply the emerging 'luxury' consumer goods market which had London as its centre.

Immediately after World War I, and before the large industrial expansion of the mid-1920s, the area was subject to a slow but continuing population growth and an increasing shortage of housing. Industrial expansion and the related movement of large numbers of workers into the area in the 1920s and 1930s served only to aggravate this housing problem, which was developing; the consequence was overcrowding and deteriorating housing standards. It was a problem that World War II did nothing to solve and although after the war slum clearance and council building began, this had little effect. By the early 1950s, it was recognised that Willesden had housing and sanitary conditions which were worse than anywhere else in Middlesex (Leff and Blunden, nd). The increasing rate of council building in the 1960s and 1970s, together with rehabilitation and improvement, may have improved the situation somewhat, but Brent Council believes that the borough will continue to face a severe housing problem for many years to come (Borough of Brent, 1977).

Our argument is then that the current housing problem in Willesden is not a recent creation: it has existed for at least fifty years and has been caused in the final analysis by the inability of private capital to meet the demand for accommodation which has accompanied the movement of labour into the borough to take up jobs in what was, until the mid-1960s, an expanding industrial area. This, however, is no longer the case and since the 1960s Willesden has experienced a considerable decline in the total number of jobs in manufacturing industry within its boundaries. However, the number of *Brent* residents actually employed in manufacturing industry has been declining since 1951 (Borough of Brent, 1977). The major part of the decline has been in those industries that provided the industrial basis to the growth of Willesden: the few 'replacement industries' (e.g. warehousing) are far less labour-intensive. But it is only recently that unemployment has risen substantially in Willesden, primarily because of the national economic recession. The area's continuing dependency upon manufacturing industry for employment means that the continuation of the recession will have an increasingly disproportionate effect on this area. It is important to note in this context that black workers in Brent have, since the mid-1970s, constituted well over a third of the number of registered unemployed (Borough of Brent, 1977).

It is therefore possible to trace a process of industrial development and decline in Willesden which is similar to that occurring in other parts of Britain. In Willesen the cycle can be traced over a relatively short period of time, some fifty years. The movement of black migrant labour into the area in the late 1950s and 1960s post-dated both the shortage of housing and the preconditions of industrial decline. Far from being the cause of these problems, black migrant workers have been the victims of economic and social processes over which they have little or no influence.

Politically, the predominantly working-class nature of Willesden is reflected in the Labour party's electoral domination of the area since 1945. The local labour movement as a whole has campaigned to combat racism locally, particularly since the electoral intervention of the National Front in 1974. The NF has remained electorally weak in the area in comparison with other parts of London: it captured only 2 per cent of the total vote cast in the local council elections in 1978.

Willesden: the data

The data we now present and discuss were collected as part of a larger study of political conceptualisation and action amongst the English and West Indian manual working class. Thus, our data does not permit a comparison with non-manual workers because it was not designed to do so. We chose as our method of data collection a combination of participant observation and in-depth interviewing in preference to a large-scale sample survey.

There were two main samples, a factory sample and a residential sample. Concerning the former, observation and interviewing took place in a large food processing firm (Food Co.) employing approximately 2400 individuals and situated on an industrial estate on the southern edge of Brent. Of the total number of employees, approximately 2000 were hourly-paid and were engaged in some form of manual job. It was from these manual workers that a sample of 72 semi- and unskilled individuals were interviewed. The sample was divided equally into English and West Indian male respondents, aged 25 to 40 years. The analysis below refers only to the English respondents (N-36).

The residential sample of 77 persons was, likewise, divided into English and West Indian respondents but differed from the factory sample in that about half of the total were women. The analysis here refers only to men and women aged between 25 and 50 years of English parentage. Although efforts were made to locate respondents in both the private and public housing sectors, an increasingly ageing population of English parentage resulted in a shortfall of eligible English interviewees in the private sector. Of the 36 interviews reported on here 31 were conducted on two new development estates with nearly the full quota of interviews being completed on the first estate to be sampled. Both estates have been built in the past six years and contain a high proportion of minority group families, mainly West Indians. Over this period of time, it has been estimated that about 50 per cent of lettings in the public sector have gone to minority group families in Brent.

Thus while there is a high degree of residential uniformity in this sample, it is occupationally diverse in comparison with the factory sample. According to our earlier definition, women home-workers and routine office workers are classified as working class. Of the 19 men reported on, 15 are engaged in semi- and unskilled manual jobs and 4 in skilled. Of the 17 women, 7 are currently engaged in full-time childcare and housework. All of these women had worked up until the time they had borne their first child, and all stated their intention to return to work when the youngest was old enough to attend a nursery or primary school. Three of the women in the sample are engaged in routine office work, another was an unemployed skilled worker and the remainder were engaged in semi- and unskilled manual work.

The ideological context of working class racism

The data we report on is drawn from in depth interviews with the individuals in both samples. None of our interviewees were aware that we were employed by the Research Unit on Ethnic Relations, nor did we indicate any special interest in their views on black people. As we have already reported (1979, p. 108), all our respondents were asked to identify what they believed to be the local problems of the Willesden area and additionally the residential sample were asked what they thought of the area as a place to live. We can now evaluate the extent to which black people are defined as a 'local problem' as against other 'problems'. Table 4.1 shows that the single most frequently mentioned 'problem' for both samples was articulated as 'coloured people/coloured immigrants'. Varied references to

Table 4.1   *Perceived local problems in residential and factory samples*

	Residential sample* (per cent)		Factory sample⁺ (per cent)
'Coloured people/coloured immigrants'	33	(M = 37) (F = 29)	39
Mugging	33	(M = 31.5) (F = 35)	8
Housing	19	(M = 16) (F = 23.5)	30
Inadequate social services, public transport, social facility	28	(M = 31.5) (F = 23.5)	14
Work	5.5	(M = 10.5) (F = 0)	28
Noise	25	(M = 16) (F = 35)	—
Kids as a nuisance	19	(M = 5) (F = 35)	3
Vandalism	17	(M = 16) (F = 18)	—
Area is rough	14	(M = 5) (F = 23.5)	—
Education	11	(M = 5) (F = 18)	—
Inflation	8	(M = 5) (F = 12)	6
Traffic/parking	—		6
Problem families	5.5	(M = 5) (F = 6)	—
Don't know	—		11

* N = 36 (Male = 19; Female = 17)
⁺ N = 36

decline were the most popular response to the question on the area 'as a place to live', although decline and coloured immigration would appear to be synonymous in the minds of some of our respondents. But the following quotes are illustrative of how respondents perceived the 'coloureds' as a 'local problem'.

The coloured people I think. I think they are taking over. Willesden's covered with them. Then there's the Asians. The Londoners are moving out into the country because it's the only place they can live nowadays .... I got nothing against them. There's too many of them. They run the transport. They can get houses from the Council. I can't. My mum said I would make a fortune if I was black.

> (Male, semi-skilled factory worker)

If I could get a job elsewhere with the money I'd move out. Perhaps I'm colour prejudiced but I see them come out of that school there 5 whites to a 100 immigrants and it affects the standard of education.

> (Male, lorry driver)

The second most commonly identified 'problem' was 'mugging', references being very prominent amongst the residential sample but less so amongst the factory sample. Many of the references to 'mugging' link what is seen as this comparatively new form of crime to the general decline of the area:

No way do I want my children to grow up here. You only have to read the local paper and you'll find out what it's like. Ten years ago you'd never hear about muggings in this area or people frightened to go out at night. It's wrong. I'm not saying it's all one people, it's six of one and half a dozen of another.

> (Male, skilled worker)

Many references to 'mugging' indicated implicitly that the respondent believed it to be a specifically black crime, though some references were explicit:

The highest place for muggings are the Brixton and Harlesden areas and around there where there are a lot of coloured immigrants. I suppose in ten years time this place will be what Harlem is to New York.

> (Male, semi-skilled factory worker)

The 'problems' of 'noise', 'kids are a nuisance', vandalism and education are also residentially concentrated and, additionally, are more likely to be referred to by women than men. Like 'mugging', these 'problems' particularly 'noise' are also often linked, explicitly or implicitly with the presence of 'the coloureds':

Well the noise and the vandalism that goes on. Out on that play area it's disgraceful in the evenings. The noise is terrible and my

boy is the only white child down there after 6 p.m. in the evenings.
(Female home-worker)

We have West Indians mainly around here and they're so darned noisy and so indifferent to other people's feelings, they have noisy night parties and things like this, you have music playing until 2 and 3 in the morning and when they play it it's really loud.
(Male, skilled worker)

Certain other 'problems' were identified by our white working class samples. Housing, work and the provision of social services, public transport and social facilities are referred to by more than a quarter of the respondents in one or other of the two samples. Housing was seen as 'problem' in a number of senses, as being low in quality, expensive and in short supply, while work was a 'problem' in the sense that jobs were difficult to find, the closing down of factories being commonly mentioned as a cause. The following quotations illustrate the respondent's concerns:

Well at the moment I should say work, with the industries moving out. I can remember when this estate round here was booming and there was talk then that Food Co. was the highest paid factory. Now it's like a ghost town.
(Male, semi-skilled factory worker)

I don't think there's much going on in this area for anyone of any age group, only pubs. There aren't any youth clubs. The kids have nowhere to go and so you see them hanging about in gangs and causing trouble. I would like to see more youth clubs in the area.
(Male semi-skilled factory worker)

Finally, many of our younger respondents (particularly in the residential sample) explicitly spoke of decline in the area in their lifetime and the departure of age cohorts:

The area is going downhill a bit now, we're getting too many problem families and that's bringing the area down. A lot of the young couples have moved to the new towns and problem families move in.
(Male, unskilled)

My really close friend moved to Scotland because she and her hubby said London holds nothing for them. She blames it on the coloured people but I don't think that has a lot to do with it all. You hear of all the young people going to Milton Keynes and you wonder if you will be the only one of your age group left.

(Female houseworker)

So, amongst our interviewees there was a strong sense of 'material' disadvantage and/or decline, whether in terms of housing, employment or social facilities or services. In addition, and this was the case only for the residential sample, there was a common belief that the Willesden area was socially disadvantaged ('mugging', noise, 'kids are a nuisance', vandalism). But the most commonly mentioned single 'problem' was 'the coloureds' or 'coloured immigrants', a 'problem' perceived to be interlinked with the perceptions of material and social decline.

Our respondents were also asked if they saw housing as a problem locally and, if so, were asked what had caused it to be a problem. As can be seen from Table 4.2, the latter question elicited a small but significant number of 'don't know' responses from the factory workers which is probably explained by a certain lack of specifically localised experience amongst members of this sample. But, taking the two samples together, it is the failure to deal with the problem of scarcity in housing which emerges as the most commonly attributed explanation. Our category of 'failure to develop and/or improve property' includes simply shortage in itself, shortage of decent housing and the failure to take action over empty houses in the area:

Well one thing is the places that they leave to stand empty for long lengths of time. Where I was living before there was places empty for three years. I don't think it was the council, I think it was a firm that bought them and moved the people out to remodernise them and left them half done for three years. When something like that happens you would think the council would approach them. That is terrible when so many people want them houses.

(Female, unskilled worker)

There isn't enough to go round and there isn't enough decent council property, people don't want to go into high rise flats. The people that build them live in a green belt somewhere.

(Female, houseworker)

Table 4.2 Explanations for the local housing problem in residential and factory samples

	Residential sample* (per cent)		Factory sample+ (per cent)
'Coloured people/coloured immigrants'	30	(M = 37) (F = 23.5)	17
Failure to develop/ improve property	28	(M = 16) (F = 41)	30
Overpopulation	17	(M = 21) (F = 10.5)	14
Modern development	11	(M = 10.5) (F = 10.5)	14
High rent/cost of property	3	(M = 0) (F = 6)	14
Abuse of the system	5.5	(M = 5) (F = 6)	—
Immigration	5.5	(M = 5) (F = 6)	—
Government policy	—		6
Don't know	—		19
No answer	8	(M = 5) (F = 6)	6

*N = 36 (Male = 19; Female = 17)
+N = 36

However, 'Asians' (particularly Ugandan) and 'coloureds' take the highest proportion of blame in the residential sample. Unlike for at least a proportion of the factory sample, there is, for the residential sample, an immediate source of conflict over a particular scarce resource – public housing, an explanation which is given additional support by the large percentage of the residential sample who believe that blacks receive preferential treatment in the allocation of council housing. Thus, while over a quarter of the residential sample are willing to admit that the problem is one of scarcity, a similar proportion attribute the cause of the housing problem to 'illegitimate' competitors for council housing. For this proportion, it is the very presence of black people in council housing that causes a high level of resentment among our respondents and results in their blaming the 'coloureds' and the 'Asians' for scarcity itself. The following quotes are illustrative:

> They should scatter the immigrants a bit more. When they took all those Asians from Uganda, they took God knows many thousands into Brent.
>
> (Female, houseworker)

> Housing is a major problem. You've got all the coloureds here and all the whites are moving out, even though its difficult to make the move.
>
> (Male, lorry driver)

The residential sample were also asked if they thought the method of council house allocation was fair. The majority thought that it was not and, again, as this interview extract shows, black people are commonly perceived as part of the reason why the procedure was unfair:

> This borough bends over backwards to help the blacks. In this borough, they have built enough houses in the last ten years to rehouse every single family here yet we still have 7000 on the waiting list. The Asians come straight in and the people who have been on the waiting list have no chance.
>
> (Male, unskilled council worker)

Other 'causes' of the housing problem were seen as 'overpopulation' (an explanation which often implicitly refers to 'Asians' and 'coloureds') and 'modern development' (only one of our council tenants actually said that she liked living on a new estate and most had refused to live in a high rise block). Thus, once more, material explanations become entwined with the perception that the coloureds and Asians are to blame for the scarcity of housing, particularly council housing.

However, as a sharp contrast to the data presented in the preceding paragraphs, it is the absence of references to blacks and the predominance of material explanations which is one of the most striking features of the explanations for local unemployment as shown in Table 4.3. The most common explanations focus on some of the factors that have stimulated factory closures and rationalisation, although it must be added that the underlying dynamics of capitalist production are not necessarily identified:

> All I can say about this area is that the rateable value of the industrial property is really high. I work for a small company and we know that if it wasn't for us renting space from another one, they would have to close down.
>
> (Male, skilled worker)

> Well, I think they want to get out to where the land, the labour is cheaper. Even if it's only one or two pounds cheaper, it's a lot of money added up over the years. They can also go to those areas where the government subsidises them and also gives them money for every person that they hire. You can't blame them: that's the way capitalism works.
>
> (Male, semi-skilled factory worker)

Table 4.3   *Explanations for local unemployment/redundancies in residential and factory samples*

	Residential sample* (per cent)		Factory sample+ (per cent)
Rates/rents too high	28	(M = 53) (F = 0)	22
Low profits/rising costs	11	(M = 10.5) (F = 12)	20
Advantages of new towns	17	(M = 21) (F = 12)	8.0
Strikes/union power/ workers to blame	11	(M = 16) (F = 6)	22
Do not believe is a problem	—		11
Government policy	5.5	(M = 5) (F = 6)	11
Bad management/ overstaffing	5.5	(M = 10.5) (F = 0)	6
Immigration	5.5	(M = 10.5) (F = 0)	—
Don't know	25	(M = 16) (F = 35)	25
No answer	11	(M = 0) (F = 23.5)	—

*N = 36 (Male = 19; Female = 17)
+N = 36

The other striking feature of Table 4.3 is that about a quarter of the two samples said they did not know how to explain this 'problem', suggesting a fairly high level of simple ignorance. One possible explanation for this pattern of responses lies in the very recent decline in employment opportunities in Brent in comparison with the more chronic long-term housing shortage. It may also be relevant that the majority of our samples was either engaged in wage labour or not actively seeking paid employment and therefore not directly involved in competition for a job.

Finally we report on the explanations for national unemployment provided by our respondents and shown in Table 4.4. Once more the balance between ideological and purely material explanation

Table 4.4 *Explanations for national unemployment in residential and factory samples*

	Residential sample* (per cent)		Factory sample[+] (per cent)
Lazy workers/abuse of state benefits	25	(M = 26) (F = 23.5)	33
'Coloured people/coloured immigrants'	19	(M = 21) (F = 18)	13[a]
Inflation	14	(M = 10.5) (F = 18)	8
Rates too high	14	(M = 21) (F = 6)	—
Capitalism/profitability	11	(M = 16) (F = 6)	14
Government	3	(M = 5.5) (F = 0)	11
Low investment	11	(M = 16) (F = 6)	3
International competition/trade	—		8
Not a problem	—		8
Overpopulation	5	(M = 0) (F = 12)	—
Don't know	—		11
No answer	8	(M = 10.5) (F = 6)	—

* N = 36 (Male = 19; Female = 17)
[+] N = 36
[a] In our earlier paper (1979), this figure was incorrectly quoted as 6 per cent. Subsequent work has shown that this was due to a clerical error.

swings back in the direction of the former with 'strikes, union power, workers and idleness' receiving the greatest share of blame. It is in the course of these explanations that another scapegoat 'those who don't want to work' becomes prominent:

> I don't think a lot of them want to go to work. I think that's what it is myself. A lot of them rely on the dole. They get the money so why should they want to work.
>
> (Male, semi-skilled factory worker)

> I think a lot of it is people who don't want to work. I don't think the situation of people not being able to find work is as bad as it appears because people have things too easy with the welfare state.
>
> (Male, unskilled council worker)

But references to 'coloured workers/coloured immigrants' were also made, although not as often as in connection with the perception of 'local problems' or the perceived explanation for the 'local housing problem'. It is less easy to explain this in terms of the material decline of the 'inner city' not least because as shown in the preceding paragraph, the local manifestation of what is also a national issue did not elicit many racist explanations. It may therefore be that this question on national unemployment has tapped responses whose origin is to be traced to 'information' received from the media rather than from the immediate experience of working class life in the 'inner city'.

In a paper of this length we cannot present case studies or draw extensively on our observational data, but two points should be clear from the still partial (but nevertheless more complete, when taken with our first analysis) picture we have presented. Firstly, despite the fact that a majority of our sample does hold some racist beliefs (Phizacklea and Miles, 1979, p. 110), not one of our questions produced a majority of responses which can be labelled racist. Secondly, our respondents articulated both racist and other explanations for perceived problems and/or material decline, a fact which our mode of analysis and presentation both here and previously has tended to hide. Thus the racism of the majority of our sample cannot be described as a consistent ideology (the small minority who did exhibit such an ideology either supported, voted for or were once members of the National Front). Rather, and here we re-emphasise an earlier argument (1979, p. 117), we believe that racist ideas

abound along with many others often as equally vague and inconsistent as the racist ones, or indeed, with self-professed ignorance.
Some of these ideas indicate a reality half grasped, while others
suggest a complete misunderstanding of the socio-economic processes
that touch and to a considerable extent determine their lives. They
reflect both their own individual and collective experience as well as
messages mediated by the television and newspapers (Hartmann
and Husbands, 1974).

Racist ideas as action

But, it might be argued, racist ideas and explanations, however
commonplace, are of little consequence because what really matters
is what people do rather than what they say they believe. In a certain
sense this 'belief versus behaviour' distinction is a false one if the
beliefs are openly expressed both to other whites as well as to fellow
black workers and residents. The open expression of racist ideas
in the factory canteens, streets and estates of Willesden, even if only
by a minority, can, purely because they are not seriously challenged
(when they are it is by a small minority who are often dismissed as
'christians' or 'political activists' or both) serve to define a feeling
of solidarity amongst 'us' (the whites) and to establish a boundary
of exclusion against 'them' (the blacks). Interviews and more casual
conversations with black workers and residents showed that a
substantial minority were aware of the existence of these ideas,
and this led them to maintain a certain distance from their white
fellow workers and neighbours to ensure that they were not
directly abused. We believe, therefore, that it is mistaken to assume
that in the absence of actual physical violence or even active
discrimination (although these *were* evident to us) there must
be good 'race relations', a view which tended to predominate amongst
the management in the factory where interviewing and observation
occurred and is often voiced about Brent as a whole by casual
observers. After all, it is claimed, black and white workers live and
work side by side and no one seems to mind. But such observers
then find it difficult to explain the tension and evident restriction
of social contacts between the two groups following, for example,
the sacking of a black male worker for allegedly striking a white
female worker. This is even more true in the residential context,
where there is very rarely contact between black and white residents

because of a high level of tension. Such segregation becomes indirectly institutionalised when, for instance, a tenants' association on an estate with a majority of black residents has an all-white membership or when efforts to introduce tenant management results in no black tenants coming forward for election to the management committee or when the caretakers go on strike for what, even the housing department admits, are reasons containing elements of 'racialism'. In these circumstances, it is surely not difficult to comprehend the extent to which *racism* and its eradication is a fundamental task for any 'inner city' solution.

Discussion

We offer no easy solutions to the eradication of racism in the 'inner city' but we believe the following points are central to any debate on this issue.

We have stressed that the racism we found among our respondents is largely inchoate (cf. Nichols and Armstrong, 1976, pp. 148–52), and, even more significantly, in our research experience is so often unchallenged. We have also stressed the significance of racist explanations for material decline for our 'inner city' residents. What is of equal importance, and this is something which we previously underestimated, is that a proportion of our sample are at least partially aware of the material forces which create social and economic decline; thus racist explanations are not the only explanations. But the presence of such alternative explanations gives little ground for optimism in that no unanimous or even majority agreement on what constituted the significant local problems or an explanation for certain of these problems is apparent amongst our sample. Furthermore, while material reasons may be given as explanations for our four 'problem' areas, taking the interviews as a whole, 75 per cent of the sample express negative beliefs about black people. Thus our sample is composed of a majority group whose racism is piecemeal and whose understanding of social and economic processes is often very confused. Set against them is a minority, whose significance lies in their constituting the largest group to share a single ideological perspective, and their view of local and national political and economic developments is consistently related to their negative views on the presence of black people in Britain. The extent to which this minority can gain increased support from the larger 'reservoir' depends upon its ability to persuade others of the validity of the racist explanation. Anti-racist campaigns might make a significant intervention in this context in that they challenge the racist perspective and offer a competing interpretation of reality. But such campaigns must contend with the following facts.

First, we reiterate that working-class racism in the 'inner city' is not simply a complex of racial stereotypes inherited from an imperial past but is also an attempt to understand and explain immediate daily experience. Against this, arguments which attempt to explain socio-economic decline in terms of much more abstract and long-standing social and economic processes can seem quite unreal. But if the process of social and economic decline in the 'inner cities' were reversed and the material basis of working-class racism eradicated, the residue of culturally transmitted racism (which is widespread in British society) would still remain. Earlier we gave an illustrative quote from a young white woman who had challenged the racist explanation for 'inner city' decline. In the course of the interview she offered accurate material explanations for that decline but later over a cup of tea and informal chat she suggested that the black tenants did not seem to mind living in the high rise flats on the estate because it was probably a big improvement on mud huts. There were many other references of this nature: for example, Jack, a senior shop steward in the factory, who believed that black people 'had just come down from the trees with no more than a fig leaf over their bollocks'. Racial stereotypes persist in our culture and will probably do so for some time to come.

Second, and in line with the implication of the previous point, 'inner city' areas are not isolated from national political processes in the same way that they are not isolated from national or even international economic processes. Indeed, it can be argued that the 'inner city' context is perhaps the context in which the economic and political contradictions of capitalism most clearly manifest themselves. The 'racialisation' of British politics is of particular significance in the 'inner city' because the speeches of Enoch Powell, MP on immigration and the activities of the National Front can so easily be interpreted as legitimating those racist ideas which are an ideological product of material decline. For instance, when one of our male respondents was asked what were the main reasons for the high level of unemployment he answered:

A. Well the population is too big, isn't it?
Q. What could be done to reduce the level of unemployment?
A. Voluntary repatriation of the immigrants. I know that's the National Front but even Enoch suggested that and he's a Conservative, isn't he? The Government should look at the coloured people not working.

Thus any campaign against racism which has an 'inner city' context as its focus must also confront head-on those political forces which do much to legitimate it. Nor should the ambivalent postures adopted by the Conservative and Labour parties to racism be ignored. Both parties are pledged to fighting racism and to introducing measures to alleviate 'inner city' decline, yet British immigration policy, despite Labour party posturing to the contrary following the Conservative party's 'initiative' in early 1977, remains racist in both intent and effect. If governments face in two directions simultaneously on the issue of racism, then should we be surprised that racism in the 'inner city', or elsewhere, remains a reality?

Thirdly, any discussion of the future development or decline of racism in the 'inner city' must take into account the nature and direction of political beliefs and behaviour within the black working-class. We have elsewhere commented on this issue and do not have the space to develop it here (Miles and Phizacklea, 1977; 1979). Suffice it to say that the apparent low-profile approach of the original black immigrants to working-class racism has not prevented its articulation and its legitimation by certain politicians and racist political parties (Schoen, 1977; Husbands, 1979; Taylor, 1979), although a proportion of their children seem to be adopting a different and more aggressive strategy (Miles, 1978). Moreover Rex (1979) has suggested that black communities as a whole are beginning to adopt a strategy of defensive confrontation. The increased willingness of the black working class to defend itself verbally and physically against racism may serve to head off the latter's development, though the opposite outcome must also be considered as a possibility. But whatever the outcome, it will be affected by the political strategies adopted by the black working class.

Thus we would agree with other commentators (Taylor, 1978; Rex, 1978) that racism cannot be countered simply by measures designed to alleviate working class disadvantage in the 'inner city',[3] but we also believe that our evidence shows that there is a reservoir of support for a political movement which had as its focus both an opposition to racism and a commitment to the reversal of the process of social and economic decline in the 'inner city'. Whether any of the existing major political parties in Britain are capable of leading such a movement is another issue, but a continuous failure to challenge the racist explanation for material decline must leave the door open for those who gain by a working class divided by, amongst other things, racism.

5   Policy without Protest: the dilemma of organising for change in Britain
Robert Kraushaar

Introduction

'Routine drives out planning' is an axiom of organisational theory. Normally it simply means that the everyday pressures of decision-making preclude the opportunity to plan ahead – a tendency which Lindblom (1959) raised to the 'science of muddling through'. In the context of this paper, however, that axiom is given a broader meaning. 'Routine' here is defined as the daily workings of the capitalist state within a capitalist system and 'planning' as the planning and implementation of collective action by the working class.

This paper is an exploration of the 'routine' of the capitalist state and how it acts to preclude collective action at the community level. It is an effort to try and understand the role the state plays in creating this 'routine', the effect of this 'routine' on everyday life, and why past attempts explicitly aimed at 'planning' at the community level failed to do so. To facitiate this, the paper is divided into two sections. The first is a case study of the frustrations experienced by the North Tyneside Community Development Project (CDP) when it attempted to organise collective forms of action. The second section is a theoretical examination aimed at explaining the inherent difficulties faced by the project as well as many other community collective struggles.

The North Tyneside CDP

North Shields is typical of many older industrial areas in the north of England. Its initial growth was predicated on traditional heavy industries centred around the port (shipbuilding, marine and heavy engineering, etc.), industries which have long been declining and experiencing job loss. Employment in manufacturing originally increased after World War II, helping to compensate for this job loss, but during the 1960s it started to decline to the point where almost 15 per cent of the male jobs in manufacturing have disappeared. Women have become an increasing proportion of the labour force, both in the manufacturing and service sectors; in the latter they are still increasing in absolute numbers – albeit marginally. The population of the area has been declining since the 1930s and the unemployment rate has been higher than the national average for the same period.

It is an area going through the process of disinvestment, both in what is left of its traditional industries (shipbuilding being a good example) and in the newer manufacturing industries which are increasingly becoming subsidiaries of multinational corporations able to look elsewhere in Britain or abroad for cheaper labour, new resources and more favourable government support. The present economic difficulties in Britain have quickened this process, increasing the rapid erosion of North Tyneside's industrial base through factory rationalisations and closures, increasing structural unemployment, and causing massive public expenditure cuts (North Tyneside CDP, 1978a).

In 1973, just prior to the realisation and first effects of the present crisis, the North Tyneside CDP was formed. The local situation they confronted, then and now, is not much different from other older industrial areas (National CDP, 1977a). The frustrations they encountered while trying to effect change given that situation were also similar. For this reason the efforts of the North Tyneside CDP to effect collective action are typical of many other attempts, both within and without the CDP structure (National CDP 1975), and represent a general feeling of which this is but one expression.

There has been much written on the history and ideological struggles of the government-initiated CDPs (Mayo 1975; National CDP, 1977b). Originally the CDPs were to be small scale experiments seeking to ameliorate the worst excesses of the economic system by establishing information flows and communication links between the state and the communities in which the local projects were situated. They were to do this within an overall framework that defined poverty and deprivation as being caused by the social disabilities inherent in poor communities or by a lack of efficiency in local authority service systems. This is a good example of the tendency of the state to define problems as individualistic and/or technical in nature, and was clearly the dominant perspective at the time. All of the local project teams adopted this framework in varying degrees, at least initially.

In this respect the North Tyneside CDP was no exception, but in less than a year it had evolved what it considered a more radical and more relevant model of action.[1] This was a 'radical reformist' model of social action.

> Radical reformism is a class model of society, it is a process that involves fairly substantial change in one aspect of society but that in the end does not challenge the fundamental basis of society. . . . Expressed crudely, the difference between radical reformism and revolutionary perspectives is that the former does not aim at challenging industrial issues.
>
> (North Tyneside CDP, 1978b, p. 10)

The project's analysis of the political environment and its major objective within that environment were indicative of many analyses put forth during the 1970s, in the decade between the rediscovery of poverty and the public expenditure cuts.

> The context was seen as one of continuing growth with the issues arising from the disposition of the resources generated by that growth . . . . The objective was to establish working-class locality-based collectives to ensure that resources went one way as opposed to another.
>
> (North Tyneside CDP, 1978b, p. 1)

It is within this overall framework that the initial efforts of the North Tyneside CDP workers to promote positive collective action must be situated. To them, their activities were legitimated by the then growing dissatisfaction caused by the economic decline of the inner city coupled with the state's inability or unwillingness to arrest that decline. Their solution was to promote collective working-class action through work that was 'issue-centred, locality-centred, and local authority-centred' – in short a solution which was the same as many of the community action initiatives taking place in the country at the time.

During this time period, between 1973 and 1975, the CDP concentrated their efforts on two types of local community activities – information shops and neighbourhood action groups. Most of the local CDPs established information shops of one kind or another. These were storefront, high street centres where individuals could come for information, advice or assistance with personal problems, usually in relation to welfare or housing problems. This was a valuable community service which assisted thousands of people in ways such as reducing the level of uncertainty in their lives or helping them receive legally entitled state services (Canning Town CDP, 1974). In addition, however, these information and advice centres were used by the CDPs as a way of becoming known in the neighbourhoods, as a way of establishing their credibility, and as a way of 'specifying issues of common concern in an area, thereby enabling some kind of collective action to begin to take place' (North Tyneside CDP, 1975a, p. 6).

In North Tyneside there was a conscious effort to bring together individuals with similar problems so that they could attempt to solve them collectively. The great majority of these efforts, however, failed to achieve this. A major reason for this was the state's ability to 'shape the way people think about their situation, to form their opportunities to act on their analysis, and to generate the rules which delimit their action' (Piven and Cloward, 1979b, p. 16). Individuals requiring assistance accepted the state's definition of their problems and appealed for help on that basis. Therefore the tendency and pressure to handle each issue on a casework basis was ever pervasive.

This tendency was greatest in areas such as welfare rights and housing allocation. There were unsuccessful attempts to establish an unemployed workers group using a newsheet *Signing on Times* as a catalyst, for example, but the difficulties of organising outside the labour process in the face of an ideology which defined unemployment in personal terms proved insurmountable. Another effort occurred in the summer of 1975 with an extensive welfare rights campaign initiated to maximise the awareness of welfare issues and the take-up of welfare services. The campaign included extensive publicity, leafleting and door-to-door surveys as well as welfare rights counselling for interested groups and individuals. This too was unsuccessful in promoting any sort of collective action.

There is no evidence that the campaign acted as a catalyst for local people to organise themselves – word about the [welfare rights] van and [information] shops may have spread by word of mouth, but few local people extended their interest once their original problem had been 'solved'. One of the aims of the campaign was to encourage the setting up of an independent claimants' union in the area. Despite the large number of claimants contacted, little interest was found, and the pressure of time and manpower meant little progress was made in that direction . . . . The attempt to use it as an opportunity to increase the involvement and awareness of local people both in their common problems and interests and in taking a more active role in the running of the information shop, was a failure. In the end, the impact of the campaign was purely on an individual, and usually short-term basis.

(North Tyneside CDP, 1975b, pp. 68–9)

So the work of the information shops never really broke out of 'the straight-jacket of the case-work approach' and this was acknowledged by the project team in their final report.

The administrative system's insistence on the individual and particular of claimants' problems (or tenants' problems in the case of housing allocation) is a crucial part of the state's method of managing the real issue involved in reproducing a reserve army of labour and if we accept this sort of analysis, then we have to devise a technique for collective work which is specifically and deliberately non case-centred.

(North Tyneside CDP, 1978b, p. 34)

One of the ways of doing this is to choose issues that are collective in nature, and in this sense the North Tyneside CDP had more success in bringing individuals together to work on a collective basis in housing and redevelopment efforts where the issues were initially defined collectively, even by the state (except for rehousing and housing allocation issues). It was around these issues that the local action groups formed with the assistance of the CDP workers. The project soon realised, however, that collective action organised around individual concerns does not necessarily lead to an awareness of or a desire to deal with the wider structural problems at hand.

State definitions are also effective in defusing collective issues by de-politicising them and making them appear as administrative issues only. The project's comments concerning its work with one action group in the project area can be generalised to cover most of its similar efforts elsewhere.

> The project to some extent recognised the problem [of trying to raise broader issues] but in working with the Western Area Group and other groups in North Shields we found ourselves continually drawn into the immediate day-to-day problems of the area and the needs in organisational terms of the groups. Attempts were made to introduce a debate about the politics of housing but this proved impossible to organise in a structured way because precedence was always given to the business matters to be dealt with at meetings. It sometimes proved possible to raise more general points but not in any consistent way. More importantly, perhaps, was the resistance from some members of the group of raising politics into what they regarded as a non-political issue. Although this view was challenged by both members of the project and the group, it was never satisfactorily resolved.
>
> (North Tyneside CDP, 1978c, p. 74)

So the North Tyneside CDP was constantly frustrated in its efforts to establish 'working-class locality-based collectives' by the structure of a system which worked to preclude their existence. In this they were no different from many other similar attempts elsewhere in Britain. (e.g. Lambert, Paris and Blackaby, 1978).

The marginality of the North Tyneside CDP's efforts was brought home to it by the growing crisis of capitalist profitability: the first effects were in the 1974 public expenditure cuts. After inital confusion, the CDP team came to realise that the nature of the political situation had changed and with it the relevant issues, strategies and organisational forms. The problem was no longer seen as 'the consequence of local maldistribution of resources, which could be corrected by a bit of organisation and consequent political strength on the part of those being discriminated against' (North Tyneside CDP, 1978b, p. 13). Instead, a broader, more political approach was needed to confront the retrenchment of state services and the resultant decline in working-class living standards.

Their response was the North Tyneside Housing Campaign, an

attempt to organise a wider coalition and to raise wider issues through
the highlighting of the local council's housing policy, its relationship
to national policies and its detrimental effects on the working class
in Tyneside.

> Tyneside set out, after its initial failure to make any real sort of
> political impact through its detailed, issue-oriented work, to
> encourage an alliance of tenants, unionists, and Labour Party
> supporters to mount a critical campaign over housing issues in
> the borough. The project had always maintained that five years
> [the life of the project] was too short a period in which to effect
> any real distribution of resources locally and had argued that
> what ideological power they did possess as a project should be
> invested in encouraging working class demands for the improve-
> ment of living and working conditions. They tended to focus their
> attention on the council as they felt that housing issues, over which
> they were already heavily involved, were ideal as a platform for
> attempting to revitalise the Labour Party, with its traditional
> local concern over housing.
>
> (Popplestone, 1976, p. 60)

The Campaign was seen as a way to politicise the housing issues
in Tyneside: it was to be an ideological battle that would put forth
an alternative to the official explanations then being expounded
at the national level and echoed at the local level.

> Better housing has been a central commitment of the Labour
> Party. That commitment is now being abandoned under 'the
> pressure of economic circumstances'. The best way for local
> and national administration to cope with this is to start redefining
> the purpose of Labour governments away from reform and
> towards control. This is made that much more difficult if the scale
> of reneging on social programmes becomes public knowledge and
> is used for the basis of political organisation and demands by
> those who are affected by the cuts.
>
> (North Tyneside CDP, 1975c, p. 3)

The Campaign started with the publication of several editions
of the *Housing Action News*, a newsletter describing the local housing

situation and the need for coordinated local action. Research reports that analysed the local history and politics of working class housing were also disseminated. These and other activities were directed towards convening a conference which brought together most of the local groups and individuals concerned with housing – residents, trade unionists and Labour Party members – in an effort to initiate a large-scale effort to oppose government cuts while at the same time working towards better housing conditions in the region.

The conference led to the formation of the North Tyneside Housing Campaign Committee which used the conference position paper as its mandate. Members of the CDP, at least initially, were to act as secretariat to the Committee. Even after this eventful start, however, the sought-after unity among the labour movement quickly fell apart.

The local unions (such as the Union of Construction, Allied Trades and Technicians) either refused to participate because they felt it was not relevant to their immediate workplace situation or engaged only in 'resolutionary' politics with little, if any, active support.[2] The local action groups tended not to be very active because the nature of the campaign was different from their own local efforts, so they devoted most of their time and energy to their own organisations. And finally, Labour party members, even though confused over the position of the party in the overall retrenchment process, still could not see themselves actively working against the policies of Labour government.

The history and shortcomings of the campaign have been documented in full by the project itself (North Tyneside CDP, 1978b). In the end the campaign did not succeed in its goal of achieving major political influence over housing issues in Tyneside. It was not able to get the council to change its attitudes or policies towards the local housing situation in specific or public spending cuts in general. It could not motivate either residents or the local labour movement enough to get them to work together, even on common issues such as the public spending cuts. It was not able to promote any mass protest about the deteriorating local conditions, even among those most adversely affected. The campaign was finally disbanded, more or less, in 1977 after being reduced, during the last six months of its existence, to working in one local housing estate.

The role of the state

As Piven and Cloward (1979a) have observed, it is the everyday experiences of people which determine, if any, their forms of collective action. In the community, these experiences are heavily influenced by state institutions. Therefore an important starting point in understanding the difficulties of collective action is the changing nature of the state within modern capitalism. The criteria defining the capitalist state are taken from the relationship between the state and the accumulation process, the development of which as analysed by Offe will form the framework here because of its emphasis on the role of the policy-making process in this relationship.

To Offe, the key attribute is the way in which the state is 'functionally related to and dependent upon the accumulation process'. Accumulation 'acts as the most powerful constraint criterion, but not necessarily as the determinant of content, of the policy-making process' (1975a, pp. 125–6). The state can only function in this manner, however, if it can conceal in some way its nature as a capitalist state. In other words, 'the *existence* of a capitalist state presupposes the systematic *denial* of its nature as a *capitalist* state' (1975a, p. 127, emphasis original).

Therefore any capitalist state has two conflicting needs: efficiency and legitimacy (1975b). *Efficiency* is not based on the state being efficient in its own internal operations, but on how efficient those operations are in maintaining and maximising the accumulation process. Its degree of success in maintaining its *legitimacy* is really its degree of success in disguising its own nature. This is because the capitalist state ostensibly bases its legitimacy 'on the postulate of a universal participation in consensus formation and on the unbiased opportunity for all classes to utilise the state's services and to benefit from its regulatory acts of intervention' (1976, p. 306). This, being a direct contradiction to its role in the accumulation process, is the source of the state's 'inauthenticity' (Habermas, 1976, p. 128).

As the state has evolved a more 'productive' rather than 'allocative' role in modern capitalism it has taken over an increasing number of functions that were previously primarily within the economic sector.

The state produces education, skills, technological change, control over raw materials, health, transportation, housing, a structure of cities, physical environment, energy and communication services. The emphasis on the productive character of these state activities is because all of them differ sharply from the allocative ones since what is needed in a given situation is not already at the disposal of the state but must be *produced* by the state in the first place. The state-owned resources (like money and legal and repressive powers) are, so to speak, merely the raw materials out of which certain outputs have to be manufactured according to decision rules (or 'production rules') that the state cannot take from its environment but has to generate for itself.

(Offe, 1975a, p. 134, emphasis original)

The capitalist state has become, therefore, a major participant in most processes affecting people's lives and, as a result, there has been a tendency for economic struggles to be transferred to the political arena. Thus the increase in political action directed against the state apparatus has meant that the legitimacy of the state has increasingly been called into question. Now that administrators have become more involved in the highly political allocation of crucial goods, such as housing, it has become much harder to sustain the idea of administration as a non-political function.

By expanding social services and infrastructure investment, the state does not only exacerabate the symptoms of fiscal crisis, but makes itself the focus of conflict over the mode in which societal resources should be utilised. That state does not so much, as liberal reformers believe, become a force of social change and social progress, but rather it becomes increasingly the arena of struggle; it provides the rudimentary model of organisation of social life that is liberated from the commodity form without being able to live up to the promise implicit in that model.

(Offe, 1975b, p. 256)

In the long run, one of the major ways by which the state defuses this conflict has been to de-politicise it through its everyday activities. Its increased activity has meant that more and more elements of capitalism that are harmful to the working class are de-politicised. This is one extremely valuable function which the state provides – its tendency to turn issues of collective concern to the working class into individual and technical – administrative problems.

The benefits of this to capitalism are obvious, but even more important are its benefits to the capitalist state. Caught between the dual and contradictory demands of efficiency and legitimacy, its de-politicisation of issues (or to be more precise, perhaps, its false politicisation of issues) decreases its legitimation pressures giving it more scope in its efforts to increase efficiency. This has been necessitated because the 'functions that have accrued to the state apparatus in advanced capitalism and extension of administratively processed social matters increased the need for legitimation' (Habermas, 1976, p. 58). In other words, the separation of administration from legitimation helps to increase the scope of action of the state. Conflict is kept at the level of institutional rationality with the choices made seen as being technical, not normative or systemic.

> In advanced systems of state-regulated capitalism, political stability can be more reliably ensured through the systematic exclusion and suppression of needs which if articulated would endanger the system, than through the granting of a politically privileged status to a minority that already enjoys economic dominance .... Consequently, consensus formation is no longer filtered and controlled primarily through positive rights granted to determinate categories of *persons*, but rather through disciplined mechanisms built into the *institutions* charged with the articulation of political needs.
>
> (Offe, 1976, p. 397, emphasis original)

So the legitimation function of the state has evolved and increased, therefore, just as the efficiency function of the state has evolved and increased under modern capitalism. Instead of promoting stability through positive, personal reinforcements to various segments of society, the state now concentrates more and more on negative, institutional means of regulating the working class. These institutional means of indirect social control are usually more effective than overt repression or more obvious forms of direct social control in that they tend to promote stability in the system and produce less collective pressure for change.

Capitalist state institutions, therefore, have evolved a decision-making process that is dominated by technically interpreted 'avoidance imperatives' (Offe, 1976, p. 419). Controversy of any kind is to be avoided or dampened. Problems are automatically defined as administrative ones with simple enough solutions that mesh with the workings and rationale of the institutions involved.

Added to this is the tendency for the state apparatus to individualise collective problems. Now this is closely related to the change from political to administrative, but it has its own benefits to the state. By itself, when political issues are defused into administrative issues, there still exists an implicit fault in the state. By individualising collective problems, the state is not only able to defuse potential protest, but is also able to increase its scope for action by establishing a 'blaming the victim' ideology. Problems caused by the contradictions inherent in a capitalist state are thereby redefined as problems caused by the very people affected. In this way, 'social conflicts can be shifted to the level of psychic problems . . . that can be charged to individuals as private matters' (Habermas, 1976, p. 129).

In the past, this tendency has been used to define poverty as the fault of the individual poor, rather than the workings of an uneven economic system and its need for a reserve labour force. Bad housing has been blamed on the people who live in it, ignoring certain factors such as the many housing estates that were 'slums on the drawing board' (Newcastle CDP, 1978). This creates feelings of guilt among those affected and causes them to hesitate and not react, thereby relieving pressure on the state.

> This ideology eats into the poor's view of themselves . . . . It accounts for the failure of people to claim their rights for 'one way to evade the unpleasantness of being dependent is to avoid getting help at all in a dependent situation'. The poor and the deprived are forced to see their situation as *their* fault. Poverty is a 'humiliating condition which most people are ashamed to acknowledge', and the feelings of guilt and shame which they experience mean that they do not *want* to act, still less to organise, for to do so implies a public admission of *personal* failure.
>
> (Dearlove, 1974, p. 27, emphasis original)

The effect of these activities by the state is to make it difficult for collective protest to occur and for organisations based on a perception of common problems to form. The state is not always successful in this, as will be discussed later, but its second line of defence, so to speak, is its ability to fragment issues among community and group interests, the workplace and the community, which are themselves artificial divisions within the working class. An example of this is the concept of 'housing classes' which has been an idea in good currency in Britain since the late 1960s (Rex and Moore, 1967). As noted by Cynthia Cockburn (1977, p. 44), it is a concept in which 'false categories are played off against each other, the "ratepayer" against the "council tenant", "council tenant" against "homeless" or "squatter"'. This is, in effect the division of the working class into several social bases which are in competition against each other for a set amount of resources.

> State intervention systematically fragments rather than unites class interests; to that extent separate *housing* classes might have some meaning. But this structure, which is the product of state policies, can also be changed by state policy, and should not be confused with class differences based on wealth, property and power.
>
> (Lambert, Paris and Blackaby, 1978, p. 168)

Finally, there is the cooptation of protest organisations that actually do get formed (as a result either of outside intervention, by, for example, community activists, or as a result of extreme local disruptions, such as large-scale urban redevelopment schemes, which encourage a collective response). The incorporation of these organisations is not the result of an organised conspiracy on the part of the local state apparatus. Rather it is the result of the need for individual local institutions, as well as the local state as a whole, (i) to offset spontaneous, but disruptive local activities; (ii) to monitor and increase its information concerning its external environment, concerning its external environment, (iii) to gain legitimacy for its activities; and (iv) to promote self-help activities to aid community socialisation as well as relieving economic pressures to provide additional services. (This aspect of state activity has been the subject of many recent reports, including Dearlove, 1974; Cockburn, 1977; National CDP, 1977b; Mason, 1978.)

These factors, then, combine to create a serious dilemma for radical community activists. As the North Tyneside CDP (1978b, p. 27) observed, 'the real problem was of collectivising in a system where breaking up politically active collectives is a function of the system itself, in terms of its origins'. It is easy to see, just from the experiences of the North Tyneside CDP, how community activists can be drawn into situations where they are working with individual claims or fragmented groups. New activist organisations, whether a state-sponsored CDP or an independent community group, are not formed in policy vacuums. They are formed to address issues that are not or can not be adequately resolved by other organisations and their continued existence depends on their ability to do so. At the same time, however, there is tremendous pressure on these new organisations to follow 'the rules of the game'; to conform to existing standards and practices. And this pressure comes not just from state institutions and state definitions of the issues, but from individuals and groups in the community who accept these institutional divisions and ideological definitions as norms upon which to base their behaviour.

But for community action to be relevant it must confront the tendency to de-politicise and individualise any conflict that arises, or any issue addressed. Already established organisations that must be dealt with (unions or local authorities, for example) have their own goals and needs which conform to the dominant ideology: this will produce inevitably conflict and tension. There is always tremendous pressure to gain security by accepting external constraints on decisional activity and by compromising original objectives and theoretical frameworks. Finally, there is the realisation that, frequently, there are few alternatives to working with these other institutions. The North Tyneside CDP (1978a, p. 185) found that 'since we had to establish our legitimacy, we found ourselves working with both the "new" formations and the old (a politically contradictory position) hoping that political gains would be made in a number of ways in a variety of contexts'.

This then is the environment of constraining pressures that the North Tyneside CDP found themselves in, an environment in which most community activists have to work. Dissatisfaction is frequently evident, but its form is such that the majority of working-class people affected interpret it individually and not collectively. Therefore, even though there may seem to be many political issues, there is not a clear list of those that can be readily organised around.

Political space
This environment is far from perfect in its ability to contain and constrain collective action. The capitalist state has yet to develop any policy-making process that can reconcile its efficiency and legitimacy functions, and in fact, because of the 'non-coincidence

of its motives and objective functions', its expansion under modern capitalism magnifies this inherent contradiction.

> Its mode of functioning has absorbed the 'anarchy' that it partially eliminated from the economy. In spite of all attempts towards urgently needed rationalisation, 'muddling through' without plan or praxis has become the official programme.
>
> (Offe, 1975c, p. 104)

As a result, the institutions that make up the state apparatus can never fully adapt to the changing nature of capital and therefore can never fully respond to the demands made upon them by the working class.

In the present British context, capital has been reorganising, moving out of traditional industries and traditional industrial areas such as inner cities, and into new forms of technology which tend to create their own disruptions (an example being the recent concern over the projected microelectronics revolution). The traditional organisations of the working class, however, do not seem capable of adequately responding to grass-roots demands to alleviate the situation.

There has been widespread disillusionment with the Labour party, especially its national leadership, because its policies have led to an increase in inequality and poverty rather than the expected opposite. The recent Labour government was increasingly a corporate state and decreasingly responsive to grass-roots working-class demands and desires. It had ceased to be (if indeed it has been for a long time now) the working-class party of collective radical action, except in a few isolated local instances.

The national unions, formed to deal with industry-wide issues, have increasingly based their policies on their influence on and interaction with the national government, especially Labour governments. The apparent total incorporation of many sections of the national union leadership by the state, through their relationship with the Labour party, has meant an increase in tension between shopfloor and official structures of the union movement. This situation has been intensified by the pressure exerted by many multinational corporations for union negotiations at the national level only.

The result has been policies and programmes that seek only to placate the working class – examples being the Manpower Services Commission's stop-gap programmes designed to keep potentially disruptive youths off the streets and the emptiness of the Inner City Programmes.

The 'Policy for the Inner Cities' White Paper and the consequent policy developments are palliatives. But they are more than just irrelevant to the causes of the present organisation of poverty, they are clearly *diversionary* tactics. The Labour Government has succeeded in controlling the unions (who see an even worse option should the Conservatives win the next election) but is becoming in the process the party of monopoly capital. Elected on a working-class vote it has managed to restrain wage demands, hold steady or cut workers' standard of living whilst embarking on policies designed to 'recapitalise' private capital.

(Paris, 1978, p. 168, emphasis original)

So people are experiencing situations that go beyond the ability of their existing organisations to handle. And it is only when established methods of solving problems fail that people begin to look beyond their present organisations. As one ex-CDP worker observed:

It is taking place in the shop stewards' committees and in the tenants' associations where people are confronting problems that they have to attempt to change because they undermine their very existence, and they don't have a clear framework or clear organisation in which to do it.

(private interview)

A useful concept towards understanding this process is that of *political space*. A similar concept, 'policy space', was formulated by Anthony Downs (1967) as a way of defining an institution's *raison d'être*, that is to say that its legitimacy is based on its ability to fill the policy space that has been created by demands from its environment. Downs's concept, however, in line with most liberal policy research, defines the environment only in terms of other institutions. It ignores the functional aspects of the state as a *capitalist* state. It is, therefore, much more useful to redefine policy space as political space and make it dependent upon the accumulation process which poses certain problems and requires certain state activities (Offe, 1975a). The relevant political space in the present context is that which the state has been unable to fill because of its inherent limitations. In other words, it is the gap between the legitimacy that the capitalist state needs and in actual fact is able to produce.

The concept of political space is not a static one. As the accumulation process changes, so do state functions and legitimacy requirements, and so does the relevant political space. For example, it is perhaps possible to note two clearly different political spaces in Britain in the last fifteen years. The 1960s were an era of state expansion and intervention caused by the demands of capital for rationalisation and infrastructure. This was the era of community action as organisations formed either to stop local disruptions or to gain a bigger piece of the cake. Most of the 1970s, on the other hand, has been an era of retrenchment as the present crisis has forced the state to cut back on real wages and social benefits. The traditional action group, created to stop or influence state expansion, is clearly inadequate to the task of coping with state retrenchment. New organisations and new theoretical frameworks for action have slowly been evolving. The experiences of the North Tyneside CDP is a good example of this phenomenon.

Other examples of these new developments include the revival of local trades councils, shop stewards committees and combine committees, as well as several new 'community' organisations that are trying to work towards what they see as a natural alliance of industrial groups and community groups for their joint interest. Community struggles are seen as lacking real political muscle; exclusively industrial struggles frequently lack the ability to expand the political horizons of the workers involved beyond the immediate issues at hand. The Coventry Workshop (a locally-based research and advisory unit for trade unionists and community organisations), for instance, has been instrumental in the formation of the Coventry Trades Council Housing Sub-committee, which has as its aims: to support community action organised to tackle some of the concrete problems such as repairs delays; to initiate a programme of education about how the costs are rising while the quality of housing for working-people in the city is deteriorating; and to sponsor local meetings to open up a dialogue about the housing problems and to build a more critical perspective about housing in Coventry within the local labour movement (Kraushaar, 1979). As one worker involved in this process explained:

> We think we are contributing towards a movement that will eventually crystallise in new political formations. I don't honestly know whether that means new political parties or a reformulation of the Labour party for instance. It's too early to judge .... The important thing seems to be that working people, at work and in the community, begin to become more conscious of the problems they are tackling and then to demand that their 'representatives' actually work on behalf of their interests. And those choices will begin to be made by them as to whether it is possible for them to gain control over existing organisations or to shape alternative ones.
>
> (private interview)

Besides the legitimacy of these new organisations, which comes as a result of people turning to them for help because of the changing nature of the system, a second key factor is the framework of analysis that is used to understand the causes of the disruptions and to show ways of alleviating it. That there is more than one way to interpret the present crisis is graphically illustrated by the National Front and its attempt to fill the existing political space with its racist beliefs.

The fact that these new community-based organisations have been attempting to develop an alternative framework for analysis is important, not only to counter the all too frequently appealing logic of fascist slogans, but also to understand the true nature of the problems encountered. An alternative framework allows these organisations to interpret the problems within a wider context and the dominant tendency to de-politicise and individualise problems is more successfully resisted – both by the activists themselves and by the people they work with in the community.

But having said that, there exists always a dilemma between that framework and the actions taken. The problem of drawing up a programme of action that relates both to an analysis of the cause of the problems and to the realities of the existing political situation is one which inevitably faces community activists. It is very difficult to translate the political understanding of the forms of action that issues imply into action itself, to the point where too much emphasis on the political understanding can lead to inaction while too much

emphasis on action can lead to cooptation and counterproductive
activities.

Conclusions

Power is to be found more in uneventful routine than in conscious
and active exercise of will.

(Westergaard and Resler, 1976, p. 144)

The purpose of this paper is by no means to be critical of the
efforts made by the North Tyneside CDP. It is easy with hindsight
to analyse what others should have done but it is extremely difficult
to combine intellectual assessment with correct political practice.
However, the North Tyneside failures to achieve their goal of collective action are important for what they represent because they
were not engaged in 'naive, evangelistic and highly personalised'
community action. On the contrary, they were trying to build
organisations that would serve as a basis for collective working-class
action.

The fundamental basis of a capitalist society is not compatible
with collective working-class action; therefore the capitalist state
seeks to preclude its existence or defuse its effect. No real attempt
at promoting collective action, therefore, can succeed without
challenging that fundamental basis. Activity that does not deal with
the anonymous social mechanisms that act to preclude collective
action is self-defeating. This is the real lesson of the North Tyneside
experience.

What is needed is a strategy that leads to 'non-reformist reforms',
that is, anti-capitalist activities that do not base their validity and
their right to exist on capitalist needs, criteria and rationale (Gorz,
1968, p. 7). Therefore any theoretical framework should be based on
the working class as a whole and not on the artificial divisions pro-
pagated by the state such as industrial issues or community issues.
This is difficult enough, but the building of organisations based on
that framework is even harder. One cannot fully escape the existing
reality as embodied by organisations already in existence such as
the Labour party and the official union structure.

The interconnection between theory and organisation cannot be
overemphasised. It is not sufficient for organisations simply to evolve

within the political space created by the functionings of the state. Without a sound theoretical perspective, even the most active of organisations have little chance of achieving long-term positive results.

The north Tyneside CDP recognised the changing nature of the political situation and attempted to cope with it by changing their organisational structures. Unfortunately, they did not change their theoretical framework of radical reformism. Therefore, even though the situation demanded a wider focus within the traditional labour movement, their response was to mount an *ad hoc* pressure campaign, assuming that the situation itself would bring together natural allies.

> The lesson here is not that it wrong in the first place to seek an alliance with the labour movement, but that it was wrong to believe that a large issue would be enough to bring together all those with a similar vested interest.
>
> (Haymen, 1977, p. 25)

They did not consider the overwhelming ideological and organisational constraints that act to keep these very same components of the working class apart. Simply put, there was no tradition locally of these various groups working together, except in support of the Labour party. The North Tyneside Housing Campaign, 'a kind of revivalist mission', had no foundation or tradition on which to base its activity and legitimacy, and proceeded too quickly to build on the dissatisfaction that was slowly developing within the community. This dissatisfaction had reached a point where people were starting to turn away from their normal institutions, but there was little consensus on what should be done. The campaign ended up confusing the issue because people could not relate their own personal experiences with the goals of the campaign, and therefore the relevant individuals and groups were relatively inactive in its activities.

The process of building the relevant organisational structures is a long one because of the background pre-political work which is needed for them to exist. Most of the community-based activities involved have rejected strategies based on 'flash in the pan' protests and are now concentrating their energy either in building upon existing traditions of industrial and community linkages (such as in London's Docklands) or in slowly developing new ones (such as in Coventry) (Kraushaar, 1979). As one of these activists explained:

The link is that there is no organisation nationally, no political organisation or political process nationally that can tackle these problems. Therefore you begin at the roots; you begin at the point of production. If your criticism is not just of the structure of capital, but also of the state, that means you can no longer work through state instruments. You have to build alternative workers' organisations, independent workers' organisations, and that is what we're all into.

(private interview)

At the moment there are at least three strategies put forth to achieve this. The first is for community struggles to be successful in their own right before seeking wider alliances with the labour movement. Another strategy is for work on community issues to be undertaken through existing organisations of the labour movement. The third strategy is the formation of completely new structures that will serve as a link between community and industrial groups, trying to get both sides to work together.

But all of these efforts, by the various CDPs and the present community-based organisations, are hopefully serving to evolve more relevant organisations capable of overcoming the present ideological and organisational constraints in order to promote effective counter activity in relation to the detrimental effects of capital on the working class.

The decisive 'crisis of the political system' does not come about simply because the ruling class is suffering from a loss of legitimation and the disintegrated state apparatus subject to manifold 'restriction' has a serious 'management problem' to report. These are only *conditions* for a political development in which class struggle is no longer waged from above: only this would be the real 'political crisis' of the bourgeois state. The process of politicisation on which this is based is indeed mediated through the perennial legitimation and functional defects of the state apparatus, but it acquires its perspective only when it is organised and practically directed against the social relations that are the basis of the bourgeois state and its peculiarly deficitary mode of functioning.

(Hirsch, 1978, p. 105, emphasis original)

6 Nationalism as Legitimation? Notes towards a political economy of regional development in South Wales*
Gareth Rees and John Lambert

Introduction

This chapter is addressed to what seem to us to be two major and related limitations of many of the analyses of urban and regional development in Britain that have been carried out broadly within a 'political economy' framework. Firstly, they have been characterised by what, in another context, Morgan (1970) has described as 'metropolitan provincialism'. Relatively little attention has been paid to 'peripheral' regions, although the work on the Northeast of England by Carney et. al. (1975; 1977) is a notable exception. Secondly, these analyses have acknowledged only inadequately the significance of class consciousness. The limits of urban and regional change are set by the conflicts of objective class interests: however, these conflicts are translated into real political processes only insofar as they are clearly perceived. It is therefore important to take account of what are very often local political traditions, moulded by quite specific historical experience, in shaping the nature of these perceptions. And, in all this, the role of the state is crucial.

These considerations come together, we believe, in any proper analysis of urban and regional development in South Wales. Events have to be set in the context not only of a particular pattern of industrial and urban development, but also in that of political domination by the Labour party. Moreover, the continuous exertion

* Earlier versions of this chapter have been read to meetings of the British Sociological Association Wales Group and the Conference of Socialist Economists Regionalism Group. We have benefited from comments made, but ultimate responsibility remains our own.

of a diffuse nationalism in Welsh politics, marked especially in the growth of distinctly Welsh institutions of government, requires special attention. Equally, the role of the state in South Wales comprises not simply the creation of 'the closest to a nationalised region that existed in Britain' (Humphrys, 1972), but also the nurturing and management of particular forms of consciousness. And, of course, seen from this perspective, any attempt to present politics as separate from the economy is simply ideological.

This chapter is an initial attempt to frame an analysis of regional development in South Wales which takes account of these issues. Following this introduction, we give a sketch of what we see to be the distinctive political tradition of South Wales. This tradition, in turn, has exerted a powerful influence upon what we term a 'regionalist consensus', orchestrated by the state, about the past performance, future goals and institutional means of state intervention in South Wales. This conventional wisdom has been remarkably stable and pervasive in its influence. In the third section, we seek to show that whatever the rhetoric of the 'regionalist consensus', the problems of ensuring capital accumulation have imposed their own logic on the location of economic development and on the specific forms that it has taken. So, beneath the increasingly elaborate structures of national identity promoted by the state, the ordinary processes of capitalist uneven development can be seen at work; and these processes, in turn, have had far-reaching effects on the structures of class formation and change in the region. Viewed in this light, the absence of significant political upheavals in the face of these massive economic changes is highly problematical. In the concluding section, we argue that it is the state's ability to manage (as well as reflect) political consciousness which lies at the centre of this paradox. Moreover, in the specific context of South Wales, nationalism has provided a major resource by which the state has ensured this political stability in the face of massive changes in the urban and regional structure: nationalism has been a means of legitimation.

The politics of the regionalist consensus

In broad outline, the course of industrialisation in South Wales is well known. The rapid growth of the iron and then coal industries in the valleys of Glamorganshire and Monmouthshire produced an enormous influx of workers throughout the nineteenth century, both from other parts of Wales and, increasingly, elsewhere in Britain. In short, South Wales was transformed into a major industrial region – urban, proletarian and ethnically diverse. It came to contrast sharply with the rural hinterland of 'inner Wales', which remained a society predominantly of peasants and tenant farmers, whose language and culture were Welsh (Hobsbawm, 1968). However, this rapid development of a thriving urban–industrial economy, albeit narrowly based upon export dependent industries, was matched by its collapse during the interwar years. Massive unemployment, crippling poverty and mass emigration from the region were the inevitable and tragic consequences.

Out of this experience developed the particularities of Welsh politics (Morgan, 1970). During the early stages of industrialisation, Wales might have become divided economically, but common to each Welsh region was a powerful nonconformity which was expressed in a radical politics, the vehicle of which was the Liberal party. However, the strain between nonconformity and the concerns of the industrial workers became increasingly marked; especially given the former's hostility toward trade unionism and socialism (and, in particular, the Independent Labour party). In the event, at least in South Wales, it was labourism which triumphed. The trade union movement consolidated its hold over the loyalties of the workers; the electoral dominance established by the Labour Party in the 1920s has scarcely been challenged since.

A third defining theme of Welsh politics, of particular importance here, which emerged from the specific circumstances of industrialisation was that of nationalism. Butt Philip (1975, p. 208) defines this theme well:

> Nationalism, defined as the belief in the supreme importance of the interests of the nation, has many sources and buttresses in Wales. Nationalist attitudes find support from people in all walks of Welsh life in all parts of Wales . . . . It is such a nationalism that colours the approach and the decisions of politicians and administrators because it is so general a feeling, and because those who feel themselves to be Welshmen often wish to see the individuality and the special needs of the nation recognised.

This nationalism, then, has never been the prerogative of a political minority: indeed, it has more often than not been expressed within mainstream British parties, as for example with *Cymru Fydd* in the nineteenth century Liberal Party; or in all-party or non-party organisations as, for example, the *Ymgyrch Senedd i Gymru* (Parliament for Wales Campaign) of the 1950s. Equally, its influence can be measured not simply in the cultural sphere, but also in the creation of distinctive political and economic institutions, ostensibly to meet the needs of the *Welsh* situation. In this sense, then, it is possible to trace a continuous development from the Welsh Department of the Board of Education, established in 1907, to the ill-fated proposals for an elected Assembly of the mid-1970s (Butt Philip, 1975). Moreover, this latter development suggests how the nationalism to which we are referring has been nurtured and reinforced by *state* policies: the Welsh *ideological* integrity which informs this nationalism has been strengthened by state recognition and the creation of distinctively Welsh institutions.

Right up until the contemporary period, the dual legacy of economic structure and political tradition has shaped the pattern of urban and regional development in South Wales. The legacy has been, we believe, a powerful 'regionalist consensus' about the problems confronting South Wales and of their possible solutions. *Regionalist* because the problems were defined in terms of the special characteristics of the region itself; and a *consensus* because it was not a perspective confined to any one sector of Welsh society: organised labour and capital and the major political parties were in general accord as to goals and strategy. The role of the state in moulding and sustaining this 'regionalist consensus' has been crucial and was most clearly revealed in the 1967 White Paper, *Wales: the Way Ahead* (Cmnd 3334). In particular, three elements of its analysis can be seen to embody the consensus to which we refer.

The first element of the consensus view expressed by the White Paper was that by the 1960s the modernisation of the economy in South Wales was all but complete. Government had rationalised the coal and steel industries; encouraged the growth of new manufacturing industry to absorb those made redundant; and had dramatically improved the communications infrastructure and the physical environment generally. Indeed, even a *Times* leader of 1963 had commented: 'The redevelopment of South Wales has been one of the great success stories of the past 30 years.'

Secondly, the major remaining problems were seen to relate to the valleys of the coalfield 'where much of the original economic base has gone and only been partially replaced by new industry' (Cmnd 3334, p. 102). The preservation of the valleys was an acknowledged and essential task, in spite of the major difficulties of attracting manufacturers to the area. Therefore, the solution was seen to lie in the planning of 'growth centres' at the mouths of the valleys (and to a lesser extent at the valley heads), thereby capitalising upon supposed locational advantages to entrepreneurs, as well as enabling valley residents to commute to their prospective new jobs. Finally, it was recognised that the continued development of Cardiff as an administrative, commercial and cultural centre was essential not only to the success of the state's plans for the region, but also in order to provide Wales with an *appropriate* capital city. An extensive programme of state-sponsored redevelopment was therefore envisaged (Cooke, 1980).

The White Paper expressed most clearly the scope and legitimacy of government interventionist policies. The role of government in the restructuring that had occurred was as crucial as its role in dealing with the remaining problems. The need for such policies was not simply a product of the 1964 Labour administration. The White Paper took over an analysis and prescription from a study set up during the last years of the previous Conservative government (Williams, 1971). However, it is undoubtedly important to note that *Wales: the Way Ahead* was published by the first Labour Secretary of State for Wales at a time when the vast majority of Welsh constituencies, for both local and central government, were controlled by Labour. So the White Paper reflected and legitimised their expectations about what *their* Labour government should and could achieve for their area. In this way, it was consistent with the labourism of the Welsh political tradition to which we have referred.

In a related way, it is also significant that the White Paper claimed that Wales had *special* needs. Hence, it was not questioned that the mining valleys should be preserved, even though other coalfield areas were, at about the same time, the object of planned population decline (see, for example, Bulmer, 1978, on County Durham). Even more clearly, Cardiff was said to require particularly grandiose redevelopment, at least in part, because of its role as the *capital* of Wales. In other words, the 'regionalist consensus' expressed in the

1967 White Paper appears to have been influenced by a further strand of the Welsh political tradition – namely nationalism.

This latter influence is, however, much more clearly illustrated in the characteristic means which should be adopted, according to the 'regionalist consensus', in order to achieve the objectives set down for regional strategy. From the 1960s onward, there has developed a powerful lobby for the creation of a devolved apparatus of economic management, through which the specific needs of Wales could be expressed. The continuity between these developments and the nationalism which we have outlined is clear. A chairman of the Welsh Council (Professor Brinley Thomas) has given clear expression to this thinking:

> It is important to recognise the fact that the regional planning machinery appropriate to the English planning regions may not be the most suitable for Wales ... there has been an increasing political, social and cultural awareness in the regions, notably in Scotland and Wales, accompanied by the demand that people of the regions should have a stronger voice in determining their own futures. And this is a view shared by all parties, not one exclusive to the Nationalists, or indeed one that has ever been their monopoly.
>
> (interview, March 1969; quoted in Williams, 1971, p. 46)

The Welsh Council itself, established in 1968, with terms of reference and an organisation quite distinct from the regional economic councils in England, was an early indication of the movement toward such devolution. Some gauge of the consensus support for this type of economic management is given in the fact that both organised labour and capital, as well as diverse other interests, were able to cooperate in the operation of this regional planning machinery.

Clearly, it is this element of the 'regionalist consensus' which has been dominant in recent years. Quite apart from the Welsh Office and Council, an extensive battery of 'regional' institutions have been established in the 1970s in Wales which have no real equivalents in the regions of England: for example, the Board for the Development of Rural Wales, the Land Authority for Wales and the Welsh Development Agency. Most distinctive of all, of course, was the proposed Welsh Assembly. And it is instructive that the Assembly was advocated, *inter alia*, in terms of its ability to improve the management of the economy in Wales.

Moreover, all the political parties, the Wales Trades Union Congress and the Confederation of British Industry had declared themselves in favour of some form of devolution, even if they could not all support the assembly proposals. Certainly, the trend toward devolved economic management is unlikely to be reversed, irrespective of the result of the 1979 Referendum on Labour's assembly proposals. As we have said, support for some form of devolution has been an element of a 'regionalist consensus' developing since the 1960s. Indeed, such developments are highly traditional responses by the state to problems in Wales, which have to be understood in the context of the Welsh political tradition.

However, whilst it is important to emphasise the continuity and stability of the 'regionalist consensus' in the terms that we have outlined, it would be quite wrong to suggest that there were no challenges to this particular conventional wisdom. At a local level, for example, the strategy formulated in *Wales: the Way Ahead* was fiercely challenged at a public inquiry held in 1972 over a proposal for a New Town at Llantrisant. More generally, quite notable electoral successes by a different form of nationalism from the one which we have sketched, in the shape of the *separatist Plaid Cymru*, occurred in the late 1960s: and in the ideas promulgated by the *Blaid*, there emerged a not inconsiderable ideological counter to the 'regionalist consensus'. Moreover, these political waves were being made in a context of mounting economic crisis. It is to these issues that we turn in the next section.

Economic restructuring

The public inquiry about the proposed New Town at Llantrisant can be seen as a key episode in the career of the 'regionalist consensus'; it encapsulated the central issues in an extraordinarily concentrated way. The formal proposal to build the new town was made by the Secretary of State for Wales in April 1971; this was, however, the culmination of many years of discussion (Edwards and Thomas, 1974). Certainly, such a development was a key part of the general 'growth centre' strategy for industrial South Wales which had been outlined in *Wales: the Way Ahead*. Llantrisant occupies a strategic,

valley-mouth location on the line of the new M4 between Cardiff
and Bridgend; even before the New Town proposal, it had been
selected as the site of one of the state's most prestigious and well
publicised 'moves to the regions' – the relocation of the Royal Mint.
The public inquiry took place during the summer of 1972. Here, the
Welsh Office's proposal was sponsored by the (then) Glamorgan
county council, but met with fierce opposition from an alliance of
district local authorities, representing declining industrial areas in
the coalfield (the Heads of the Valleys Authorities Standing Conference) and, for rather different reasons, the Cardiff city council.
These latter were able to persuade the Inspector and his decision
was accepted by an apparently reluctant Secretary of State in 1974.

In some ways, the Llantrisant public inquiry blows the gaff on
the realities of 'growth centre' planning. The Heads of the Valleys
Authorities' attack on the proposal was based on the argument that
far from preventing further decline in the valleys, as had been claimed,
it would hasten their demise. They argued for policies actively
dispersing industry to the many available sites in the valleys, especially
at their heads. They could also draw attention to achieved or planned
expenditure on infrastructure which would be wasted if development
at Llantrisant were encouraged. Equally, for Cardiff, recent years
had seen the decline of its already narrow industrial base and, by the
early 1970s, it could have no great confidence in the long-term future
of its major steel plant (East Moors, with 4000 plus jobs at stake). The
prospect of New Town-style managed urban growth, in a Special
Development Area only a few miles from the city boundary, was, not
surprisingly, unwelcome.

Of course, these attacks upon the Llantrisant proposal have to be
located within a context of what was seen by many as a deepening
economic crisis in South Wales during the 1960s. This period had
witnessed the intensification of pit closures by the National Coal
Board; moreover, the fuel policy announced by the Labour government in 1967, with its priority for gas and nuclear energy, gave a
bleak prognosis for the mining valleys. In the case of the steel industry,
whilst things were by no means as bad, there had been persistent
underutilisation of capacity and intensifying international competition during the 1960s. By the early 1970s, although there were
reconstructed steel plants at Port Talbot and a brand new one at
Llanwern (Newport), the future of East Moors and Ebbw Vale

looked decidedly uncertain. In the years between 1965 and 1970 the unemployment rates in Wales were running at nearly 80 per cent above the average for Great Britain, with a number of 'black spots' in the southern coalfield. Not surprisingly also, rates of population movement out of the region had been extremely high; whilst, in spite of some particularly conspicuous investment in the refurbishing of the housing stock, the urban environment of much of South Wales remained exceptionally poor (Humphrys, 1972).

This is not to say, of course, that all parts of the region were affected equally badly. New jobs have been flowing into South Wales, but, for the most part, they have not been located in those areas which have lost jobs from coal and steel. On the contrary, they have been going to precisely those valley-mouth locations which Llantrisant epitomised. Hence, Manners (1964) has shown that between 1945 and 1962, 35 of the 40 million square feet of new industrial building in South Wales was approved in the coastal belt/valley-mouth area and 93 per cent of the privately financed industrial floor space was also situated in this enclave. Moreover, the major settlements of the coast (Cardiff, Newport and Swansea) have benefited significantly from the growth of employment in the tertiary sector. In short, although South Wales has done well relative to other regions of Britain in terms of job gains, this expansion of employment has not benefited the communities of the region uniformly.

In addition, it would appear that it is jobs of a *particular kind* that have been created. It is remarkable, for example, that many of the new jobs which have become available have been filled by women; this is true of both manufacturing (and especially industries such as electrical engineering) and, to a much more marked extent, of services (McNabb, 1980). The general trend that emerges, then, is one of employment losses in the traditional, male dominated industries being counterbalanced by gains in new, female dominated ones. There is also some evidence to suggest that many of these new jobs are semi- or unskilled (Davies and Thomas, 1976; Lovering, 1978). Indeed, the admittedly partial picture that emerges appears to accord very well with 'the emerging form of the spatial division of labour' described by Massey (1978).

Viewed from this perspective, what was remarkable about the Llantrisant public inquiry was that the attacks upon the strategy embodied in the New Town proposal were so very limited. The whole affair was conducted, in effect, *within* the 'regionalist consensus'. Hence, it was never questioned that government intervention provided the only appropriate means of tackling the problems facing the region. Furthermore, the definitions of the nature of these problems were held in common by the protagonists: government policies had achieved a partial modernisation of the economy in South Wales since 1945, but the inevitable decline of the coal industry (and to some extent, steel as well) because of market conditions meant that there would be residual problems in the valleys. Indeed, the only contentious issue was whether the best solutions lay in planned growth at a limited number of centres or in a more dispersed pattern of economic development. Moreover, it proved possible for the Secretary of State to accept the Inspector's recommendation not to proceed with the proposal, whilst not, in fact, deviating from the 'growth centre' strategy. In announcing his decision, he ignored calls for a detailed study of alternative strategies and announced that development at Llantrisant would be supported within existing local authority powers. Ironically, Llantrisant has since enjoyed one of the most rapid rates of growth in the whole of South Wales.

However, a more forceful challenge to the 'regionalist consensus' was made during the late 1960s and early 1970s by the Welsh nationalist party *Plaid Cymru*. It is probably true to say that the real significance of the *Blaid*'s challenge lay not in the extent of its electoral success in South Wales, which has always been relatively small, but in the fact that the Labour party's dominance was being contested at all. Hence, Butt Philip has commented in the following terms on the effects of the significant advances made by *Plaid Cymru* in a series of by-elections held in valley constituencies between 1967 and 1972: the *Blaid* was actually victorious in none of them.

> The moral for the Labour Party in Wales was made clear. Labour hegemony in the Welsh valleys had become blurred in the face of the continuation of pit closures, economic insecurity, and of the continuation of high rates of unemployment under a Labour government. Plaid Cymru appeared to offer a socialist alternative, a modern and a Welsh alternative too, to the valley people.
>
> (1975, p. 110)

This latter point is, of course, a significant one. *Plaid Cymru* had emerged during this period as a party which had moved away from its previous preoccupation with linguistic and cultural matters into the domain of economic development; moreover, it has been argued that within the party the dominant group were adopting increasingly socialistic lines on economic policies (Rawkins, 1979).

In effect, then, the *Blaid* was able to draw attention to the manifest inability of government to do what was being claimed for it within the mainstream of the 'regionalist consensus'; official development strategy was quite simply not protecting many communities in South Wales from the consequences of quite massive economic change. Moreover, it could also offer a set of policies of its own which rejected *some* of the key assumptions embodied in the 'regionalist consensus'. The crucial point here is that *Plaid Cymru* set the economic problems of South Wales within a Welsh, rather than British, framework: instead of taking the central government's role in regional development as given (as did *Wales: the Way Ahead*), it started from an estimate of the number of jobs that would be needed to maintain Welsh communities and tied its proposals to this estimate. This led to a much closer focus upon the organisation of production in Wales and, hence, to proposals for a National Development Authority, with control over industrial investment and profits, to implement a programme of highly dispersed economic development (Plaid Cymru, 1970).

Even here, however, the threat to the conventional wisdom of the 'regionalist consensus' was not a fundamental one. Admittedly, the focus of South Wales's problems was shifted; but only as far as the way in which British government was organised. By creating an independent Welsh framework of economic management, it was argued that solutions to the familiar problems could be found. In brief, then, Welsh government could do what British government could not.

Therefore, it is perhaps not surprising that the most tangible result of *Plaid Cymru*'s advance was a focusing and strengthening of the already existing trend toward devolved economic management, especially within the upper levels of the Labour party organisation in Wales (Jones and Wilford, 1979). Certainly, the very limitations of *Plaid Cymru*'s challenge is indicated by the ease with which it has been safely absorbed in a devolution massively more limited than that being advocated by the nationalists. Viewed in this light, the reverses suffered by the *Blaid* at the General Election of 1979 can be seen as marking a success for the 'regionalist consensus'.

The effective absence of any more thorough-going challenge to the conventional wisdom of the 'regionalist consensus' is all the more surprising given the key role played by the state in generating the massive economic changes that we have sketched. Hence, as Morgan (1979) has shown, the difficulties experienced by the British coal industry during the postwar decades (and particularly since the late 1950s) have been attributable to the pricing policies imposed by successive governments: in short, cheap fuel has been deemed essential to the interests of private industry and, in particular, to its international competitiveness. A similar rationale underpinned decisions by the state to convert Britain from a virtually single fuel economy, dependent upon coal, to a multi-fuel one, using gas, oil and nuclear energy as well. One of the results of this sort of policy orientation was, of course, the massive programme of pit closures in South Wales, which we have described. The story of steel is a more complex one. At one level, the postwar reorganisation of the industry benefited South Wales in that the region remained a major focus of both sheet-steel and tin-plate production. Moreover, part of the explanation of the decision to maintain the Welsh industry was the pressure exerted on the steel companies by the government, so as to avoid the acute social and political repercussions of closures in the region. However, equally, the steel companies were themselves anxious to pursue a policy which involved the least disruption to the pre-war organisation and locational pattern of production. It is, of course, much more difficult to assess the extent to which this postwar, state-mediated decision affected the long-term viability of the industry and resulted in the extended programme of plant closures that was initiated after nationalisation in 1967 (Morgan, 1979). What *is* clear, however, is that the reorganisation of steel *within* the region, culminating in the 1958 decision to site the new strip mill at Llanwern, yielded a clear geographical concentration on the coastal belt/valley-mouth area. This pattern, as we have seen, was repeated to a very large extent for the rest of manufacturing industry.

The introduction of new manufacturing industry to South Wales has been the third key element in the postwar restructuring of the region's economy. And, it has been claimed, especially within the 'regionalist consensus', that the government's role – by means of its regional economic policy – has been central. It is important, however, that regional policy has operated with any vigour only during the immediate postwar years (until the national economic crisis of the late 1940s) and from around 1963 through to the mid-1970s; for the remainder, it was in abeyance or virtually so (Morgan, 1979). Now, it is true that both these 'active' periods did see considerable growth of new manufacturing capacity in South Wales (Humphrys, 1972). However, it is important to acknowledge that the region offered manufacturers a pool of (female) labour, willing to accept low-skill jobs at low-cost to employers (particularly attractive given the absence of union organisation amongst these workers). At a minimum, this set a context in which regional policy was likely to be extremely successful. Alternatively, it could be that the effect of regional policy was to improve an already attractive proposition for industrial capital because of the particular circumstances of these two periods (Morgan, 1979; Massey, 1979; Pickvance, 1979).

Furthermore, it is a point of some significance, as we have shown, that new employment opportunities have been massively concentrated at coastal belt/valley-mouth locations. The point here is that it is precisely these sorts of locations which were the most attractive to capital. Moreover, whatever the 'regionalist consensus' rhetoric of the *impossibility* of attracting manufacturers to the industrial valleys, the overwhelming weight of the state's activities has actually been directed at making the coastal belt/valley-mouth locations more attractive. And this has been a discernible and consistent policy throughout the postwar period. Hence, for example, the state has undertaken a massive programme of infrastructural investment – overhauling the communications network, providing factory buildings, establishing the facilities of collective consumption – most of which has been located off the coalfield itself. And, of course, this investment has been *necessary* to ensure the continued profitability and competitiveness of industrial capital.

In effect, then, the restructuring of the economy in South Wales illustrates with considerable clarity the way in which the state has functioned to reproduce the conditions necessary for successful capital accumulation (Carney and Lewis, 1978). The activities which we have sketched are testimony to the role the state has played in co-ordinating, channelling and facilitating the advance of the capitalist mode and its relations. Uneven economic development, both within and between regions is an inherent feature of this mode. And, certainly, whatever the claims made, the state has proved itself incapable of reshaping this development by directing investment to locations deemed unsatisfactory for successful capitalist production.

Conclusion

In the preceding pages, we have presented what amount to two contrasting views of the pattern and process of urban and regional development in South Wales since World War II. On the one hand, there has been the view from within the 'regionalist consensus' that, aided by government intervention, the modernisation of the economy of the region could be pushed forward to its ultimate goals of balanced economic development, full employment, revitalised physical environment and so forth. Moreover, the machinery of such government directed development was vested in special Welsh agencies, which were the means for a measure of devolved management of the Welsh economy, based on a regional governmental apparatus in Cardiff, the growing status of which as a 'proper' capital city was a further element in the cementing of a national identity for Wales.

On the other hand, there is evidence from the effects of economic restructuring that suggests a pattern of development that contrasts the 'modern', relatively affluent coastal plain with the continuing dereliction of the valleys of the coalfield. Moreover, in this pattern the role of the state can be seen to be crucial in promoting and facilitating those very changes and shifts which from the viewpoint of the 'regionalist consensus' are the *problems* faced by the region.

We would not wish to suggest that these outcomes of state policies were in any way inevitable; rather, they need to be seen as deriving from political processes reflecting a given balance of class forces. It is not simply a matter of *paradox* between appearances or claims or policies and realities. We need to explore how, despite the manifest consequences of state policies and the major disruptions and hardships they have entailed, the 'regionalist consensus' has held sway and *political* upheavals and conflicts have been minimals.

The answer would appear to lie in the examination of the role of the state. Not only has it operated at the economic level to ensure the conditions of successful capital accumulation, but also at the political and ideological levels to maintain the stability and cohesion of the social formation. In short, through its orchestration of the 'regionalist consensus' it has legitimated the form and framework of its interventions in South Wales. However, here again, this has been no automatic or inevitable process. The state has worked within and reflected a particular configuration of classes and a particular political tradition, with its own consciousness and preoccupations. In turn, the state's actions have affected both these in ways that have yet to be fully worked out.

We think that the ideological effect of the nationalism we have sketched has provided a powerful element in this process of legitima-tion. On the one hand, the nationalism which pervades the Welsh political tradition has provided the state with a powerful resource. It has served to direct attention away from the conflicts inherent in Welsh society and to emphasise common interests and objectives. More specifically, nationalist responses by the state at the political and administrative level, typically emphasising the particular nature of Welsh problems and the need to establish particular Welsh policies and institutions, have diverted attention from the thorough-going integration of the economy in South Wales into the mainstream of British and world capital and from the necessary implications of that integration. Moreover, the symbolic power of this nationalism has derived from the fact that it has a strong ideological and political presence within Wales: a presence which, in turn, is at least partly dependent upon the state use of it. In this sense, then, nationalism has been a significant factor in determining the *form* of state inter-vention in South Wales. The essential *functions* of that intervention have been the equivalent of those in other, similar regions.

However, because those functions have involved the sorts of economic changes that we have described, there has also arisen the rather more vigorous nationalism represented in *Plaid Cymru*. Indeed, Poulantzas (1975) has suggested that this kind of nationalist resur-gence is a typical response to the effects of the internationalisation of capital; whilst other commentators have argued that the rise of such nationalist political parties have potentially grave destabilising effects on established social formations (Carney and Lewis, 1978; Nairn, 1977). As we have seen, at least in the Welsh context, it is difficult to reconcile *Plaid Cymru*'s limited threat with this sort of analysis; it has all too easily been defused by the state's devolutionary strategy. Nevertheless, it is important to recognise that nationalism is highly complex and, as Miliband (1973) has pointed out (in a rather different context), it may be either a stabilising or a destabilising influence, depending upon its form.

Moreover, to consider the issue of destabilisation simply at the level of nationalism, as, rather surprisingly, Nairn (1977) is prone to do, is to ignore the necessity of complementing analysis at the level of consciousness with that of the objective processes of class formation and change. Quite simply, analysis in terms of the plain 'nation' (still less 'region') is not enough. It is clear that we just do not know enough about what is happening to the particular configuration of classes that characterises South Wales. However, we can only suggest that the effects of the economic changes that we have outlined have been to divide the working class of the region into a relatively affluent stratum, able to capitalise upon the new employment opportunities that have become available, and an increasingly marginalised and impoverished stratum, unable to 'make out' in changed economic circumstances (Rees, 1980). Moreover, the increased penetration of South Wales by multi-regional and multinational companies and the general growth of white-collar work may well be leading to the increasing *embourgeoisement* of areas within the region. And, of course, changes such as these will, in turn, profoundly influence the character of the regional political scene.

Clearly, all of this remains tentative: we have attempted no more in this chapter than to outline an appropriate framework within which to analyse urban and regional change in South Wales. However, we hope that we have demonstrated that the most fruitful avenue of future research is the interrelationship between the nature of this development, the processes of class formation and change and the role of the state in facilitating the former and managing the consequences of the latter.

7 Urban Development on the Periphery of Industrialised Societies
Robert Moore

Introduction

In the early stages of capitalist industrial development the resources of the countryside and the colonies were appropriated for the benefit of industry in towns and cities. The industrial provinces were also expropriated; for example, County Durham had its main resources exploited in the nineteenth and early twentieth centuries, the profits from this were invested in banking, property or new industries elsewhere in Britain or overseas. Thus a county which generated considerable industrial wealth was by virtue of its social relations to capital deprived of benefit from that wealth.

Peripheral areas have again become attractive sources of labour. Industry seeks to reduce labour costs: it may do this by replacing men with machines, importing migrant labour, employing women or relocating in an area of plentiful and/or less expensive labour. The deprivation of the provinces has become known as the 'regional problem', and a host of ameliorative measures have been designed to encourage industries to relocate away from the overcrowded and overemployed areas and back to these peripheral areas. The interests of the state and industry may coincide in this. Thus one 'solution' to the problem of Liverpool or Glasgow may be to encourage foreign multinational companies who may make, assemble, tranship, market or store their goods in these 'Development Areas'.

Peterhead is a small town on the northeast coast of Scotland: its three largest employees are a branch of General Motors, a canning factory for a Swiss-based transnational food corporation and an engineering works belonging to an English conglomerate based upon the electrical trade. The reason for conducting research in this town was that whilst being part of a Development Area (Scotland), it has become an asset to multinationals and to the state by virtue of its proximity to the North Sea oil and gas fields. In the course of research on the social effects of the arrival of the oil industry, it became clear that the actual impact was mediated by the intervention of the state, both directly and by virtue of the evolution of a body of regional development and planning policies. But the policy framework within which oil industry developments took place was not one designed to cope with primary extraction industry but with conventional regional development problems; unemployment, emigration and low rates of investment. The disjunction between needs and policy nicely highlighted the role of the state and its response to the problem of peripheral areas. This paper is intended as a description of this significant disjunction.

North and Northeast of Scotland contain 14 per cent of the population of Scotland and 1.4 per cent of the UK. In the small towns heavy unemployment is measured in hundreds. This has to be contrasted with the chronic unemployment of many thousands and the industrial dereliction of the populous midlands. One altruistic Peterheadian suggested that in 'the national interest' even a 'St. Kilda solution' (evacuation of the whole population) was acceptable if it saved the British economy and brought benefits to the more populous regions thereby. Drastic as this may seem and given that Peterheadians are neither a rare nor a migratory species, such a policy could be seen as acceptable for the greater good in a programme either of accelerated capital accumulation or of socialist reconstruction. It is suggested later that it may be misleading to think in terms of an homogenous 'national' interest in this way. But crucially it remains a fact that what happens in the Northeast is relatively unimportant to most Scots or to the UK population at large – and this is part of the problem we have to address, in attempting to understand what was happening there.

In observing Peterhead the sociologist is not looking at a town which is as unique as it is to a Peterheadian nor at a location which simply has problems of planning and policy, as an administrator might see it. Theoretical issues are raised by events in Peterhead, and it is the questions raised by these to which the sociologist primarily applies himself, believing that whilst he may not immediately satisfy either the Peterheadian or the planner he will be able to offer them a wider and more general perspective upon the events that interest them and thereby help them to a fuller understanding.

Theoretical problems especially gather around the notions of *industrialisation* and *development*. Our image of industrialisation is rooted in a stereotype of the English industrial revolution; we think of the forced-movement of rural population into rapidly expanding towns and of the rise of mass employment in large-scale extractive and manufacturing industry. This primary industrialisation was then followed by a growth in retailing and services, the rise of business and municipal administration, the expansion of banking, insurance, the City and the state. (A number of these features might also be preconditions for industrialisation, rather than the effect.) This growth of industry is accompanied by the rise of new classes; a property-owning entrepreneurial middle class and an industrial working class, the latter starting from a condition of economic and political dependency organises its interests in the trade union and the Labour party, and through them begins to transform the relationships between the classes.

When we say that large-scale industry comes to North and North-east Scotland as a result of oil we must not imply a repetition of this history. Nevertheless politicians and some policy-makers seem to adhere to the stereotype and equate industrialisation with the development of manufacturing and the creation of large numbers of jobs. Is this just a simple mistake or does the historical model serve an ideological purpose in concealing the interests served by the development policies adopted?

Theories of industrialisation and development

The discovery of North Sea oil and the decision to exploit it commercially was greeted euphorically in the region:

> for generations we watched our youngsters pack up and drift south looking for work ... if we can build up a proper industrial base ... all the rest will follow. And that means jobs: more important it means careers, some kind of fulfilment in the north. It may even mean colleges and teacher training schools. Let the London newspapers, the gentry and the southerners bleat all they like. North Sea oil represents a way out of generations of neglect, decay, demoralisation and exploitation.

(Rosie, 1974, p. 56)

But the euphoria was not universal: sociologists responded more cautiously because of their knowledge of the social process of economic development, both historically and in other parts of the world today. We had *theories* about developments which enabled us to connect events and make sense of the course of events. These are discussed briefly in the book I have written about Peterhead (Moore, 1981) and in a paper (Moore, 1978). Importantly, we had theories which disconnected ideas of industrialisation from development and suggested outcomes to the current course of events that were unlikely to reinforce the euphoria.

Industrial enterprise is not new to North and Northeast Scotland, and the current changes are not rooted in a primal industrialisation process. The optimistic view of oil appeared to be based on an idea that these areas of Scotland were non-industrial or pre-industrial regions needing capital and a change in traditional attitudes for industrialisation to take place. Oil would provide the economic base, foreign capital the opportunities and the oil men an injection of new ideas; and a hitherto backward part of Britain would take off with high employment into affluence and modernity. Even social problems were foreseen in terms of an urban industrial society – strained social resources, family disruption and the collapse of traditional social controls.

The theory implicit in this outlook and elaborated in much of the classic economic and sociological literature explains very little. Ian Carter has argued that the Highlands are not backward in relation to industrial areas. They have developed (or underdeveloped) in response to the needs of the wider society. The crofting system was itself a response to the economic opportunities created by industrialisation in the eighteenth and nineteenth centuries and the incorporation thereby of the Highlands and Islands into capitalist society: it is a system highly deleterious to agriculture and resulting in decreased agricultural productivity. Like many contemporary underdeveloped societies the Highlands and Islands now has to import food, having once been self-sufficient. Similarly the area around Aberdeen could have been considered not pre-industrial but post-industrial, a previous base in textiles, quarrying and (more debatably) paper, having largely collapsed. According to the critics of the classic theories the North of Scotland has always been an integral part of the British economic and social structure but its position in that structure has been dependent and subordinate (Carter, 1974). In spite of some quite large 'development' schemes there has been no autonomous self-sustained growth in the North which therefore has remained economically dependent.

The main weakness of traditional theories was the division of the world into sectors at different stages of development. Critics of these theories stress the oneness of the world economic system and the interdependence of the parts. The most productive theoretical developments that take account of this have concentrated on the idea of 'dependent development'. Dos Santos has described dependent development in the following way:

> When some countries can expand through self-impulsion while others being in a dependent position can only expand as a reflection of the expansion of the dominant countries.
>
> (quoted in Oxaal et al., 1975, p. 12)

The word 'dominant' is significant because Dos Santos is not discussing the functional dependence of equal members of a social structure all on the same path to development, but relations of domination and subordination.

One problem with the notion of dependent development has been its generality. We can, after all, readily agree that the world is one system of interaction, but this tells us nothing at all about the structure of social relations among and within particular societies or the consequences of particular social arrangements for specific populations. But current work is now more precisely specifying the institutional characteristics of dependent development. Possible approaches can be illustrated in borrowing a formulation from Galtung by examining dependent development in terms of an international vertical division of processing, of capital and of labour (Galtung, 1971).

The division of processing involves the dependent region in low levels of processing and the dominant in higher levels of processing. Autonomous industrialisation in the dependent region is usually precluded because dependent development is geared to the production and export of relatively primary goods, so that the maximum value may be added to them in existing industrial areas near large markets. This was a fact of life in many colonies and is still a fact of life in many ex-colonies. Opportunities for local entrepreneurs are found mainly in servicing this kind of production. Peterhead would be *industrialising* on the basis of oil if it were moving into, say, plastics manufacture and pharmaceuticals. But it is a long way from the market for plastic goods or highly processed petrochemical products. Most of the region's oil products will be inputs for industries elsewhere. The only exceptions we might expect to find are dangerous, polluting or processes otherwise unacceptable in industrial areas might be sited there.

The division of capital needs no comment. The UK itself could not provide the finance needed for North Sea oil exploitation and the Northeast and Peterhead certainly could not provide any. Normally profits accure to capital. Will, then, all the profits migrate, perhaps to where the maximum value is being added to oil, in manufacture? We cannot answer decisively because state intervention is an important factor and furthermore the government can not be changed by the direct intervention of foreign companies as is the case in some Third World nations. It is to be expected however that neither a Westminster nor an Edinburgh government will give Peterhead priority when large-scale social and economic problems of a politically damaging nature press elsewhere.

Under a dependent division of labour the research, planning and control of production comes from outside and the region provides unskilled, semi-skilled and service workers only. Key questions we have to ask include how long it takes local men and women to move into more skilled and managerial posts, how long it takes educational institutions to provide training for advanced and specialised scientific and engineering skills – and how long it takes young men and women to motivate themselves to acquire these skills? Will it all take longer than the profitable life of the oil fields? The life of the oil fields is dependent on economic and political forces outside local control.

This last set of problems is crucial because if what prove to be the relatively transient demands of the oil industry draw men and women out of existing industries, the effect may be that of permanently disabling industries that would otherwise be main sources of future employment. If this were to happen we could say that the region had been actively *underdeveloped*, because its latter state would be worse than its former. This could be aggravated by accelerating emigration if young people and educational institutions adapted themselves to conditions that no longer held; indeed the region might once again provide skills for other parts of the world on a large scale, as it is the last resource to be exported from underdeveloped countries that always seem to be its potentially most valuable, namely its man and womanpower.

Dependency theories do not suggest a simple division of the world into exploiters and exploited. There *are* opportunities for local entrepreneurs to start or expand businesses. And these native supporters of intruding economic and political interests may come to constitute a politically important class. A significant part of the local working class enjoys high wages for a portion of many working lives. We referred to the 'transient' demands of the oil industry; if the demand is for labour for twenty-five years, then it clearly does not seem transient if you are 20 years old and unemployed. *Average* wages in the Northeast are now around 95 per cent of the Scottish average, having been only about 75 per cent for many years.

Two features of this local prosperity have to be noted. First, new inequalities overlay or replace old ones – not the unequal relations of master and employee or differences of class but inequality between those who are in the progressive sector of the international economy of oil, enjoying relatively high income and perhaps high prestige, and those who are in the now stagnant or declining sector, with lower incomes and prestige and perhaps employed in businesses made precarious by oil. Thus while wages go up, differences between the highest and lowest widen and consumption patterns and styles of life may become conspicuously differentiated. It was changes such as these, but perhaps not so clearly perceived, which underpinned fears of irreversible and undesirable changes in a 'traditional' way of life in Peterhead.

Second, benefits enjoyed are not based on any indigenous and autonomous economic activity but on activities outside local control. The traditional economy of the Northeast has been based largely on local industries largely locally owned and connected to the rest of the British economy mainly by markets only. This is changing at strategic points. Work by Hunt (1978) has shown that whereas in 1969 the majority of companies in industrial manufacture and the servicing of manufacture were locally controlled in Aberdeen City, the control passed out of the area by 1974. It seems that in Peterhead too major *new* employers are not local, and in some cases not even British. New kinds of economic enterprise are locating themselves in

the region in order to exploit offshore oil. The techniques and organisation of the extraction, processing and marketing of oil are the
province of multi-million dollar transnational corporations which
are in the most technically advanced sector of capitalism. The
relation of these corporations to the governments of nation-states
and the enormous economic and political power they wield has
given rise to a set of problems, 'the power of the multinationals'.
Part of the basis of this power lies in the relationship between the
corporation and the states of the advanced industrial societies,
notably the USA.

Theories of industrialisation and theories of development help us
to understand much of what is happening in northern Scotland and
this would be the case if the region was neither industrialising nor
developing. However, these theories have been used in a way that
stresses the uneven economic development of regions and highlight
the *spatial* or geographical distribution of costs and benefits of
economic change. Capital has been extracted from both the British
regions and colonies overseas without being invested locally or
replaced. Northern Ireland and the Scottish midlands developed
textiles, shipbuilding, coal, iron and steel at particular phases of
the British imperial economy. Now both experience major industrial
decline whilst Southeast England and the European industrial
triangle flourish. The state has, meanwhile, evolved policies to redress
the uneven spatial distribution of industrial changes. But has the
whole population of Southeast England, or Birmingham, so enriched
itself at the expense of Scotland, Northern Ireland and the English
regions that there is now no poverty, no poor housing, no deprivation
of any kind in the Southeast? The suggestion is absurd.

The decline of one region may be the necessary condition of the
development of another but the costs and benefits are unevenly
distributed *socially* within the regions. There are people unemployed,
lacking adequate housing and with poor educational opportunities
in Ballymena, Stonehaven, Spennymoor and Stepney. Fortunes are
made in the City of London at the expense of people in all these
locations, just as there is a local class in each place which benefits
from local deprivation. The unemployed, the poor and the affluent
each have common interests which cut across region or locality and
have more in common with people like themselves elsewhere than
they have with those in better or worse social and economic positions

in their own neighbourhood. The extent to which they actually recognise these common interests is highly problematic as is the concept of the 'national interest' looked at in this way.

It is certain *classes* who are the beneficiaries of the relative deprivation of the declining areas or the growth of the growth areas. The state intervenes here too to effect a degree of redistribution between classes, but it does not act in a neutral way. The crucial point is that an analysis centred upon the causes and effects of events upon a region or locality misses the class aspect, which may be much more significant. Thus parts of our analysis of Peterhead focused upon possible transformations of local classes and the ways in which they articulate with the wider class structure. Of special interest was the possibility of the emergence of a new intermediary fraction of the old local middle class of small businessmen and professionals who will stand between incoming interests and the local community. Equally important would be the development of a more organised working class augmented and mobilised through the introduction of large-scale 'industrial' construction and service activities, national trade unions, and more aggressive, non-local employers. In other words we tried to understand Peterhead not as a location with different interests from Edinburgh or London but as the focus of particular facets of class conflict: This helped shape the line of sociological enquiry into oil-related developments in Peterhead.

State policies

Economic change is social change. It is in considering the *political* impact of oil that we see the sharpest contrasts between theories based on the idea of *industrialisation* and *dependent development*. A discussion of power and control in the town formed a major part of the study of Peterhead. In this part of the analysis, as in all others, the role of the state was again of major significance. In common with every other town in Britain, Peterhead is subject to the authority of 'the state' in its various manifestations. The policies adopted by the state are usually orientated to national considerations and how these impinge upon any one locality is a matter for empirical enquiry. Three aspects of state policy have been especially influential upon Peterhead, those policies concerned with the economy at large, with planning, and with regional development. This would be true whether Peterhead was an 'oil town' or not. But the state also intervened quite directly in the affairs of the town. What is the state's interest in oil that makes Peterhead so much more significant in its plans than it was four years ago? The answer lies in Peterhead's strategic location in the recovery of oil. North Sea oil will enable the UK to become a net exporter rather than importer of oil and natural gas will be a substitute for other imported fuels. Gaskin and MacKay reckon that this will entail a balance of payments benefit of between £5000m and £6000m a year by the early 1980s (1978, p. 28). Secondly oil and gas are sources of taxation revenue to the state worth between £3000m and £4000m per annum in the early 1980s (Gaskin and MacKay, 1978). The revenues accruing to central government are described by the authors as 'the major benefits from North Sea oil and gas production' (Gaskin and MacKay, p. 16).

Thus although the taxation regime brings enormous benefits to the oil industry itself, the major beneficiary in the UK is the state. How then does the state relate to a small town caught up in oil developments? Part of our analysis concerned economic policy and the effects of wage restraint upon local firms trying to compete with in-comers accustomed to paying high wages. Local authority expenditure cuts also prevented the provision of certain infrastructural items (such as adequate sewage treatment) and, quite importantly, prevented the growth of the research activity that was necessary for local and regional social policy development. Another part of our analysis focused upon planning where state intervention took one crucial planning decision out of local control because it was a matter of 'national' importance. We also explored the implications of the lack of power to prevent speculation in land (prior to the Community Land Act) and the problems of planning in situations of almost total uncertainty. We might also have looked at the dependence of the state upon the oil industry for technical advice in planning (an even more acute problem for the British National Oil Company, BNOC).

How do existing policies engage with present changes? The state has a range of policies quite specifically geared to the perennial problems of the peripheral areas. Regional policies are designed to help identifiable areas but there are other policies concerned with counteracting the uneven distribution of wealth, income and social capital. Rating policy is a case in point; the Exchequer operates a scheme for balancing the rates between richer and poorer authorities. One of the major claims of those locals who sought to encourage development in Peterhead was that projects such as the Scanitro Ammonia Plant, the Natural Gas Liquids plant to be built by Shell/Esso and the offshore bases generated high rateable values and therefore high rate incomes which would benefit the locality. It is true that higher rate income would be generated but the argument is spurious because a *pro rata* loss of rate support grant would keep the net income the same. In this case therefore arrangements to help poorer areas also prevent them from benefiting from economic development by redistributing away the increased rate income.

When we turn to regional policy as such we find that Peterhead is part of the Grampian Region which is part of the Scottish Development Area. Incoming companies may, therefore, qualify for any of a range of grants, tax allowances or loans. The grant and loans are as follows (as of early 1979):

Regional Development Grant   This covers 20 per cent of the building costs and 20 per cent of the cost of new plant and machinery. It is available for enterprises in manufacturing and processing.

Removal grants   Projects moving into a Development Area may qualify for up to 80 per cent of the cost of removing plant and materials and of the employer's net statutory redundancy payments at the previous location.

Selective Investment Schemes and *Interest Relief Grant*   Although the first is available only for projects costing at least £0.5m, both contribute to the cost of interest charges, at a level to be negotiated.

Transferred Workers Removal Assistance   Under this scheme grants are made either for moving key workers in, or for sending local unemployed for training at a parent plant. The payments cover travel, removal, disturbance, etc.

Industry schemes   Certain industries (including machine tools, wool textiles and redmeat slaughter) qualify for grants and loans to cover the cost of new plant and equipment necessary to modernise or rationalise production.

Service industry grants   These cover a grant of £1500 for employees moving to the area, a grant of £1000 for each new job created and a grant to cover rent for five years. To qualify the firm must create at least ten new jobs and it must have a genuine choice of location.

Tax allowances   In the first year in a Development Area an enterprise may claim 100 per cent of capital expenditure on machinery and equipment and may write off 54 per cent of the construction cost of buildings (and then 4 per cent per year).

Incoming industry therefore seems to attract very considerable state subsidies in a Development Area. Because the whole of Scotland has been a Development Area wherever Scanitro or Shell/Esso located themselves they would at least have received 20 per cent of their capital costs from the state, 54 per cent of these costs allowed against tax and the whole of their equipment costs in the first year. The most that local employers could have hoped for was a cash grant or loan towards modernisation. This seemed unfair when local employers had weathered economic difficulties in the local community, were 'loyal' to Peterhead and then had to watch a newcomer, only after rich pickings and already forcing wage rates up, gain state aid on a big scale. At least this was how locals expressed it during planning enquiries.

A sociologically significant point about the array of grants and loans is that there is a theory underlying it. It is a very simplistic theory of economic development based upon the classic development of industrial capitalism. The development areas are either 'backward' and therefore need modernisation (through Industry Schemes) or in need of 'development' and this is equated with the growth of manufacturing or processing. Why else exclude service industries unless they have a genuine choice of location? Obviously oil-related service industries do not have this choice, they are where the oil industry needs them. So perhaps the logic is if an industry will come anyhow, why subsidise it? The same logic could be applied to Scanitro and Shell; they will be sited in a technically and commercially suitable location in order to carry on a highly profitable activity. Should they therefore benefit from the inducements offered to encourage other manufacturing and processing companies who might otherwise not choose to come to a Development Area?

The policies described not only rest upon certain theories, they support particular interests. Capital intensive industry stands to gain the most, even though the policies are ostensibly designed to create employment. A recent report made a similar point with reference to the Scottish Development Agency. The Agency is charged with the pursuit of social objectives, including the generation of employment for example, but has to do so according to the normal commercial criteria of profitability, efficiency and modernity. None of these factors favour the generation of employment as such and they may discriminate against small, new and indigenous firms (Fraser of Allender, 1978, pp. 34–6). The fact that commercial criteria do not dictate high employment may be the reason why we are expected to become accustomed to mass unemployment and full employment is no longer an objective of policy.

The logic of regional policy no longer fits Peterhead because it was not policy devised to cope with the situation now found in the oil affected areas. Processing provides few jobs and most of the locally recruited personnel would work in unskilled occupations. The servicing and maintenance of offshore installations will be a long-term undertaking outlasting the development and construction phases of work offshore and onshore. It is an activity which uses a lot of labour and which has to upgrade the skills of locally recruited employees; it therefore provides jobs and training. If offshore servicing attracted state aid Aberdeen's loss of full development area status might have favoured Peterhead and offset some of the disadvantages of distance from the railhead and poor roads. Furthermore existing bases might have taken on additional employees and made innovations in anticipation of developments in the future if they could have raised funds or obtained tax relief from the state.

It is certainly anomalous that the sector most likely to sustain economic growth, long-term employment and the stimulation of small scale engineering and electronic works does not qualify for development aid. If the provision of jobs and skills has been a major objective in the Northeast then the equation of development with manufacturing with jobs in the present circumstances is likely to subvert that objective because manufacturing and processing in petrochemicals are capital intensive, not labour intensive, whilst 'service' activities create jobs, skills and spin-off developments. Service activities will perhaps have a stronger multiplier effect than processing, in pulling more money into the local economy through wages and the creation of extra demand for consumer goods and services. If it is agreed that private economic enterprise should receive state aid in Development Areas it seems illogical to exclude the kinds of firms that are likely to operate in Peterhead. Meanwhile planners and councillors think in terms of finding factories for industrial estates or encouraging petrochemical processing.

In the context of the Northeast the notion of 'service sector' is itself anomalous and confusing. Service enterprise is seen as *following* industrial activity: it is a *tertiary* activity dependent upon primary or secondary production. But the term 'service' has more than one meaning. The 'service sector' includes retailing, banking, insurance, hotels, catering and so on; these are services to industry and consumers but not producers of goods in themselves and therefore 'non-productive'. The servicing activities in Peterhead do not produce goods either but neither are they services in the sense of non-productive. If oil production is primary production then offshore supplies and servicing are part of it. They might even be defined as a pre-primary sector. It could be argued that banking is a similar service, but the location and type of bank (or indeed the source of capital and 'banking' facilities) is unimportant from the point of view of facilitating production. To make oil production possible bases can only be situated in certain locations and onshore bases are an integral part of offshore work. If oil companies were also base operators it seems probable that the costs of running a base would be tax allowable as a cost of production. That they are operated by servicing companies as such puts them in a non-manufacturing, non-processing sector and therefore outside the category of enterprises qualifying for state aid – even though, paradoxically, the state had to go into business to promote offshore servicing itself. The use of categories like 'servicing industries' or 'tertiary sector' is relatively meaningless where one company may encompass a wide range of production and (traditionally) service activities or another may provide only a service without which production is not possible. Each enterprise is treated separately for aid purposes and not seen as part of an 'industry' in which sub-contracting is normal. (By not integrating servicing into their own activities offshore operators sub-contract financial risks and fluctuating employment to other companies. They also sub-contract some 'non-progressive' industrial relations.)

In choosing examples of the way in which national policies fail to match the situation in Peterhead we are not suggesting a conspiracy against Peterhead. The state develops policies to cope with what is defined as a regional problem, and it is within the limits of such policies that regional and local governments have to deal with particular local contingencies. The problems of Peterhead would not cause the state to alter national policies and in this sense Peterhead is a peripheral location subject to policies devised to cope with problems elsewhere. The wry observation was made by a number of informants in Peterhead that had oil been struck in the English Channel there would have been no wage restraint. In other words the interests who would have experienced 'unfair competition' for labour in the Southeast would have had sufficient political influence to change the course of incomes policies. As a corollary to this observation, Peterhead would have fallen even further behind in wage levels.

The incoming multinationals have therefore stood to gain much from regional policies, especially financial incentives. Yet they are companies which could afford their North Sea developments without recourse to state aid and which were brought by geography and geology not financial incentives to a Development Area. In recognising this the state has compounded the problem. Aberdeen has been removed from Development Area status. This penalises all the non-oil firms who have to compete with oil, and further it makes it more difficult for them to modernise or expand. And yet these local non-oil industries will be increasingly important as the significance of oil declines in the 1980s. Once oil is excluded from the calculations, manufacturing is declining in Aberdeen, as in the UK as a whole (Gaskin and MacKay, 1978). It would have made more sense according to the logic of development aid to impose a 'choice of location' condition upon manufacturing and processing rather than making a wholesale change to the area's status. The way in which the state intervenes also underlines the whole problem of the notion of 'region'. Regions are just lines on maps dividing the country up for management purposes. Administrators, planners and policy-makers deal with problems on a locational basis, but this does not mean that they deal with an entity (called a region) which has its own problems; instead they treat aspects of wider problems that may seem to have geographical locations. In the case of Aberdeen the problems have been confused with the location so that when oil does well it is assumed that Aberdeen is doing well. The extent to which the *location* of problems makes the problems different or peculiar is an empirical problem. Similarly the extent to which social, economic and political relations in particular locations have a discrete and significant autonomy which enables us to use a notion like 'region' for analytical purposes has to be established and not simply assumed.

The development of Peterhead

We have dealt for some time with 'the state' in stressing the dependence of a town like Peterhead. It would be a mistake to see the state as monolithic and omnicompetent. The planning enquiry to consider the building of the Shell/Esso Natural Gas Liquefaction (NGL) plant showed the corporations and the state to be inefficient and unable to make sense even of the data they had (Moore, 1981).

There are also examples of conflicts within and between state agencies and between levels of government that have consequences for Peterhead. This is clearly seen in the failure of the Secretary of State to develop 'an oil and gas strategy for Scotland ... and to indicate the role of the Buchan area in that strategy' (*Contingency plan for petrochemical industries in Buchan, para 1.1*). The Secretary of State for Scotland, for example, is operating in a position similar to that of a local authority: he needs to develop resources and technical skills for research and the evaluation of policy working from the same poor data base in the same conditions of uncertainty. There is uncertainty about the technical means of recovering oil resources, disagreement over the magnitude of profitably exploitable resources and arguments over the effects of taxation on profitability. The oil industry does not proffer neutral technical advice on these questions and yet the Secretary of State is largely dependent on the oil industry for information: the industry is therefore in a strong bargaining position and especially so given that the oil companies are the main agents for realising the government's economic goals. Thus, for example, 'recent predictions of delay or even a rundown in North Sea developments, resulting from the tax and participation proposals, amount largely to a negotiating posture by the oil companies' (Francis, 1974, p. 22). The establishment of BNOC may reduce this dependency of the state upon the companies while tying its financial interests more closely to theirs. And will BNOC be staffed by 'oil men'? Certainly many will be trained by the oil industry under agreements with BNOC (Wybrow, 1978).

Policy decisions by the Scottish Office directly concerned with Peterhead relating to the management and use of the harbour and provision of a site for a supply base upon land retained by the Crown were a direct intervention by the state in the town. Both were to be developed in the national interest and with little reference to local interests or even local knowledge. It was assumed that the locality would be able to adapt advantageously to these projects. Had the Shell/Esso proposal for loading NGL's in Peterhead Bay Harbour gone ahead, however, there would have been substantial physical and operational changes in the harbours which may have had an adverse effect upon fishing. This potential conflict of interests was not fought out to any conclusion because the applicants withdrew in confusion. But it could arise again either with the natural gasoline pipeline which must be provided or in the event of Shell/Esso deciding to use Peterhead Bay Harbour for the export of NGL's after all if the Mossmorran project fails to materialise.

Peterhead has moved therefore from being a town based on small local firms and branches of national firms in a politically remote location to being a centre of activities for multinational firms in a world economy and a town where the state has intervened over and above the normal provision of welfare state benefits, taxation, law and order, etc. to aid the activities of the multinationals. The implications of this are worth spelling out in a little more detail and in terms of the interests of local capitalists, the 'new' capitalists and the government.

The old capitalists in Peterhead benefited from low wages and low rates. For the incoming oil-related companies operating in Peterhead in a world-wide range of locations and dealing in vastly capital-intensive production, wages are not the most important factor. They are prepared to pay to get a job done on time, and they are relatively uninterested in their influence upon local wage rates. The government however wished to encourage development whilst controlling wages. This discriminated against local employers who could only raise wages to compete with incomers during the brief relaxation of wage restraint. Incomers could set their wage levels on arrival and then improve them through offers of bonuses and overtime or by subterfuge. The government seems to have turned a blind eye to this. Plainly there are exceptions to this rather simple 'rule'. Incoming firms such as British Oxygen Company and Aberdeen Service Company who intend to operate offshore supply and service bases in Peterhead for some years have an interest in reducing wage inflation both to limit their own costs and to reduce the hostility of the local employers alongside whom they have to work. The local capitalists were accustomed to a dependent workforce, grateful for jobs, unorganised and willing to accept relatively low wages. The local myth of sturdy independence helped sustain their interests. They were anti-trades unions. The incoming firms were accustomed, in Europe and the USA at least, to dealing with organised workers and the unionisation of workers offered a further means of control, or at least rational communication with their employees. (See Chapter 8 in this volume for a discussion of the role of the state and national trade union leaderships in aiding the large construction companies by undermining the power of locally organised labour.)

This is very much the view of both major political parties – namely that the unions should control the workforce and their senior officials police the pay policy currently in force. The 'incorporation' of the working class into the institutions of capitalism so that they accept market relations and the logic of capitalism, rather than having them dependent and in opposition, would seem to be the desirable outcome for the state. The local capitalists wanted low rates and taxes and managed to keep the area from becoming a welfare state as evidenced by low rates, high council rents and poor urban facilities in the days when Peterhead was an 'independent' burgh. The big corporations also prefer low taxes but by and large accept the logic of taxation which provides the revenue for the state to support the families that will raise new workers, the schools that will train them and the medical service that will keep them in good health. The welfare state and the nationalised industries provide good services to the most advanced sectors of capitalism. The state taxes as a matter of course and depending upon its political complexion and the pressures to which it is subject shifts the costs of producing and sustaining labour either towards labour itself or capital. With the decline of political consensus and the faltering of the world economy from the late 1960s onwards, Labour governments have, in fact, cut the 'social wage', namely that part of total household income which comprises the consumption of welfare state benefits or services. But they also needed to maintain the electoral support of organised labour. It is in this kind of conflict of policy that one sees the class conflicts within which governments are locked. Mrs Thatcher's variant of conservatism is very much in tune with that of the Peterhead petits bourgeoisie and Mr Callaghan's corporatism is in tune with that of the large corporations – except in so far as even they now feel the wages policies to be unduly restrictive upon them.

Peterhead is not simply a new locus for developments in the national and international economy. It is a location in which national class conflicts can be seen to be fought out in a way that was not possible with labour dependent and unorganised. If the working class had been organised in Peterhead they would have redefined the housing issue from one of keeping rates down to one of the distribution of resources. However questions of the distribution of resources are no longer decided at the burgh level. Thus Peterhead's incorporation into larger political and administrative units has coincided with the raising of wider political issues of power and the distribution of social resources. Alongside such questions the local problems of a small town and the misalignment between policy and needs is of very minor interest to the state. The state's avowed policy has been to favour the periphery but when the periphery offers such potential benefits to the state and the corporations, absolute priority is given to transferring the benefits to the centre.

8 Industrial Relations in the Wilderness: working for North Sea oil*
Dan Shapiro

Introduction

The main theme of the research that Robert Moore and I have been engaged in is that of migrant labour and occupational change in the North of Scotland.[1] This arose from the nature of oil-related activity in this area, one of the most straightforward aspects of which has been the creation of jobs. Thus in May 1977 – the peak month for that year – nearly 26,000 people were wholly employed in directly oil-related jobs in this area; this is close to 10 per cent of the employed population. Of course this employment is not evenly distributed; for example, for the area of West Ross and the Western Isles at this time the percentage of the employed population was not 10 but 29. If those who are *partly* employed in oil (e.g. some engineering workers) or employed indirectly as a consequence of oil (e.g. hotel and transport workers) are included, then this general total rises to nearly 15 per cent of the employed population. That the vast majority of these jobs have appeared since 1970 – indeed, more than half of them since 1975 – demonstrates the pace and scale of what has happened.[2] The creation of these new jobs entails either a large migration of workers into the area or a significant shift into new forms of work, or (obviously) a combination of both.

Within this general framework, one of the aspects that I have been involved with is the observation of industrial relations and a variety of industrial disputes at the principal oil-related sites in the North of Scotland, excluding Aberdeen (which has seen relatively little large-scale manufacturing and construction activity) and Peterhead

*A longer version of this paper appeared in the *Scottish Journal of Sociology*, vol. 3, no. 1, November 1978 and was reprinted in Parsler and Shapiro (eds.) (1980).

(which Robert Moore has been studying in depth, see Chapter 7). In this chapter I examine what happens to a major locus of conflict – industrial conflict – which typically occurs (and is typically studied) in an urban environment, when it is translated to the relative wilderness – physical and sociological – of the North of Scotland. It has often appeared that the parties to industrial struggle – experienced workers, unions, managements and companies in the construction industry, for example – have initially brought with them the rules and institutions of industrial conflict developed in an urban context. This has been followed by periods of bitter redrawing of the lines of battle as the structural implications of the new situation are realised. This setting holds out the promise, then, of casting some comparative light on these rules and institutions and the conditions that maintain them.

However, to attempt simply to list distinctions between industrial relations in urban and remote settings would not only be dreary but also vacuous in the absence of a theoretical principle around which such distinctions could be organised. One apparently promising avenue towards such a principle is to consider oil-related activities in the light of theories of development. It is clear from their scale, concentration, technological sophistication and novelty that these events do constitute development in some sense; certainly they are presented or propagandised as such where they occur. Nevertheless their status as 'development' remains problematic, and has been discussed by Robert Moore elsewhere (Moore, 1978). The exploitation of North Sea oil is being undertaken by multinational corporations within a global context of alternatives, so it is hardly surprising that several researchers in seeking to analyse these events have tried to make use of current theories of 'dependency' (implying, at the simplest level, the shift to outside the 'area' of control over the presence, pace and nature of advanced production) (Dos Santos 1973) or of the 'development of underdevelopment' (implying the weakening, through externally controlled 'development', of such independent productive capacity as the area previously enjoyed).

But if a 'state of dependency' is to have explanatory value as a sort of 'umbrella' concept under which oil activities may be characterised, then it must eventually manifest itself in changes in concrete social relations. To the extent, that is, that 'economic relations' is a euphemism or shorthand for particular forms of social relation, then a state of economic dependency must be mirrored in a variety of 'dependent' social relations. It ought, if this is so, to make sense to speak, for example, of dependent political relations or dependent industrial relations arising in a situation of dependent development. Indeed, as I have indicated, it would be hard to see just what 'dependent development' meant at all if it did not mean some of these sorts of things – and that has, perhaps, been the tenor of some of the criticisms of the generality and vagueness of dependency theories (O'Brien, 1975).

It is from this direction, then, that I wish to pursue the topic. It would be possible to approach the industrial relations of oil in a variety of ways and there is no shortage of themes in the literature that might fruitfully be taken up in this context. To do so would be to use the context of oil in the North of Scotland as a set of relatively arbitrary examples. But my intention in this chapter will be to see how far we can get in giving more priority to the particular setting, in treating it as more than arbitrary – to see, that is, whether it does make sense to consider the industrial relations of oil as 'dependent'.

But just what might be meant by 'dependent industrial relations'? The term dependent has often been used very loosely just as a synonym for 'exploitative'. This usage is of dubious validity as the term exploitation can only be given precision as a relation between *classes*,[3] and it cannot, in any case, be satisfactory here. Dependency in industrial relations cannot rest simply on exploitation for this would imply that non-dependent ('advanced', 'metropolitan') industrial relations are not exploitative. Following Kay (and others) we would in fact be more justified in concluding the reverse.[4] Dependent industrial relations must then, if it means anything, refer to particular *forms* of exploitation distinct from, and perhaps interacting with, those inherent in the labour market, in the treatment of labour power as a commodity.

Put this way, the question clearly relates to another issue which has figured centrally both in discussions of dependency and specifically in relation to the North of Scotland: the delineation and interrelation of capitalist and pre-capitalist modes of production. The orthodox approach and that which leads to the most straightforward theoretical scheme is to regard the capitalist mode as relying purely on market relations for the exploitation of labour. Modes of production prior to capitalism, by contrast, rest on social relations of production which are not those of the market but rely on other, ascriptive relations and on non-market constraints. And it follows from this that where relations of production are not purely market relations, the mode of production is not a purely capitalist one but incorporates at least some pre-capitalist elements.

One of the difficulties with this simple formulation is that it does less than justice to situations where relations of production are clearly pre-capitalist and yet whose very existence is intimately connected with capitalist developments and capitalist economic relations. How this is treated will depend on whether relations of exchange or relations of production are allowed primacy. Thus, for example, A. G. Frank's argument (1967) that economic relations in Latin America have, since the Conquest, consisted of a chain of metropolis–satellite relations with the final metropole located in Europe; hence that Latin America has had a market economy from the beginning; and hence that Latin America has been capitalist from the beginning. And in his renowned reply Laclau (1971) criticises Frank precisely for taking relations of exchange rather than relations of production as the basis of his analysis, insisting that the feudal regime of the haciendas has survived – indeed been strengthened by – the insertion of Latin America into the world market.

This general question finds a particular reflection in the North of Scotland. The persistence of a particular form of peasant agriculture – crofting – and particular forms of manufacture – e.g. the Harris Tweed industry[5] – has led to the characterisation of the Highlands as pre-capitalist, or partially capitalist, by many, including agencies of development such as the Highlands and Islands Development Board. But this 'dual economy' model of the Highlands has been decisively challenged by Carter (1971, 1972, 1974), drawing explicitly on Frank, who shows that the capitalist market had penetrated every corner of the North of Scotland; and by Hunter (1976) who shows how the crofting system of agriculture, or, more accurately, labour reserve economy (Corrigan, 1977), was itself the *product* of this market penetration.

The analytical problem of the conjuncture of these elements remains, however. The traditional solution has been to regard the coexistence of capitalist market relations and pre-capitalist relations of production as transitional – a process of primitive accumulation necessarily encompassing the breakdown of feudal relations. Indeed, this notion of transition can be made to transcend its sometimes rather lame, residual status. Thus, to stay with a local example, Carter, in discussing the inter-penetration of capitalist and pre-capitalist agriculture in the Northeast, gives real point and elegance to the notion of a complex and extended transition (1978). But there are very many instances where the conjuncture is not to be explained away as transitional[6] and it is precisely around these that theories of dependency and their successors were born. I will not attempt to pursue this question directly here,[7] but it returns our attention to the problem raised earlier. For if the persistence of pre-capitalist forms is to be seen not just as a transitional anomaly but as the actual result of a world capitalist system operating normally, then it follows that non-market social relations and hence industrial relations – Miliband's 'polite euphemism'[8] – are as much a product of capitalism's normal working.

This is precisely the point made by Philip Corrigan in the article referred to already (1977). Drawing on a very wide range of sources from over the last twenty years he calls on us to recognise that ascriptive constraint, non-wage coercion and the un-freedom of labour far from being feudal relics characteristic of the early stages of industrialisation are entirely compatible with the expansion of capitalism and indeed frequently *increase* with its penetration. And once the point is put it seems immediately absurd to deny to capitalism the panoply, the full, rich variety of coercion and constraint of which it is capable – in whatever way we may subsequently decide to analyse it. The principal examples that Corrigan uses are bonded service relations in Britain in the eighteenth, nineteenth and early twentieth centuries; slavery, neo-slavery and debt-bondage; and labour migration. In a very direct parallel with dependency theorists he criticises the evolutionary paradigms of both conventional sociology and Marxism which blind them to the continuity of coercion (1977, pp. 436–7).

Corrigan emphasises the centrality of un-freedom to the capitalist labour process in *all* its forms – indeed, of un-freedom as constituting the labour process, of ascription as '*the manner in which* [the] division and circulation [of labour] is accomplished' (p. 449, original emphasis) – citing Aufhauser's demonstration of the structural analogy between slavery and Taylorism, and pointing to the extra-economic social and ideological coercion inherent in the fragmentation into different labour markets (1977, pp. 449–51). His main *illustrations* however remain either historical or 'marginal' from the (obviously) myopic viewpoint of Europe-centred development models. By focusing, in this paper, on a peripheral region of the 'mother of capitalism' and on fully enfranchised, unionised labour, I hope to bring these points a little closer to home.

When we embarked on the research we conceived the study of migrant labour along lines similar to those which Corrigan urges, and a paper by Robert Moore given to the 1975 British Sociological Association conference spelt out in detail the necessity for an approach to migrant labour in terms of its international class dimensions. We thought it likely that we would be following the latest north European wanderings of a super-exploited sub-class of 'guest workers' whose subordinate position would be constituted by their political and civil disenfranchisement, expressed in such things as work permits tying them to particular employers and particular sites and the threat of expulsion for trouble-makers, and by their exclusion from the protection of 'native' trade union organisations. In view of what has happened in Norway, for example, this was not an unreasonable supposition. That is, we anticipated that there would be differential access of different groups of workers to rewards, conditions, security, etc. and that struggles would occur between oil employers and groups of workers over workforce composition for just this reason.

This turns out to be not so much wrong as incomplete. What we find is not a unified market within which some groups of workers are more advantageously placed than others; rather, there is a variety of alternative 'labour markets', the specificities of which are contributed to by varieties of non-economic constraint. Employers, though obviously subject to constraints of their own, still largely retain the initiative in using these alternatives tactically in the industrial relations struggle. Thus in considering the differential access of different groups of workers it is not so much that there are 'winners' and 'losers' relative to each other but, rather, that there is a variety of ways of losing.

The industrial relations of oil
What I would like to do, then, is to look at this intertwining of forms of constraint using examples taken from 'the industrial relations of oil'. It will be necessary to describe these very cursorily and schemati-

cally and so to state baldly interpretations that really require detailed substantiation: a fuller treatment will be offered elsewhere (Shapiro, 1981). The examples I shall use are two particular strikes – one at the concrete production platform fabrication yard at Kishorn in Wester Ross in November 1976, and one at the steel platform yard at Nigg on the Cromarty Firth in March 1977 – and some aspects of industrial relations on offshore exploration and production rigs.

One of the key issues in studying the industrial relations of oil has been the extent of unionisation. Before oil, union activity was with few exceptions narrowly confined to the Aberdeen area and at the start of the research it seemed a completely open question what the effect of oil activity would be. In fact, there have been virtually no 'guest workers' in oil activities onshore (and I should point out that, perhaps contrary to popular belief, something in the order of 78 per cent of directly oil-related employment in the North of Scotland is onshore). Unlike other oil sites in northern Europe, the supply of natives has been quite adequate. And, in terms of sheer numbers, the record on unionisation has been a triumphant one: there has been massive unionisation of oil activites onshore to the extent that there are hardly any major sites which are not *de facto* closed shops, meaning that there has been heavy recruitment among local as well as migrant workers. This is the case both at Kishorn and at Nigg.

Kishorn: November 1976

I have no space to describe the fascinating background to platform fabrication at Kishorn – indeed I can only give a grossly reduced account of the dispute itself. Work started in earnest at Kishorn – a fairly remote part of Wester Ross – in 1975 and by mid-1976 roughly 2000 workers were employed there – about half of them by the main contractor, Howard-Doris. During the first, dry-dock, phase of the construction, until September 1976, the workforce could be classified into three groups on the basis of home location: those living in the general vicinity of the yard (roughly 21 per cent, in mid-1976); those who were 'local' in terms of Highland geography, i.e. including East Ross and the Inverness area (22 per cent); and 'travelling men' from further afield (57 per cent). Of these, the third group lived in a work camp on the site; of the second group some were also in the workcamp but the majority commuted to work by company bus or train, involving journey-times for some of from four to five hours per day. Though virtually all the employees had (or laid claim to) experience in construction, most of those who regularly worked in large-scale industrial construction were in the third group.

The achievements of this workforce, with respect to the terms on which they sold their labour, were considerable. The site had been entirely unionised from the beginning, virtually all Howard-Doris employees belonging either to the Union of Construction, Allied Trades and Technicians (UCATT) or to the Transport and General Workers' Union (TGWU). Although work conditions were often very arduous and hours were long – twelve-hour shifts, seven days per week – earnings regularly (in 1976) topped £300 per week for all grades of construction workers, leave comprised one week off for every three worked (unique, at the time, in the British construction industry), and the (free) board and accommodation were of a high standard. In September 1976 the second phase of construction began when the platform was towed out from the dry dock to its first 'wet site', an anchorage three miles away. For those working on the wet site the working day now increased from twelve to thirteen or fourteen hours on account of the boat journey to and from the rig, but leave was now one week off for every two worked.

A strike of Howard-Doris workers began on Monday, 1 November 1976 – to vastly oversimplify a complex skein of issues – over a cut in the rate of bonus from around 90p per hour to 40p, a measure imposed by the management without consultation. This was in response to technical and weather problems which had halted production, but the men claimed that as the lost production had not been caused by any failing on their part, the level of bonus should be maintained, as had been done in a similar situation shortly before. The men reacted to this as a straightforward, unilateral cut in pay [I argue elsewhere (Shapiro, 1981) that this is an entirely reasonable interpretation in the context of the civil engineering industry], and it is clearly a 'perishable dispute' (Eldridge and Cameron, 1968), that is to say, one that is lost unless action is taken without delay. My purpose here, however, is not to legitimate the strike but to look at its consequences. It was not – as industrial disputes go – embarked on in a precipitate or ill-considered manner. The shop stewards had eight meetings with management over this issue, reporting back to site meetings in between, but could not persuade the management to alter their position: the subsequent site meeting voted to strike.

The strike began on Monday. On Wednesday dismissal notices were issued to all those on strike; on Thursday they were ordered off the site and out of the accommodation. No arrangements for alternative food or accommodation had been made, though the stewards did have the use of a caravan outside the site. Even the nearest pub is eight miles away. There was nothing for the men to eat and nowhere for them to stay, so the stewards had no option but to send them home. No arrangements were made to involve any of the men in picket rotas, not even those living locally. Over these few days it was raining and sleeting, with bitter cold winds.

Full-time officials from UCATT and the TGWU arrived on Thursday afternoon. They met with senior management who were now adamant that they would not reinstate any of the men. All strikers had been sacked as being in breach of contract, and they were recruiting an entirely new workforce. Everyone dismissed would be entitled to re-apply and each application would be considered on its merits – in other words there would be no protection against victimisation. Finally, on Saturday morning, management allowed it to be understood that they would give all of the shop stewards their jobs back *but* that they would *not* recognise them as shop stewards. They would be allowed back on the understanding that they did not seek re-election. Meanwhile, there had been sporadic, disheartened and ineffective picketing of the main gate. Saturday midday, the officials advised the stewards to lift the picket and fill in application forms for their jobs: the strike was over. For taking part in the strike 440 men had been dismissed: about 400 applied for their jobs back, and of these about 300 were re-employed.

In discussing this dispute elsewhere I have focused mainly on two issues: what we can learn from it of the ideologies of industrial relations being employed by workers, site unions and management; and the nature of relations between workers, shop stewards and the full-time union hierarchy. But the point here is to emphasise the contribution made by the specific environment to this crushing defeat. There can, I think, be little doubt that it was the credibility of the company's threat to 're-man' – recruit an entirely new workforce – which was the crucial factor in their victory. This was, of course, in part a result of prevailing unemployment in the construction industry (194,000, or 13.6 per cent, in August 1976; as compared with 5.4

per cent general unemployment) but this would not have been sufficient were it not for the geographical setting. We have seen how the two largest sections of the workforce were completely dispersed at the outset of the strike, leaving behind an unorganised rump of workers from the immediate locality, themselves the most dependent on employment provided by the company. In this fragmented condition the workforce would find it difficult even to know about, let alone prevent, the company's re-manning efforts.

Now, the ability to re-man is not, of course, a distortion of the 'market'. On the contrary, it is a triumph of the market which posits precisely this sort of fragmented relationship between employer and employee, mediated only by laws of supply and demand (and contract). But it is also very unusual, indeed almost unthinkable in an urban environment, and this directs attention to one way in which solidarity regularly succeeds in defeating the market – by exercising some control over it in a strictly *local* context. We can hardly doubt the force of this achievement when we look at what happens in its absence, as at Kishorn – a major defeat on a fundamental issue of principle from which the workforce never fully recovered. But this defeat was inflicted, not by any hidden hand but by power directly wielded by the company. What happened at Kishorn, then, was that one particular 'distortion' of market forces – the organisation of labour – was countered by other forms of non-market constraint: company control over food, accommodation and transport and its ability to use these as weapons to disperse and fragment the workforce. The result looks very like the hegemony of market forces of early industrial capitalism (to the extent that this hegemony is not itself largely mythical).

However, of equal interest from the point of view of this chapter is what happened to workforce composition in the aftermath of the dispute. I have mentioned above the proportions in which the workforce was divided in terms of home location: 21 per cent from the surrounding area, 22 per cent more broadly 'local' and 57 per cent 'travellers'. This can be contrasted with the Nigg steel platform fabrication yard of Highlands Fabricators at which, in September 1974, 68 per cent of all employees were local,[9] and this within a very tight geographical definition of 'local'.[10] It used to be my habit to use this contrast to argue that workforce composition was determined for the companies once certain fundamental decisions were taken, and hence that it would be naïve to regard the distribution of employment opportunities between migrant and local labour as being principally a matter of overt recruitment policy. Thus, both these platform fabricators, Howard-Doris at Kishorn and Highlands Fabricators at Nigg, have a 'policy' of preference for local labour. But, I used to argue, for the companies the problem of recruiting local labour is partly one of numbers available but is more importantly one of skills, and the intention to employ local labour means relatively little unless it is backed up by an effective training programme and facilities. At Nigg Highlands Fabricators established a training school at the beginning of their operations and many hundreds of men passed through, receiving full paper qualifications and union ticket after six weeks' training in trades that are normally time-served. Howard-Doris at Kishorn, on the other hand, did not set up significant training facilities.

This is a fairly obvious determinant of the composition of the labour force[11] but it has further and less obvious corollaries. If a company here is not prepared to train men on any scale then it must rely on attracting skilled migrant labour – 'travelling men'. But if it is to do so successfully it must implement an appropriate working regime. Thus travelling men, who are working away from home and families, 'travel' precisely in order to maximise their earnings. They work in the context of an effective grapevine and will move to wherever the terms are best. This, in the construction industry, means abundant overtime and, preferably, a seven-day week. The local man, on the other hand, may have religious objections to working on Sunday, or be subject to pressure from his own community not to do so, and may also need weekends and other days off for working his croft or other primary activities. Ordinary working hours in the new industry may offer far higher earnings than previously, and his loss of leisure time is a real one to him.

Thus the company must choose which group of workers it is going to please, and if it is reliant on travelling men, then its choice is already made. Thus, as I have described above, working hours at Kishorn rose from twelve to fourteen per day, seven days per week. Concessions on free time took the form not of shorter hours but longer leave periods – one week off for three worked, subsequently increased to one for two. At Nigg, by contrast, the yard started by working two ten-hour shifts a day, subsequently reduced to two (sometimes three) eight-hour shifts. Since then maximum hours per week have rarely risen above forty-eight and there have been many months when this was reduced to forty. Hence at Kishorn the employment of local (and especially semi-local) labour becomes problematic even for those categories where skill and experience are not perceived as essential, and this is borne out by very high turnover rates for these workers.

This account again, I believe, turns out to be not so much wrong as incomplete: the area of strategic choice remaining open to the companies has been underestimated. For a dramatic change in the recruitment pattern at Kishorn occurred in the aftermath of the strike. Suddenly, the company started to recruit workers from the Isle of Skye. Skye lies off the mainland directly opposite Kishorn, which is just ten miles, measured in a straight line, from its main ferry terminal at Kyleakin. To the observer, this sudden switch was electrifying: it was as though Columbus had just discovered the place. One month, the necessity of recruiting only men skilled and experienced in continuous pouring of concrete in industrial construction and the problems associated with hiring local labour were being stressed; the next, a special ferry had been laid on to transport workers from Skye directly to the platform (now three miles nearer at its 'wet-site' anchorage) who rapidly grew to form a significant proportion of the workforce. It was not long before an Employment Service Agency official was estimating that one in ten of the employed population of Skye was working at Kishorn.

The recruitment of workers from Skye mitigated a number of problems for the company, including that of transporting workers in the 'second' category which had become well-nigh impossible with the introduction of a fourteen-hour day: it had previously been intended to cope with this by increasing work-camp accommodation. But the timing and other evidence suggest that it was the strike which prompted a reconsideration of the possibilities of workforce composition. There might be disadvantages associated with insufficiently experienced labour; but these might be judged to be outweighed by the advantages of a docile, local labour force with reliance on militant, organised 'travellers' reduced. The validity of these stereotypes is a different matter, but it is an obvious avenue of ideological representation for management.

To the lessons of the defeat over the strike, therefore, may be added those of the company's strategy over recruitment. The labour market can be seen not to be continuous but segmented and, although benefits and penalties attach to each, the company retains the initiative in being able to select from these and wield them to its own overall advantage.

What is it, though, that constitutes this segmentation? The obvious distinction, that of level of skill, is precisely the one the company had just dispensed with. Nor was there any evidence either at Kishorn or at Nigg of an association between skill and militancy. It is, rather, its very 'localness' which marks it out, in conjunction with the desperate shortage of local work. At one level this is a routine labour-market phenomenon, but it could not operate except in the context of an ascriptive attachment mediated through the locality. This attachment is an exploitable commodity; it can be exchanged for a price and forms part of the basis of a dialectic of deference.[12]

Nigg: March 1977

A strike in March 1977 at the Highlands Fabricators steel platform fabrication yard at Nigg in East Ross, forty-five miles by road north of Inverness, also concerned bonus payments and involved a very intricate and complex argument as to the men's entitlement. However, it will not be necessary to explore this argument in detail – whether the position of the men or of the company was more formally 'correct' as an interpretation of the bonus agreement between them – and the fact that this is not necessary is one of the key points of this example. For the company and its allies succeeded in preventing this substantive issue from ever figuring centrally in the process of the dispute.

In barest outline, then, the point at issue was this. Work on the third platform to be built at Nigg – for the Chevron oil company's huge Ninian field off Shetland – started in September 1975 and was scheduled for completion on 17 March 1977. Following the very successful completion of the first two platforms (for British Petroleum) negotiations took place over wage rates for the Chevron platform, but this was at a period of tight wage control limiting the direct increases possible. However, an alternative acceptable to the Department of Employment was found in the form of a 'completion bonus' which would be payable to each man if the platform were completed on time. The full bonus would be a maximum of £1560 for skilled grades, but the amount would reduce rapidly if completion were delayed. The importance of this element of earnings can be seen in relation to a normal week's pay which, at around £60 even for skilled grades, compares very unfavourably with earnings at Kishorn. At the end of February 1977 the company announced that, on the basis of current calculations and the amount of work remaining, work would finish about one month late and the bonus eventually payable would only be about £1200. Any further delay would result in an immediate drop to about £650. This was contentious – apart from the historical status of the 'completion bonus' as a way around incomes policy – because since the original agreement a variety of design changes and technical problems had arisen which had caused delays in production through no fault of the men and which, they claimed, had not been adequately taken into account in adjusting the target completion date. Moreover, the previous December some 450 men had been laid off *by the company* because of the then satisfactory progress.

This is also a clear example of a 'perishable' dispute: the target completion date was fast approaching and if the issue had been allowed to run its course through the various stages of the grievance procedure, it would probably be too late to take action: the platform would already be completed and the case lost by default. Site meetings of the various shifts voted to strike, and the strike began on Wednesday, 2 March 1977.

The result was the immediate unleashing of a campaign against the workforce and shop stewards on the part not only of the company but of trade union delegates and officials, backed up by government officers. The three basic premises of this campaign were firstly, the damage to the national interest involved in delaying the completion of oil installations; secondly, the threat to British participation in oil-related contracts, and hence the threat to employment in Scotland, posed by the 'trouble-proneness' of British oil workforces; and thirdly that the strike, if continued, could only have one outcome which would be the closure of the yard and the cessation of platform fabrication at Nigg with the loss of 2500 jobs. Two features of these premises of the campaign for a return to work seem to me most significant. Firstly, their total independence of any consideration of the substantive grievance behind the strike: if the shop stewards ever succeeded in getting the very complex arguments considered in detail, no sign of this emerged in discussions or in reports to site meetings. Secondly, their wild implausibility – with the *possible* exception of the second, an unmeasurable quantity always subject to propagandist use. There was no question of the dispute delaying the completion of oil installations as the platform could not in any case be towed out until the mid-summer 'weather window'; the platform would, then, be completed considerably sooner than necessary. Indeed, it is for precisely this reason that the company was able to sit out a four-week strike with equanimity.

The third premise, the closure of the yard, was certainly the most effective and so deserves to be considered more fully. The sum immediately at issue for the company was around £350 per man for a workforce of 2500 or £875,000 in all (deductable, of course, against taxable profits). In view of differing levels of bonus for different skill grades, deductions for absence, and fluctuations in the workforce, the total would probably be less. To set this in perspective I have made some necessarily very rough estimates of other aspects of the company's costs. The weekly labour bill, including national insurance contributions etc., would have been about £200,000. Hence the total projected wage bill including bonus (if the platform were completed on the target date) would be of the order of £21.5m, taking *no* account of any supplementation for design changes etc., which would certainly have been made and charged to the client. The 'extra' the company would have to pay would not be the bonus, which was already budgeted, but the wage bill for the period of the delay – roughly £800,000 for the projected month. This constitutes some 3.7 per cent of the total wage bill. The total value of the contract for this platform was around £45m, of which the disputed payment would constitute some 1.8 per cent. The total value of capital invested by Highlands Fabricators as Nigg is especially difficult to estimate as it is spread out over time, but it probably exceeded £30m. In this context, the suggestion that an otherwise profitable operation would be abandoned over this bonus payment must appear wildly unlikely. Even more unlikely is the idea that it would be abandoned without first attempting some negotiated compromise on the level of bonus payment. Yet this is precisely what was suggested, and indeed more than this. For agreement in principle had already been reached in February between Highlands Fabricators and its client, Chevron, for another platform to be fabricated at Nigg following the float-out of the current one, and some materials for this platform, principally steel, had already been delivered. Thus the cancellation of this order would immediately involve both company and client in specific costs which could easily exceed the value of the disputed bonus.

From the first day of the dispute the hierarchy of trade union delegates and officials identified themselves unequivocally with the company's position and made very considerable exertions to persuade the shop stewards and the men to abandon the strike and return to work. In the first week of the strike a mass meeting was addressed by full-time officials of the principal unions involved – the Amalgamated Union of Engineering Workers (AUEW) Engineering and Construction Sections, the Boilermakers and the Electrical, Electronic, Telecommunications and Plumbing Union (EETPU) – who urged a return to work, and large advertisements appeared in the local and national press and signed by national union officials declaring the strike unofficial and instructing the men to return to work. Local officials participated with the company in calling a mass meeting for 8 March to consider a return to work – although properly only the shop stewards' committee was empowered to convene such a meeting – and Jimmy Milne, General Secretary of the Scottish Trades Union Congress (STUC), was flown up by plane and helicopter to address this meeting. In the event this meeting was adjourned by the shop stewards' committee and Jimmy Milne, a much respected leader of the Scottish trade union movement and clearly embarrassed by the irregularity of the situation, did not attempt to speak at the meeting. Negotiations continued for all of that day among management, Milne, union officials and shop stewards' representatives. Towards evening these parties were conveyed to Aberdeen for discussions with Chevron, the clients for this platform. Chevron dutifully reaffirmed that the terms of their contract with Highlands Fabricators were established and no more money would be forthcoming from them. Later on these negotiations moved to London, involving national union officials who attempted to persuade the shop stewards to recommend a return. In an interview on local television the full-time delegate for one of the principal unions involved, and himself a former convener of shop stewards at Nigg, solemnly announced that if the men did not go back, the yard would close.

It is hardly surprising that the shop stewards' committee had difficulty in resisting this concerted pressure. In the second week of the strike they voted to recommend a return, but their resolve was stiffened by mass meetings on 10 and 15 March which voted to continue the strike. Eventually a meeting on 24 March was addressed by John Baldwin, General Secretary of the AUEW construction section, again threatening closure unless the workforce returned. There followed a confused vote and Baldwin's declaration of a majority for a return to work, after which he only managed to leave the site with police protection.

These events clearly constitute an ideological struggle, but one conducted at an astonishingly crude and explicit level, with the battle lines clearly drawn. And although the abandonment of workers by their trade union hierarchies is not a particularly unusual event there are features of this dispute that seem amenable, at least, to analysis in terms of dependency. One aspect of this is dependence on the state and the use made of 'reasons of state': the recovery of North Sea oil must not be allowed to falter and this demands sacrifices of trade unions and workforces to the exclusion, if necessary, of serious consideration of grievances. An example of this can be seen in a resolution passed in June 1978 by the Offshore Industry Liaison Committee chaired by Dr Dickson Mabon, Minister of State for Energy:

> The Committee has been considering the effects on the industry of claims for extra payment at the termination of offshore related fabrication contracts. It is concerned lest conceding such claims could reduce the number of orders coming to the UK and so affect adversely continuity of employment at our sites.
>
> The Committee recommends that contractors, trade unions and clients should act jointly to ensure that claims for termination payments in violation of existing agreements are rejected.

Dr Mabon reinforced these remarks in interviews for radio and the press and it is likely that Nigg was uppermost in the minds of the Committee. In defending the resolution Dr Mabon pointed out that trade union, TUC and STUC representatives comprise almost 40 per cent of its membership!

Another aspect of dependency is discernible in the notion of oil-related production as *privilege*. That Britain should be participating in oil-related production, that associated employment in an advanced productive sector is located in a remote peripheral region with severe job and economic problems, that training is provided to enable some locals to participate in this employment – all these are vulnerable privileges dependent on 'good behaviour' and liable, indeed likely, to be withdrawn as a consequence of 'irresponsible action'. And 'responsibility', of course, means driving a poorer wage/effort bargain than you otherwise might. It would therefore seem reasonable to add a dimension of ideological dependency in industrial relations to the material (though non-market) dimension discussed in relation to Kishorn.

Offshore work

It was pointed out above that some 22 per cent of directly oil-related employment in the North of Scotland in this period is accounted for by work offshore – installed production platforms, pipe-laying barges, supply boats, drillships, but particularly exploration rigs. It is here, though, that the 'ethos of oil' achieves its most marked expression: the glamour of the interface between man-and-technology and a hostile environment, the fabulous wages, the 'machismo' life-style and rugged individualism of those who work there. The most remarkable and enduring feature of work offshore, however, is the extreme disjunction between this myth and the reality it conceals: dangerous and degrading working conditions, management skulduggery, very low pay and homelessness ashore.

Roustabouts and roughnecks – those who do general duties around the rig and who man the drill floor – are referred to as 'slave labour' by the oil industry throughout the world: they are nearly always locally recruited and the Scottish experience has not been different. In October 1973 an executive of a drilling company admitted the obvious in stating that all the drilling companies (most of them US-based) had agreed among themselves to fix the wages for local labour. In 1972 the agreed wage for roustabouts was about *30p an hour*. By the end of 1973, in response to 'severe labour shortages' the rate had been fixed at around 54p and great displeasure was voiced at the fact that a 'renegade' was paying as much as 58–60p. At this time crews would have been working three weeks on and one week off, twelve hours per day and seven days per week, with *no* pay during the week off. By 1977 the rate had risen to about £1.10 per hour which is roughly comparable to average rates onshore, but it is less favourable when one considers that there are no bonus or other fringe payments, as in construction. The contracts that the men had to sign absolved the employers from responsibility with regard to illness and injury: no sick pay and no compensation, and instant dismissal in the event of injury. The notorious phrase which encapsulated this was, 'Fall off that derrick, son, and you're fired before you hit the deck.' Attempts at unionisation were, and mostly still are, ruthlessly supressed: anyone suspected of joining or of recruiting for a trade union is instantly dismissed. This situation is reflected in the harrowing tales related by rig workers, and fully supported in our own studies of work and safety conditions on the rigs, and in the astonishing labour turnover figures, often as high as 600 per cent per year. Very few British nationals have been promoted to 'contract' positions where the high earnings begin. These are reserved for those of the same nationality as the parent company and form part of its 'permanent' crew. A rig returning to drill in US coastal waters, for example, would be prevented by US legislation from employing any foreign nationals.

It is in the case of work offshore that we do find the situation that we originally anticipated would be more general – the super-exploitative use of foreign labour. This applies especially to pipe-laying barges and a (reducing) proportion of supply boats. Figures for a particular barge show that rates of pay for Lebanese and Indian cooks and stewards, Spanish welders, British engineers, and US contract men were in the ratios 3:10:30:45. With regard to leave, Lebanese and Indians worked one year on, one month off; Spaniards worked six months on, fifteen days off; British and Americans three months on, one month off. This also applies to the boats that supply pipe barges. One of the largest operators of these recruits seamen almost exclusively from Spain and Portugal. They are flown over direct for six-month tours of duty and paid from Rotterdam through a Channel Islands bank. All employment contracts are signed at sea outside territorial waters – Masters have explicit instructions on this. Some operators of rig supply ships also only employ foreign crews. One case which received some publicity involved a company – Star Offshore Service – which the government, to its subsequent embarasment, chose to supply fishing support vessels in the last Icelandic 'cod war'. This company only employed Portuguese seamen on several of its ships. Work offshore is also exceptional among oil-related activities in its resistance to unionisation – though just why is a complex matter which I have no space to consider here.[13]

The point is that the maintenance of this situation has very little to do with 'labour market' forces – except insofar as, with $1\frac{1}{2}$ million unemployed, there are always more people prepared to travel to Aberdeen and embark on the, by now, ritual procession around the drilling company offices and to endure, at least for a few weeks, the conditions they encounter. Rather, its maintenance is only achieved by an unremitting struggle in which the companies managed, sometimes narrowly, to keep the upper hand. By controlling a closed and tightly policed environment management has largely succeeded in selecting, excluding, confusing, indoctrinating, insulting and rotating workers in such a way as to prevent their combination and maintain their fragmented, isolated condition. This is little short – and sometimes not short at all – of physical coercion. The 'ethos of oil' is the ideology which reflects this condition: the propagandist use of capitalism as pure theory involving the notions of free competition and enterprise, each person carving out his own destiny in accordance with his abilities and his guts. The underlying reality, of course, is one in which his rate had been 'fixed' and his promotion prospects are nil.

In the various instances cited by Corrigan (1977) – migrant labour, bonding, allotments, serfdom, slavery – coercive power is being used in order to pay the worker at (or, it is sometimes argued, below) the cost of reproduction and maintenance. In the case of oil-related employment wages offshore have in the past been not greatly above subsistence; and there is now plenty of evidence that employers, in their haste to secure orders and start production, underestimated the vulnerability of their workforces and have since recouped some of their earlier generosity. Nevertheless, it is clear from, for example, the level of earnings available at Kishorn that this is not the main focus of employers' power. What is being affected is the other side of the 'effort bargain' which has been equally, historically, the object of struggle: the amount and duration of effort and control over the labour process. That is, it reinforces both the formal and real subordination of labour, only imperfectly achieved especially in the relatively primitive and craft-dominated construction industry. In this particular 'product market' the rewards are sufficiently high for the depression of money wages to be far less salient. And this in turn is supported by the very high capital requirement and hence oligopolistic position of producers. This is easily illustrated for the three examples I have cited. The defeat at Kishorn was followed by the rigid enforcement of a quite Draconian policy on lateness and absence. If a man were absent without a medical certificate more than once, or late more than twice, in a five-week cycle – that is two consecutive fourteen-day tours of fourteen hours per day with one week's leave in between – he was dismissed without further question. Following the defeat at Nigg a new productivity agreement was put into effect – drawn up in secret negotiations among management, client, union officials and shop stewards – which laid down a 40 per cent increase in productivity and tighter discipline, for no specified return.[14] The company's previous undertaking on retaining the 'local' component of the workforce in employment between contracts was also relaxed. In the case of work offshore, a considerable proportion of the work done would either be impossible, or would be very much more expensive, or would involve protracted and hence extremely costly delays if management were not able to expose workers to danger and difficulty to a degree that would be considered completely intolerable onshore.[15] This seems to be a far more important component in management's determination to retain control in the North Sea and to resist unionisation than the relatively insignificant cost of higher wages.

Conclusion

I have tried to show that there is some value in approaching the industrial relations of oil in the North of Scotland via the notion of 'dependency'; that doing so highlights specific features which they have in common and which are related to their particular environment and peripheral status. However, I think I have also shown that – in this context at least – there is no such thing as 'dependent industrial relations'. This is certainly the case if the notion of dependency is promoted as a rival dimension of dominance and subordination. For the elements out of which this dependency in industrial relations is composed are not analytically distinct from those of industrial relations elsewhere. These structural and ideological elements of ascriptively based power and non-market coercion occur – with greater or lesser effect – in all work situations. So, for example, the position of garment workers, particularly women and especia` immigrant women, is not very different from that of workers offshore. The position of workers in inner cities may be much the same as that of workers at Kishorn – a point nicely illustrated by the fact that the Kishorn employer, John Howard Construction, had used the identical tactic of re-manning to break a strike in Liverpool a few years previously. And the ideological pressures from state and union no doubt feel much the same to workers at Nigg as they do to engine tuners at Cowley.

9 Towards a Comparative Approach to the study of Industrial and Urban Politics: the case of Spain
Ignasi Terrades

Introduction

My aim in this chapter is to question some of the generalisations made about the role of the state in contemporary urban–industrial development. I will use the case of the Spanish state and industrialisation in Catalonia because it is, in so many respects, a deviation from the experience of the countries of northern Europe. Within Spain, national identities have remained strong, and these nationalisms are based within some of the most dynamic economic regions of Spain. Also, unlike the situation in many northern countries, it was the centre of government – Madrid – that, for long, remained peripheral to modern industrial development. This government was often indifferent or even hostile to industrialisation. The industrialisation of Catalonia and the growth of Spain's major commercial and industrial city – Barcelona – within this region thus took place with little help, direct or indirect, from central government. This historical legacy of an 'absentee' state has left its imprint on the contemporary pattern of development and on current political issues. To understand these, it is necessary to identify the contrasts between Catalonia and other advanced industrial regions.

Most interpretations of urban–industrial systems in terms of capitalist development have the tendency to posit a common theoretical level based on a wide variety of contexts. There is a convergent interpretation in which the different varieties of urban–industrial phenomena are explained in terms of the contradictions and crises involved within a unique and general type of capitalist development. This interpretation produces a level of abstraction in which cities and industrial settings are difficult to compare and contrast, because the level of abstraction is common for a wide range of situations. Thus, for example, in the model presented by Castells the logic of urban–industrial development is reduced to the logic of a theory of capital; that is, the criteria used to analyse urban–industrial questions consists exclusively of basic elements of the capitalist mode of production. Thus, any urban system is explained by the general classification production–circulation–consumption–public management. But the dynamic, historical characteristic of capitalist development is precisely its differential character: the fact that the capitalist world arises from differential costs and rents and differentials in the integrations between economic activities and their political conditions. The economic differentials serve to define the market structure, and the way in which this structure is politically integrated defines the social formation. Thus the market structure and its political integration are key points to consider when comparing social formations.

Some of the comparative features of this development are taken up in Bryan Roberts's chapter (Chapter 10), in which he explores the different ways in which the industrial economy is organised in terms of production markets and of the social and political order. Indeed, the absence of a strong, industrially minded central state in Spain and the relative weakness of the internal market are perhaps the major factors accounting for the particular organisation of Catalan industrial production. However, my own concern is with using the Catalan case to explore the specific significance of such phenomena as urban planning and the participation of local populations, local economic units and regional interests in it.

In the Spanish context, these practices have come to have an ambivalent attraction to many interests, including the currently dominant ones, as a means to economic and political development. One of the ways in which I will explore this ambivalence and its implications for urban development is by stressing the specific historical role that planning and participation have had in Spain. Thus, I will look at the phenomenon of the privatisation of state functions by industrial enterprises – a process which, in Catalonia, has often been the preferred way of handling the dilemmas of industrial development. Privatisation is the more interesting because, in some ways, it represents an anti-urban bias in industrial development, leading in the case of Catalonia to a centrifugal development in which industry disperses, with economic growth, to rural locations.

Initially I will consider comparatively some of the general features of recent Spanish developments as they have affected both state policies and the industrial economy. I will then consider the specific consequences of the historical legacy for Catalonia and for Barcelona, ending with an analysis of the significance of contemporary attempts to resolve social and economic problems.

Spain in a comparative context

I will begin by looking at the *forms* in which the central state relates to local populations in terms of coordinating economic and administrative activities. Principally there are two types of relations: *centralisation* and *privatisation*.

By *centralisation* I mean the relationship between the state and the economic structure where both the extraction and the assignment of superstructural resources (i.e. public assets) are organised in a pyramid-like fashion; that is to say that all the important decisions and procedures must be referred up to, or passed down from, the top of the pyramid. Centralisation is a form of relationship between the state and the economic structure. This can take two forms. The first is *interventionism*. Interventionism means a discontinuous and fragmented use of centralisation; that is, the state 'intervenes' in cases specifically judged eligible for a state action and through the channels of centralisation. The second is *planning*, the opposite of interventionism. Planning means that the centralised structure is responsive to specific needs of the economic structure and not the reverse (conversely interventionism responds to the exigencies of a centralised framework). Thus, in a sense, planning involves the participation and integration of local population and local and regional economic activities in the central institutions. (So planning is not necessarily evidence of a socialist relation between the state and private economic activities.) Planning means essentially a close integration between the levels at which economic enterprises develop and state policies are implemented (Fernandez-Cavada, 1975). Since Keynes and the development of a mixed economy, planning basically means a systematic, not sporadic, intervention in market mechanisms, especially with respect to capital goods and labour. Thus planning has to do with a concerted attempt to coordinate market forces in a period in which growth has slowed down.

Privatisation is the opposite of centralisation. Privatisation means the appropriation of state concerns by those directly involved in economic activities (i.e. private initiatives). But there is an alternative that stands between privatisation and centralisation. This mode, which is currently experiencing a revival, consists in *regionalisms* or *nationalisms* within the orbit of the central state.

In the nineteenth century, the contraction of the Spanish economy (as a result of colonial failure and the lack of development of a national market) brought about a state structure which was isolated from the dynamic productive forces of the country. The state relied on traditional sources of income: public debt, regressive taxation and the exploitation of national wealth. It was unable to integrate the varied economic activities of the whole country and, especially, unable to encourage actively the growth of a dynamic bourgeoisie such as was arising in Catalonia. This relative isolation brought about political fragmentation, and the struggles that undermined the nineteenth century Spanish state (the Carlist wars) weakened its effectiveness at the local level. From this situation there emerged a politically fragmented structure in which economic activities were politically integrated at the local or regional level without a further integration with the central level. The expression of this structure was *caciquismo*. The maintenance of the Spanish political unity was ensured, not by the integrative functions of the central state, but by the outcomes of political confrontations at the local level (but in some cases this led to civil war, particularly between Carlists and liberals). In Spain, the state has traditionally been subservient to interests that are alien to large sections of those who are economically active within the country. And so the state has only provided intermittent support for the peripheral bourgeoisie rather than in any planned, systematic action. Catalonia provides the most representative and developed case of this situation.

Catalonia, a manufacturing country, has been subordinated to the agrarian and commercial interests of a section of the Spanish bourgeoisie which was closely linked to the central Spanish state. So development of the central institutions of the Spanish state was unrelated to the economic activities of large parts of the country. Thus, there has been continuous friction between the exigencies of an alien centralised network and local economic activities. The continuous policy of centralisation has been more a means for prolonging political immobility than a means for exerting effective control. So instead of planning there has been interventionism, the discontinuous and fragmented action of the state in respect to social problems. Interventionism results in fragmented, patchy changes rather than global reforms. Basically, interventionism is the prescribed role for the state in a 'social market economy', a response to extreme cases of 'diseconomies'. In Catalonia, interventionism has mainly affected the manufacturing industry. In the urban sphere it has been confined to housing and not extended to land use planning. In summary, in Spain the exclusively political (or state-economic) aims of central intervention have negated planning. This type of control has not been concerned with curbing market mechanisms, and in fact the centralised state structure has been very ineffective in coordinating and implementing economic planning.

This failure of political centralisation in the economic field is illustrated by the fact that this non-participatory and non-integrative centralised state did not have sufficient knowledge or competence to implement the development plans that it drew up in the 1960s. In fact the state was designing policies for populations whose development was already established by themselves in a fragmented fashion. The four development plans produced in the 1960s and early 1970s were too general and ambiguous to be a useful basis for the establishment of policies which would integrate the Spanish market. These plans stressed isolated developments, having as their basis a 'growth pole' strategy which, in the conditions of Spain, merely sharpened regional inequalities and the disproportionate growth of the urban metropolis. The lack of planning and the inefficiency of centralised control have been compensated for by privatisation. Precisely because of the monolithic, introverted and limited structure of the Spanish state the private sector has taken over public concerns. (I tried to depict elsewhere [1978] the origins of privatisation in the Catalan textile industry.) The contribution made by the private sector to developing the industrial and urban infrastructure and to social welfare has been an extraordinary burden on the Catalan bourgeoisie, especially when contrasted with the modern development of the public sector in advanced European countries.

Development in England and Spain
Spain and England can be contrasted as follows. Firstly, there is

the crucial part played in shaping industrialisation by the Spanish failure and, in contrast, Britain's colonial success in shaping industrialisation. The colonial failure weakened the Spanish state and gave it an ambiguous and tenuous relationship to industrialisation. In contrast, English industrial development was relatively rapidly integrated into the political system.

Secondly, there is the contrast between the British and Spanish systems of centralisation. In Britain centralisation has stimulated a more systematic development of industrial conglomerates and planned administrative action; there have been close links between economic development and its political integration. However, in Spain centralisation, as already noted, has been essentially a political phenomenon largely dissociated from economic development. The latter is characterised by fragmentation and by small-scale private sector economic activities.

Thirdly, the participatory, negotiatory style of political integration in Britain (although more so in form than in reality) contrasts with the adjudicatory nature of political integration in Spain. In this sense the Spain–Britain comparison illustrates the two extremes for political action concerned with industrialisation. The British case is characterised by a democratic style in dealing with the political implications of industrialisation and urbanisation and the Spanish case is characterised by a dictatorial, adjudicatory style which later became an 'unplanned centralisation'.

Such contrasts are very relevant today, because Spain is now experimenting with the path to economic and political development which is now being increasingly questioned in those countries, such as England, which first adopted it. This path involves developing a mixed economy under a system of parliamentary democracy. To adopt this path implies fiscal reform, the development of public welfare, the reduction of unemployment, the development of public consumption, the dynamisation of the public sector, and the development of a representative and participatory administration. But when England undertook these changes, mainly in the 1950s, it could draw upon the surpluses of an expanding industrial development. This permitted the 'welfare state' to be developed without damaging the confidence of private investment. Spain, however, is contemplating change in the course of the world economic crisis of the 1970s and without the level of state development that was present in postwar

Britain. Thus, the democratic path is made hazardous by the scarcity of the resources necessary for such a development.

The measures required to install a democratic system in Spain have to be accommodated with the present pattern of private investment, which demands an adherence to the 'original purity' of the market economy, the stimulation of private investment via tax allowances and consequent cuts in public expenditure. This market approach to economic development also relies on securing 'public order' by having available 'authoritarian practices' (and by using unemployment as a hidden weapon in industrial bargaining to counter the growing influence of the unions). Also, among business interests there is a clearly felt ideological need to stress the virtue of private initiative in reaction to the growth of state intervention, planning and centralisation in response to the economic crisis. The present situation is thus characterised by the alternatives of either following more or less genuine democratic policies but running the risk of losing control of the political forces that have been unleashed, or of maintaining the premises of the previous regime with a changed facade. So the budgetary and tax reforms recently initiated by the state thus face enormous obstacles.

In the Francoist period the potential effectiveness of expenditure in terms of costs and benefits was not a predominant factor in influencing budgetary decisions. Rather the adjudicatory principle worked, so the budget did not result from a planning exercise in which central resources were allocated in a systematic fashion to further local development. This is also one of the reasons for the rise of nationalisms and regionalisms within the Spanish state. The aim of the current tax reform is to create more direct taxes to provide for investment in public welfare. The 'Pacto de la Moncloa' (the Spanish social contract, agreed between the government and the parliamentary opposition) established the required tax increase as 25 per cent. However this reform which, together with the democratisation of government, would lead to increased welfare, faces the restrictions imposed by the present economic crisis. Thus the limits of effective planning and of public entrepreneurship are established by the same economic forces (i.e. private initiative) that have created the conditions for the political democratisation of the country. My argument is that the mixed economy runs in a developmental fashion, so that it can rarely withstand a balanced or stagnant situation (Harvey,

1978). Once the development of the state's resources through welfare and planning do not result in an increase in productivity or in cost reduction, private investment boycotts the further development of the public structure and it begins to be viewed as parasitic on, rather than contributory to, returns on investments.[1]

Barcelona

Planning in Spain under Franco was no more than a public mystification of private interests, a superficial touch of public management applied to the anarchic development of private initiatives. One of the most striking cases of such a process was the development of Barcelona under Mayor Porcioles (1957–73) (Banco Urquijo, 1972; Marti, 1974; Tarrag, 1975). Plans were prepared but they were ignored in practice. The plans were the 1945 Comisión de Ordenación Provincial de Barcelona (to organise the settlement of immigrants), the 1953 Plan de Ordenación Urbana de Barcelona, which acknowledged the 'urban disorder' of Barcelona and tried to improve communications, establish leisure areas, facilitate decongestion and the specialisation of different areas and the 1960 Municipal Charter, which attempted to establish a sound municipal tax base. The result has been commonly depicted as chaotic (Circulo de Economia 1973), bringing to Barcelona an urban framework similar to that of third world countries. A characteristic case of this situation is provided by the district of La Mina in S. Adrià de Besós within the core of the metropolitan area of Barcelona. La Mina has a density of 864 inhabitants per hectare (Barcelona as a whole has 221). The average number of inhabitants per house is 5.6 (that of Barcelona is 3.3). There are 1500 children whose mothers work and only 500 children are at school. There are no collective services for over 800 retired people. In 1975 12 per cent of the adult population were illiterate. Some streets are unpaved and watchmen and police behave badly in an area which has a 'bad name'. Taxi drivers do not like to take people there and firms are reluctant to hire or give credit to people with addresses in La Mina. Unemployment is high (López, 1978). (Another area of Barcelona is described in Huertas-Claveria, 1973.) In short, in Barcelona economic growth has not been urbanised successfully and the city is overcrowded. The city generates a tax income similar to those of other European cities, but the public authorities are unwilling to distribute these resources to cope with the urban consequences of economic growth more successfully.

It is in such circumstances that Barcelona has continued to grow as the premier industrial centre in Spain. A third of the foreign capital invested in Spain is in Catalonia and 90 per cent of this is in Barcelona. The city contains 5 per cent of the Spanish population and Barcelona province 11 per cent. Average immigration to the province is 60,000 people per year and the city has experienced a considerable informal urbanisation: shanty towns have grown up and been rapidly converted into so called vertical shanty towns (*barraquismo vertical*). Large-scale housing units have been developed on the periphery by state agencies. These bodies have built some 50,000 houses. The use of 'partial plans' has helped building companies and other financial interests to change land use fragmentarily without any overall planning (Ferras, 1976).

Changes in the location of the factories in Catalonia must be understood in the light of this unplanned growth of the metropolitan area of Barcelona, with its lack of co-ordination of industrial and residential growth. As a result there is often little *overt* rationality in the location and relocation of firms within the metropolitan area. The report on the '*Localización de actividades en el area metropolitana de Barcelona*' (n.d.) concludes, for example, that in periods of economic recession there is a tendency for firms to change their location in order to obtain a substantial profit from the land sold, or to have an excuse to restructure the company by staff reduction. And, overall, this report showed that firms which were leaving the city left for three main types of reasons: first, because a profit could be obtained from selling urban land and buying cheaper new land; second, to avoid the dangers of a militant working class; and third, as a result of the increase in pollution and noise control in the centre. What results is an expansion of unplanned peripheral areas.

I want now to argue that this uneven and scattered pattern of metropolitan development is closely related to the existence of a strongly centralised government. Under this centralised system resources are allocated on the basis of centrally determined priorities and an inadequate knowledge of the needs of the periphery. As a result in Catalonia many matters, which elsewhere would be of public concern, are left to be resolved by the 'prodigality' of the Catalan bourgeoisie, who have often felt obliged to take initiatives of a public character (Serra Ramoneda, 1968).

Political fragmentation, unplanned centralisation and local heterogeneity

The variety of local economic and social situations in Spain demonstrate the limitations of state planning and intervention. The interstitial and fragmented nature of much Spanish economic activity, reinforced by market fluctuations, has stood in the way of systematic and generalised state action. Every government action that aimed to standardise economic processes has been hindered by a privately owned economic system fragmented into small scale units. This Spanish situation contrasts with the more integrated, centralised and systematised structure of the British economy. Thus, from a British socialist point of view,

> In the British economy mergers and takeovers have created an institutional framework well adapted for central planning. At present the top 100 industrial firms account for more than half of all industrial output, and the proportion is rising fast. Many of the remaining firms are little more than sub-contractors. Hence a takeover of the top 200 firms would bring virtually all industrial production under public control.
>
> (Cambridge Political Economy Group, 1974)

The interstitial and small-scale nature of urban businesses can be seen in Barcelona. In the metropolitan area much construction was required during the course of growth. But even the massive demand for building that occurred in the 1960s did not generate large firms. The arbitrary growth of the metropolitan area, determined by land speculation, did not create the basis for the emergence of large-scale, integrated construction firms. Rather, a system of sub-contracting developed. Thus in Barcelona 22.7 per cent of construction firms have no hired employees, 39.4 per cent have between 1 and 5 employees, 25.5 per cent 6 to 25, 7.6 per cent between 26 and 50, 2.8 per cent between 51 and 100, 1.2 per cent between 101 and 250 and 0.4 per cent between 251 and 500 (Organización Sindical, 1976). And 84.3 per cent of the employees are unskilled and semi-skilled workers. Yet because of inflation, capital development and, possibly, for political reasons, both private and semi-private (i.e. publicly subsidised) working class housing was mainly for sale. Housing has been seen by the public authorities more as a profitable private undertaking supported by the state sector than as an item of social expenditure (for indirect profits). Thus, poor materials have been used by the private building companies, for instance the use of concrete instead of brick walls to save labour, with resultant problems of condensation and lack of acoustic and thermal insulation.[2]

Construction workers, who were mainly new immigrants, bought much of the housing built in the 1960s when the materials employed were usually of poor quality. Six to ten years later many complaints were voiced about the deterioration of these houses. Many of the immigrant construction workers lived at first with their relatives and used materials taken from the company for which they were working to build their own houses in their spare time. The companies allowed such activities to go on, viewing them paternalistically.[3]

More generally too, most industries in the centre of the metropolitan area have a high proportion of small firms within them. Thus, of all the firms in the area 34 per cent have no paid employees, 38 per cent have from 1 to 5, 22 per cent from 6 to 25, 6 per cent from 26 to 50. From a total of 144,680 workers, 12 per cent work on their own account, 28 per cent in firms of 6 to 25 workers, and 16 per cent in firms of 26 to 50 workers (Organización Sindical, 1976). Of all these workers about 40 per cent were unskilled. In contrast the average number of workers per factory in the Upper Llobregat and Ter areas ('rural' areas of Catalonia) is 400. The fragmentation of employment in the urban centre may be politically useful for the bourgeoisie;[4] it is also a 'rational' response to the chaotic urban structure. On the other hand, fragmentation raises costs.[5]

Conclusion

The historical absence of an efficient and organised Spanish government able to affect local developments has created local political structures that are impermeable to the changes now taking place in central government. Centralisation in Spain has not been based on economically integrative and participatory planning but on naked political control, so changes in superstructural control have not significantly disturbed the local base. Local initiatives have, in fact, been the usual means by which different activities have been integrated and local interests have had effect. This has led to a situation similar to that of *caciquismo*, for the local political structure has been left to determine issues that are normally centrally planned in modern industrial states. So the recent political convulsions in Spain must not be allowed to obscure the fact that most of the changes that have taken place are superficial.

The recent abolition of the institutions and practices of the Franco period has been made without any noticeable change in the effective political structure. The new regime has left untouched, as did the previous regime, the real distribution of political and economic power. The political regime of Francoism was represented at the local level by the official trade unions, the *diputaciones* and the town halls. But these institutions were more passive than active; the regime was based on police power – banning rather than encouraging actions, for instance. So, local initiatives were developed on a piece-meal basis in the absence of any clear and common plans of action. Local industrialists, merchants, administrative officers, bank managers, etc. developed economic activities without much attention to supra-local integration. Localities became highly disarticulated even when they were involved in activities that extended beyond the local sphere. On the one hand, small and medium-sized economic activities were not integrated at the supra-local level; on the other hand, large-scale economic undertakings were often directly tied to the interests of centralised (and often foreign) powers. Few schemes were developed to establish and encourage systematic initiatives: the result was the development of officially controlled processes which served private interests. Because most state institutions were restrictive and did not encourage initiatives, the recent withering away of such restrictions has had little positive influence on local frameworks of economic activity, whose management is to a great extent privatised as a result of the limitations of the previous regime which have been described.

The lack of an effective central state action has contributed to the fact that political arrangements differ greatly between differing regions and towns. Local political systems have been formed mainly as a result of the action of local resources and demands rather than as a result of the interaction of the local resources and national demands. The resultant fragmentation has given rise to nationalist, regionalist and localist movements. These movements must be primarily interpreted (although our research experience refers only to Catalonia) as forms of public management.

In Catalonia entrepreneurs and other sectors of the population have often complained about the disproportionate tax burden on Catalonia and the lack of public expenditure there. Nationalism and regionalism are not just *potential* alternatives to the Spanish state, but a considerable part of the currently existing reality, for in face of the restrictive nature of the Spanish administration, private enterprise has provided many public services. Thus regionalisation or Catalan nationalisation of public management would involve the public organisation of concerns that had been privatised in face of the inefficient centralisation of the Spanish state.[6]

Urban–industrial growth in Spain stands between the two models of centrifugal and centripetal growth. Although Spain has the resources to develop centralised planning, the characteristics of its state have contributed to centrifugal patterns, with anarchic and poorly integrated patterns of metropolitan growth. Though changes now occurring aim to correct this situation, the economic crisis makes the further development of the state sector difficult. Consequently, privatisation, combined with piecemeal interventionism, is seen as the 'moderate' solution to the present chaos (according, for example, to most Catalan economists). We suggest that this solution is far from being the cheapest available (as they assume), because the fragmentation of economic activities that such a policy involves increases in production costs and adds to price inflation in general. So, if the extension of planning is limited by the economic crisis, economic growth itself will be limited too by the costs associated with the persistence of fragmented and discontinuous economic activities.

Migration and Industrialising
       Economies: a comparative
       perspective
       Bryan R. Roberts

Introduction

I will examine three examples of the role of rural–urban migration
in countries undergoing industrialization. These examples are taken
from different contexts – nineteenth century Manchester and Barcelona and Lima in the contemporary period. These examples will be
used to examine the migration patterns that accompany industrialization and to explore the significance of these patterns for urban and
industrial organization. My general aim is to explore the factors
that differentiate industrialisation in ways that significantly affect
the pattern of a nation or a region's development.[1]

   This chapter differs in its approach from those analyses of migration
that are mainly concerned with the range of migration patterns
present in particular situations and which identify the individual
reasons for migration, the characteristics of migrants, the type of
movement and the nature of migrant careers in the city.[2] In contrast,
I shall concentrate on comparing the contexts within which different
patterns of migration and industrialisation emerge. At one level,
this context will be the position of the industrialising nation or region
within the broader economy. At the local level, this context will be
the social institutions that shape industrialisation, particularly those
affecting the labour process.

   Implicit in the choice of the examples is a distinction between
industrialisation taking place in countries occupying three types of
structural position within capitalist development.[3] It is these differences in structural position which I see as the main explanations
for the differences in the patterns of migration. The first, that of
nineteenth century Manchester, is industrialisation in a country that
was at the centre of the international economy in terms of technologi-

cal superiority, available capital and political power. The second is industrialisation within a semi-peripheral economy. The semi-peripheral position is one in which there has been some development of national capital, in which the internal market is moderately developed and in which agriculture is increasingly organised along capitalist lines. However, the country remains unevenly developed. Foreign capital is important in trade and in the control of production. Also, there is dependence on the advanced capitalist world for the technology needed for industrialisation. This second case is that of Barcelona, though the analysis could be extended to some contemporary Latin American situations, such as that of São Paulo. The third type, that of Lima, is of industrialisation in a peripheral economy in which the internal market is weakly developed. Agriculture is, in great part, still under peasant production and national capital has scarcely developed. These distinctions will be used in the subsequent analysis to examine the different patterns of industrial organisation that develop in the three situations and thus the differences in the 'demand' for and absorption of migrants.

The organisation of an industrial economy is also likely to be affected by the characteristics of the available supplies of labour, capital and technology. In this paper, I will concentrate on labour, partly for reasons of space and partly because it brings out clearly the importance of social institutional factors in industrialisation. Rural–urban migration is an interesting topic for exploring the role of labour in differentiating industrialising situations. Migration is part of the relocation and reorganisation of labour consequent upon industrial concentration. Migrants are likely to have little experience of factory industry or of the urban–industrial milieu. Depending on the situation, they are made into industrial workers and urban residents through processes which include the experience of class struggle and state intervention and coercion. Our three cases show interesting differences on these dimensions. The Manchester case is predominantly that of a one-way migration of workers, many of whom had previous industrial experience, who became permanent residents of industrial communities. In Barcelona, migration did not lead to residential stabilisation. Migrants have been mainly unskilled and semi-skilled workers from rural situations. In Lima, migration has included a high degree of pendular migration and lively economic and social exchanges between the city and the rural areas.

The study of the mobility of labour has a general significance for understanding the political and economic changes brought about by industrialisation. The creation of a mobile labour force that can be disposed of flexibly to meet fluctuations in market demand and changing technology is essential to the labour process of industrial capitalism. The mobility of labour, its social flexibility, the political, legal and social institutions that make labour available to industry and the particular form that industrial capitalism takes, are, however, interconnected variables.[4] Thus, whether the supply of labour is skilled or unskilled or both, the degree of socialisation and/or coercion required to adapt the labour supply to factory production, whether labour is scarce, sufficient or 'over-abundant' – all these are factors that can influence the technology employed in industrial production, the sector of industry that develops most rapidly and the character of political and legal institutions.[5]

The social characteristics of the labour supply become an important part of the labour process; at times this works to strengthen worker organisation, at others, it serves to strengthen employer control and factory discipline. Thus, kinship, religious affiliation, place of origin or literacy can become factors in recruiting labour. They may also serve to differentiate internally the working class and may serve as means to maintain order within the workplace. Thus, ethnic or gender divisions can become associated with different positions in the factory hierarchy, dividing workers and facilitating employer rule. Industrialisation will be differentiated on these dimensions because of the specific character of the industrialising situation such as the density and economic differentiation of the available rural populations and the degree to which these populations are tied to the land.[6]

I will argue that differences in these local contexts will differentiate industrialisation through the labour process and through the set of relationships between social institutions, associated with the labour process, which develop within space. These relationships, such as those among patterns of residence, of work, of ethnic and religious affiliation and of political organisation, give a definite character to industrialisation. These 'horizontal' relationships among institutions can be used to assess the extent to which a particular city or industrial economy has an identifiable character which becomes a factor in analysis.[7] Such a character when it exists is a historical phenomenon which develops through time and should not be identified with any fixed boundaries, either geographical or administrative. The extent of the linkages among social institutions must be a matter of empirical research. Horizontal linkages – the community aspect of industrialisation – are constantly being modified by vertical linkages, such as those with the international economy. These vertical linkages can be viewed as forces for economic centralisation, such as the degree and kind of integration into a national or international economy. The strength of these forces vary from one situation to another. The stronger they are, the more likely it is that local identities will have less significance for social organisation than will national ones. It can be hypothesised that where vertical linkages are strong, for example, class identities become more salient than regional or city identities in determining the life chances and political reactions of workers or employers.

Finally, we can use the three cases to explore the conditions for state intervention during industrialisation. Industrialisation depends on political and economic centralisation for the provision of laws and regulations that enforce contracts or regulate markets. Centrally provided economic infrastructure, such as communications, also facilitate industrialisation. The pattern of state intervention is, however, not likely to be uniform. One difference that is illustrated by the contrast between Manchester and Lima is that between early and 'late' industrialisation. Later industrialising countries develop in the competitive context of an already developed world industrial economy. The scale and cost of technology required, as well as the importance of regulating the external competition through tariffs and other devices, mean that the state becomes a direct participant in industrialisation. Its role becomes more dominant to the extent that local capital is relatively scarce and that regulation and even coercion are needed to develop internal markets and make labour available. Thus, in many underdeveloped situations, agriculture is only partly commercialised and labour is tied to the land.

Our cases are also interesting in demonstrating the wide range of local conditions that can affect the pattern of state intervention.[8] The two factors that will be examined are the nature of the labour process and the strength of the industrial bourgeoisie. The Manchester case allows us to explore the implications of the situation in which capital is able itself to provide the necessary conditions for industrial expansion without much direct state intervention. Barcelona presents a situation in which the locally dominant classes have required state intervention, but in which the state has often been controlled by interests opposed to those of the industrial bourgeoisie. Finally, Lima shows what happens when there is neither a strong native industrial bourgeoisie nor a strong landed class opposing industrialisation.

The reason for examining Manchester, Barcelona and Lima as individual cases is to stress the importance of the contextual inter-relationship of the variables considered. It is important to keep in mind that the variables should be seen in their particular context and abstracted from that context only with great care. The aim of this paper is to clarify the rationalities of particular patterns of industrialisation, not to establish universally valid correlations between variables. The discussion of each case will begin by considering position within the international economy and its implication for the organisation of production. I will mainly use scale of enterprise to identify the main characteristics of this organisation of production. Then, the consequences for rural–urban migration are examined; this is followed by an analysis of the social relationships that underlie the labour process. Finally, the implications for state intervention are considered.

The Manchester case

The first point to make about Manchester is the familiar one of its position as the first great industrial city; but in the present context it is worth reminding ourselves of the implications of this position. For most of the nineteenth century, Manchester's increasing industrial production could count on expanding markets and faced relatively little technological competition. Production expanded both by bringing more labour into the factory system and by increasing fixed capital. Thus, between 1838 and 1856, there was a 56.3 per cent increase in the number of employees in cotton manufacture (to a total of 340,944), compared with a 72.4 per cent increase in motive power and (between 1850 and 1856) a 35 per cent increase in the number of spindles and a 23 per cent increase in power looms (Fong, 1930, p. 44). Large engineering firms, such as Platts of Oldham, employing some 900 workers, emerged in the same period. In addition, another important local industry, coal mining, was highly labour-intensive.

A combination of large-scale, relatively labour-intensive industries and, from the mid-century on, a relatively stable demand for the industrial product meant that employment was increasingly dominated by the factory system: outworkers and smaller units of production were absorbed by this expansion. This description is more accurate for the industrial towns surrounding Manchester than for the centre city itself. Manchester centre, as the location for the organisation of the textile economy, had a more pronounced service character. It was in Manchester centre that outworking, as in the garment trade, and small enterprises concentrated. By the end of the nineteenth century manufacturing employment was dominated by fairly large-scale enterprises. Even in the contemporary period, it is the relatively large-scale industrial employment which predominates. In the Manchester industrial township of Oldham, 72.2 per cent of manual workers in 1966 were employed in enterprises of 250 and more people. By 1975 the proportion employed in enterprises of 250 and more people had dropped to 61.2 per cent.

The labour input into this economy was provided mainly by short-distance migration from the industrialised rural areas; by the early nineteenth century this migration generated an abundant supply both of skilled and unskilled labour. The main source of long-distance migration was Ireland. The Irish were predominantly of rural background and their initial work was usually as unskilled labour, or in crafts such as tailoring and shoemaking. The Manchester area had, for long, been a centre of the outwork manufacturing system and of cottage industry (Roberts, 1978). This was true not only of textiles, but of other such relatively large-scale industries such as hat-making. In 1841 there were, for example, 5546 persons employed in hat manufacture in Lancashire; the organisation of the trade was predominantly a merchant–employer system in which several branches were carried on by men in places attached to their cottages, while the finishing processes were done in an urban factory (Fong, 1930, pp. 12, 185).

Steam power gradually concentrated this labour by increasing the size of the factories and the advantages of integrating operations within them. It also became more difficult for outworkers and independent craftsmen to secure an adequate subsistence. In the period up to the mid-century, there was considerable mobility amongst the urban population, as well as movements from the rural districts to the towns. Factory employment was not predominant even in the industrial townships of Manchester before mid-century and sweated labour systems of outwork flourished in the city as well as in the country districts. Biographies of workers of this period suggest that for the 'independent' craftsmen, such as reed-makers, inter-town mobility was essential in order to pick up one temporary job after another.

This first period of labour mobility and the existence of an industrial reserve army for the growth of factory production was followed by a period of gradual residential stabilisation. Rural-urban and inter-urban migration contributed a smaller proportion of the area's growth; natural increase increasingly accounted for town growth (Lawton, 1962). By the end of the century, there is a clear trend to out-migration from the industrial areas – an out-migration which may have gone predominantly overseas. Slow population growth and concentration in factory employment meant that the industrial reserve army was absorbed quite directly into fairly stable, factory employment. Some data on the occupations of the Irish in Oldham of 1871 are indicative of this: whereas 88 per cent of the fathers work as labourers or, in a few cases, as craftsmen, 76 per cent of their sons and daughters were working as cotton operatives.

What this second population trend meant, in fact, was the settling down of a previously mobile population in streets and neighbourhoods which became the home of families from generation to generation. In Oldham, as probably elsewhere in the industrial areas of Manchester, the turnover of families in different streets of the town dropped steadily from the last quarter of the nineteenth century onwards (Bedale, 1978). It is more difficult to trace the extent that a similar process was occurring in the job field. However, Chapman and Abbot's (1912/13) analysis of the likelihood of children entering the same occupation as their fathers, shows that at the beginning of the twentieth century over 60 per cent of male children did so in cotton textiles. This process of stabilisation in occupations and residence was the basis for the emergence of distinctive working class cultures in the Manchester area. These cultures were the basis for effective organisation, especially in defending jobs and in improving the conditions of work. Indeed, they are likely to have been a contributory factor to the slow rate of technological innovation in textiles in the early twentieth century, as unions fragmented by craft

and gender, fought against labour and skill-saving innovations
(Habakkuk, 1967, p. 143; Landes, 1970, pp. 340–8). In any event,
because of this ready supply of skilled labour and the relative stability
of markets, employers had little incentive to innovate.

This brief survey does not do justice to the complexity of Manchester's growth pattern, but it provides the necessary background
to understanding the role of the state. What is striking about the
growth of the world's first great industrial metropolis is the relative
absence of state intervention in either the economic or social infrastructure. Service employment in the Manchester area was by
1901 42.1 per cent of total male employment in the centre and 21.7
per cent of male employment in an industrial township (Oldham).[9]
This employment was concentrated in commerce and distribution,
so that personal and social services provided only 8.3 per cent of
the centre's male employment and 5.2 per cent of the industrial
township's. During much of the nineteenth century, the administration of this spatially complex area was, to say the least, chaotic and
inefficient. Indeed, until 1832 Manchester, with a population of some
160,000 people, was governed by a court leet as a manorial village
(Redford and Russell, 1940). The regular full-time police force was
few in number and bore no comparison to the numbers that São
Paulo required to control a similar population (Shirley, 1978).
Though administration had improved considerably by the twentieth
century, its evolution was hindered by the fragmentation of local
jurisdictions and was characterised by local suspicion of the attempts
of central government to extend its jurisdiction. Local government
tended instead to be amateurish and based on volunteer services,
and it tended to find *ad hoc* short-term solutions to pressing problems
of urban planning and expansion.

It is not a sufficient explanation to attribute this relative lack of
state intervention to the competitive stage of industrial capitalism.
The fragmentation of Manchester's industry into a large number of
medium-sized firms, the absence of large combines and the predominance of family capital in industry, were important, of course,
in explaining the resistance of Manchester's dominant classes to
political and economic centralisation. Yet part of Manchester's
problem in making the transition to the monopoly stage of capital
was precisely because of this failure to develop an overall strategy
of change. Educational provision lagged behind that of Germany at

this period. Manchester and its townships were slower to develop innovations in urban transport technology and electric lighting than were German of North American cities. An additional explanation for the slow development of effective centralised administration is to be found in the characteristics of a residentially stabilised labour force.

I want to argue that stabilised labour creates the possibility of privatising the control and administrative functions, usually exercised by government, which ensure the social order required for the expansion of industrial capitalism. By privatisation, I refer to the process whereby private individuals such as industrial entrepreneurs, or non-government institutions such as kinship groups or religious bodies assume state-like functions by regulating behaviour to be compatible with the prevalent industrial order (Terrades, 1978). It is, in fact, during the most mobile period of Manchester's population growth – up to the mid-nineteenth century – that the issue of the collective provision of order is most acute in the urban milieu. The army was constantly at hand at this period and had to be used to suppress meetings such as Peterloo, to stop machine-breaking, factory burnings and so on (Foster, 1974). It is in this earlier period that industrialists often 'opt-out' of the problems of urban concentration by building their own colonies in which most services are provided for workers, citing the advantages of this paternalism for labour stabilisation (Marshall, 1968).

In the late nineteenth century, the problem of urban order becomes less acute. In part, this is the result of the triumph of liberal capitalism in that the profits of industry are sufficient to enable higher wages to be paid. Also, private initiative with some government intervention begins to develop an adequate urban infrastructure for Manchester. The working class housing stock had expanded considerably by the the end of the century, eliminating severe overcrowding, the worst health hazards and reducing population densities. Thus, in Oldham from 1841 to 1871, for example, the average number of people per house had declined, even in a sample of centrally located streets, from 5.6 to 5.1, despite the population increase in the township. This housing stock was built by small-scale private initiative in which local tradesmen, professionals and manufacturers invested capital, commissioning small blocks of cottage-type housing from one of the many local construction firms (Bedale, 1978).

Accompanying this trend was the increasing efficacy of privatised forms of establishing the urban-industrial order. Keith Burgess (1977) provides a detailed analysis of how the family economy and family structure of Lancashire households provided an effective underpinning to the authority and work relations of cotton manufacture. The division of labour in the factory with the senior minders in charge of piecers and less skilled workers was reinforced by the family economy. Though more detailed research is required, the suggestion is that the senior workers were the heads of the family and often of extended kin groups, and the subordinate workers were members of the household, contributing to a joint household budget. This family and kinship organisation is also likely to have underpinned the rapid spread in the area of friendly societies, savings banks and cooperative stores: the trust developing out of close social interaction contributed to the success of these more formal organisations (Burgess, 1977).

Religion, too, is likely to have been part of this privatised pattern of collective order. The hierarchy of the factory was replicated in the different positions of responsibility that owner, overlooker, senior minder and less skilled workers occupied in church or non-conformist chapel. These closely interacting groups of kin, workmates and neighbours were the ones that enforced notions of respectability, of respect for superiors and, for example, of the virtues of keeping a clean rent-book.[10] Religion and ethnicity became sources of differentation within the working class. Thus, the Irish were, to a certain extent, residentially segregated in Oldham, occupied a distinct set of job positions and, argues Foster (1974), were the foci of dissension within the working class at times of economic crisis.

The argument, then, is that employers had little need in this context to rely on state intervention or state provision of social or economic infrastructure to establish the appropriate urban-industrial order. Partly because of the stabilisation of labour in residential communities, a set of relationships developed between social institutions in the Manchester area which gave a definite and special character to this pattern of industrialisation. A working class developed that was internally differentiated and tied to certain job traditions. Industrial crises were faced through mutual aid, as much as by political organisation. Indeed, this population seems to have developed and internalised the values and patterns of behaviour that

discouraged technological innovation and made for a slowly expanding industrial capitalism. Low rates of technological innovation in
the cotton industry and the tendency to expand production by
labour-using rather than labour-saving innovations meant that
employers were unusually reliant on the cooperation of their workers
to increase output. Thus, in the face of increasing competition at the
end of the century, employers were to agree in the Brooklands
Agreement to procedures for collective bargaining which strengthened worker organisation but gave especial power to the senior
workers – the aristocracy of labour (Burgess, 1978).

The imprint left on urban institutions by the traditions of residentially stabilised labour continues to be a significant factor in the
contemporary period of extensive state intervention. This intervention became more pronounced after World War I and even more so
after World War II. The increase in intervention was part of the
increasing centralisation of the British economy, as joint stock companies began to predominate in most sectors of British industry.
Publicly provided collective services now dominate the urban milieu
in housing, education, health and so on. In many of the townships
of the Manchester area, 40 per cent or more of families are housed
in public housing.

The relationships between the state and urban populations are not,
however, as conflictive as is reported, for example, in France or Spain
despite extensive and often ill-conceived interventions in the British
case. In Manchester, state intervention has occurred *after* the matura-
tion of the urban and industrial structure. The pressure on the state
is thus less that of resolving the contradictions of an expanding
capitalist economy through regulating land prices or providing
infrastructure. Rather, the state has come to replace the private
provision of housing or jobs by capital which has withdrawn to more
profitable investments elsewhere. State intervention in the Manchester area has, in the contemporary period, thus been more
comprehensive and negotiatory in scope than in the other cases we
will consider. Existing populations and existing industrial infrastructure have been incorporated into the planning exercise, taking into
account firmly rooted job and location preferences, investment
decisions and so on. With an extensive programme for the clearance
of central city slum housing, Manchester has rebuilt working-class
housing in the centre, and has, for example, few working-class

suburbs in comparison with European cities such as Paris or Barcelona.

The counterpart of this is the evident paternalism that has developed between the state and local populations. Council tenants have less rights in law than private tenants; they also become dependent on housing and welfare bureaucracies. The files that are kept on these populations are cumulative ones, which record not only information related to housing such as movements and failures to pay rent, but also reports of moral failings such as letters of complaint from neighbours and newspaper clippings of delinquent actions.

The Barcelona case

Barcelona is, in many respects, the image of Manchester's growth, but in the context of a semi-peripheral economy. Catalan factory industrialisation began early in the nineteenth century. In terms of the introduction and spread of steam power and other technological innovations, it was as 'advanced' an industrialisation as that of Manchester (Terrades, 1978). The fundamental restraints on industrialisation were the weakness of the Spanish internal market and the absence of a strong and stable state commitment to industrialisation. Though the British state gave relatively little internal help to industrial development in the nineteenth century, its external policy laid the foundation for industrial expansion. In contrast, the Spanish state, at best, vacillated over and, at worst, negatively sanctioned industrial growth.[11] The external weakness of Spain was eventually to lose Catalan industrialists some of their best markets when the last colonies won independence.

Within this context, Catalan industry tended to organise itself in terms of vertical integration. A large commercial company would, for example, provide cotton to factories. Also, the different stages of the production process (spinning, weaving, finishing) were frequently carried out by different enterprises, but these were linked by relatively stable relationships among the firms. Thus, a merchant employer might act in organising all the processes of production, selling the finished cloth through his own retailing network; or independent firms might simply enter into stable relationships of supply with others. Market insecurities also meant that few of the units of production were large-scale. This limitation on growth is clear in the case of engineering, the other major industry of the area. Thus, one of the largest of these firms, the *Maquinista* company was founded in 1855 to make textile machinery, steam engines and boilers for the navy and merchant marine, railway engines and gas and water-powered motors (Garcia, 1978). This diversification was necessary in face of limited, fluctuating markets, but the size of the firm could only approximate the size of Platts, the Oldham textile machine manufacturers (approximately 1000 workers). Textile machinery was ultimately to be built on licence from Platts, while collaboration with other foreign firms enabled *Maquinista* to produce diesel and steam engines, rolling stock for the railways and tramways and so on.

This pattern of industrial growth has continued, with some modifications, until the present. Thus, on the one hand, industrial expansion has taken place less through the increasing concentration of capital and labour in single units of production than through the complementary expansion of large and small-scale firms. On the other, the dominant enterprises in the economy are, in their majority, closely linked to foreign companies. In the case of the largest enterprises, the head offices of the company are, in more than half the cases, located outside of Catalonia, and a majority also have a significant element of foreign capital. One consequence of this type of industrial economy is, I suggest, an unstable and unpredictable pattern of urban–industrial development. The location and expansion decisions of dominant enterprises are only minimally constrained by local commitments and are subject to national and even international criteria of the type and scale of operation that it is profitable to develop. Also, while industrial growth encourages the proliferation of small-scale enterprises to service the largest ones, it also increases the likelihood of subsequent closures in times of recession. Indeed, periods of industrial expansion increase the volatility of the economy, with small firms popping up here and there, but closing down equally rapidly.

In the period from 1964 to 1974, which was, in general, a period of expansion in manufacturing employment (from 723,757 to 906,072) there was also a *decrease* in the average size of industrial establishment in some of the most important industries (Banco Urquijo, 1972, pp. 376–84). Thus, the average employment in textile establishments decreased from 37.2 to 33; in the metal industry, the average number of employees declined from 22.3 to 19. A similar picture emerged from our recent case study of industrial growth in a working-class suburb of Barcelona, S. Adriá de Besos. S. Adriá is the location of some of Barcelona's largest industries: energy, textiles, glass manufacturing, chemicals and engineering. Six firms employ over 250 people each, 2086 workers in total. Of the 8680 jobs in manufacturing industry in the suburb 39 per cent are, however, in firms of fifty workers or fewer. Indeed, the most rapid expansion in the 1960s in S. Adriá was in small-scale engineering firms, employing fifty people or less; these increased from 127 to 279 firms, despite the closure of others. The other most rapid expansion was in chemicals (from 102 to 176 establishments) and again through the proliferation of small firms. In fact, the general picture of industrial employment throughout the Barcelona area is that of the proliferation of small-scale establishments which contribute a large proportion of the area's industrial employment. Thus, in 1976 there were 210,399 jobs in textiles throughout the Barcelona region, and, of these, 35 per cent worked in establishments having fewer than fifty workers and 47 per cent in those having fewer than 100 (information from Sindicato de Textil).

It is in the context of this 'small-scale' industrial economy and its pattern of growth that migration to Catalonia must be understood. Catalonia has, for centuries, been the most economically dynamic area of Spain, especially in terms of the expansion of job opportunities. Migration is thus not a new phenomenon: there has, for long, been a stage migration process in which families moved in from neighbouring regions such as Aragon, often to the agricultural regions of Catalonia, while those of the interior provinces of Catalonia moved towards the most economically dynamic areas, such as Barcelona. Barcelona, from at least the late nineteenth century onwards, attracted successive waves of migrants from the other regions of Spain – from Valencia to the port and fishing areas of Barcelona; from Aragon, Old Castille and Murcia with the construction and public works booms of the 1920s. Many of the Murcians came from the industrial (mining and port) areas and found work in Barcelona's growing industry. More recently, the heaviest influx of migration has been from Andulusia so that, by 1970, 11.61 per cent of Barcelona's population has been born in Andulusia, as compared with 49.86 per cent born in the city and 10.91 per cent born elsewhere in

Catalonia (Recolons, 1976, pp. 141–2).

Unlike Manchester's migration pattern, movement to Barcelona, especially in recent years, is not predominantly short-distance; it is also the movement of people of village rather than town origin. For example, we obtained the records of all workers employed in *La Maquinista* since 1939 and found that almost 60 per cent of the workers were immigrants from villages and small towns, compared with 8 per cent who had come from the larger towns and cities of Spain. *La Maquinista*'s workforce is almost entirely a skilled one and, indeed, these immigrants were predominantly recruited as unskilled or semi-skilled workers, who learned their trade in the factory itself. While the immigrants to Barcelona and its area had higher levels of education and were more likely to have had non-agricultural work experience than the populations of their regions of origin, they are, in contrast to Manchester's 'industrial' migrants, predominantly a supply of unskilled labour. This pattern of migration is the result of the uneven development of the Spanish economy and the consequently low levels of economic diversification in the agrarian structure.

The massive influx of migrants to Barcelona was not, however, simply a question of the attraction of the better economic opportunities there.[12] These migrations were, in many respects, the result of the political situation of Spain and, in particular, state intervention in the agrarian structure. The power of the large landowners and the agricultural export interests both precluded any effective agrarian reform in Spain and lent the support of central and local government to the economic domination of landowners and merchants throughout provincial society. The Civil War and the Francoist regime consolidated this rural power system. The out-migration of villagers was a convenient means of maintaining an impoverished rural labour supply without increasing rural discontent. Seasonal labour away from the villages supplemented local incomes, while permanent migration acted as a safety valve chanelling out the most ambitious and discontented. Indeed, it can be suggested that the Spanish state increasingly lent its support to the organisation of migration as an enduring feature of the Spanish economy by permitting the growth of squatter settlements around the major cities, facilitating international migration and so on.

On these dimensions there are some interesting similarities with the situation in São Paulo in which state policy towards the rural sector of the region has contributed to rural out-migration (Brant, 1977). Many of these migrants in São Paulo come to reside in the towns and cities, but work as temporary agricultural labour. Both in São Paulo and in the Spanish situation, agriculture is an important economic sector for export earnings and for the domestic urban market. One characteristic of the semi-peripheral situation, then, is that the forces commercialising the agrarian structure and thus creating a rural surplus population are much stronger than in the peripheral situation.

This type of massive, predominantly unskilled migration interacted with the industrial economy of Catalonia to exaggerate the tendencies present in both the migration pattern and in the economy. The supply of unskilled labour, but the shortage of skilled labour, meant that it was convenient to expand the economy through units of production which could most easily use such labour. The construction industry expanded through very small units (an average of 6.2 workers per unit in 1960 and 18.2 by 1970) to provide 20.12 per cent of the city's non-service employment by 1970. Our own survey in S. Adriá indicates that construction workers, especially the unskilled, are predominantly recent immigrants. The small, more informally or-ganised industrial establishments could also feed on the abundant supply of unskilled labour: small *talleres* can, for example, use apprenticeship as a means for paying low wages while the new worker 'learns' routine work. Conditions of safety and job security tend also to be lower in the small establishment, while the close supervision of the owner and weak worker organisation inhibits effective protest.

This employment pattern has also contributed to increased migra-tion, both by facilitating the entry of new migrants who are frequently sponsored to a local *taller* or construction firm by a relative or fellow-villager and by its volatility, encouraging the onward mobility of those migrants (and city-born) already in Barcelona. Thus, though there is a considerable immigration to Barcelona, there is also a large out-migration. From 1962 to 1970, just over a million move-ments into the province of Barcelona were registered, but in the same period, 406,000 movements out were recorded, with the proportion of out-migration increasing in the last years. Movement within the province is also considerable, being estimated at some 147,535 movements between 1962 and 1966 (Recolons, 1976, Tables 15 and 16). The out-migration is not a return migration to regions of origin, but a movement to other industrial areas of Catalonia, to other large Spanish cities or to foreign countries. The role of rural–urban migration in Barcelona's industrialisation has thus not been that of a permanent one-way migration leading to residential stabilisation and the development of identifiable communities, but a continuous process of inter and intra city mobility.

Barcelona's population is thus highly mobile; but it is also a population totally dependent on the urban environment for its subsistence and reproduction. Though migrants come disproportionately as young people without families, they soon marry in the city or, in the case of those already married, the rest of the family joins them in the city. Our survey of S. Adriá showed a clear trend for households to become increasingly composed of nuclear families during the period 1965–75. In the earlier period, young single migrants were frequently found lodging with relatives or friends, but in the latter period this was less true: the many households of this kind that left the area were replaced increasingly by nuclear families, while other households 'lost' their single additions.

Though region of origin may retain a sentimental attraction for migrants, there is little evidence that it has any concrete economic or social significance. Migrants in S. Adriá commented on the practice of their parents in making sentimental return journeys to villages in Andulusia, while remarking on their own relative lack of interest in returning. Frigolé's studies (1975, 1977) of Calasparra and of Calasparra migrants in Barcelona also show the gulf between the urban migrant and the ongoing life of the village; their actions, when there, indicate the finality of the separation. For example, the priest the migrants chose to honour on one return visit was not the contemporary parish priest, but the priest who had encouraged them to migrate some ten years earlier.

Migrant identity is, in terms of the Catalan/non-Catalan distinction, a significant feature of the social structure of Barcelona. Its significance is, however, much more a product of the class divisions of the city than of continuing attachment to region of origin. Those born in Barcelona are more likely than immigrants to have skilled and white collar jobs; this class difference is exhibited in, and at times enforced by, differences in language between Catalan and Spanish

speakers (Esteva Fabregat, 1973). For our purposes, what is significant is the absence of any stable basis in rural–urban linkage for
consolidating urban kinship or social networks. Indeed, the sponsorship of cultural associations based on region of origin was un-
successfully tried by right-wing political interests as a means of
weakening the control of left-wing parties over the immigrant
populations through neighbourhood associations and labour unions.
The social institutions creating internal differentiation within the
working class are, it can be suggested, weaker than in the case of
nineteenth century Manchester. In the Barcelona case, differentiation
is based on the heterogeneity of the labour process through different
types of work situation or skill hierarchy. The absence of strong
institutions of status differentiation shaping residential preferences
or regulating aspirations also means that the consumption patterns
of the urban population are relatively homogeneous.

It is in the context of a mobile, 'unattached' population that state
intervention acquires its significance in the Barcelona area. On the
one hand, the potential demand for state welfare services by the mass
of the population is great since work is unstable and movement
precludes the development of stable bonds of social interaction and
mutual aid. On the other, industry has little commitment to the
reproduction of a stable urban labour force. The predominant
pattern of small-scale enterprise means, also, a generalised interest
among employers in saving on infrastructural costs. Noisy workshops
in the middle of residential streets and, indeed, in the middle of
blocks of flats, are a common source of complaint in the city. The
abundant supply of workers also means that these employers have
had little reason to want to stabilise their labour by sponsoring the
provision of more adequate urban facilities, whether in housing,
schools, health and so on. Instead, unstable markets and the consequent speculative nature of much of this small-scale enterprise
makes taxation a major threat. Owners of small enterprises have also
been the group that has predominated in the control of municipal
institutions in the Barcelona area under Franco. Thus, in S. Adriá
owners of small construction companies, of commercial establishments and of workshops have been mayors and councillors since 1939.

This issue must also be analysed in terms of the historical tendency
of the Spanish state to abstain from direct sponsorship of industrial
capitalism (Terrades, 1978). From the nineteenth century onwards,

Catalan industrialists received little help from Madrid in terms of the infrastructure of industrial development. Thus, Terrades notes the way in which those industrialists who developed large-scale enterprises were often forced to privatise state functions. The largest of the textile factories were located in the rural areas of Catalonia and organised as industrial colonies in which the order required for their smooth functioning was maintained by the meshing of kinship structures, religion, household economy and the authority and reward structure of the factory.

An explicit reason for the industrial colony in Catalonia was, in fact, the difficulty of maintaining stable production in urban milieus in which dense and volatile populations were easily organised against the employers and in which the state had not developed an adequate repressive apparatus. This political economy generated a spatial structure for industrialisation in which large enterprises, which could afford the costs, moved to peripheral locations and provided their own collective infrastructure. Smaller enterprises concentrated in the urban centres and relied on an abundant supply of labour and on their intimate control of workers to maintain the necessary order. The interests of small enterprise entailed an anarchic development of urban infrastructure.

Terrades documents the extent to which these tendencies can still be observed. Thus, large, capital-intensive enterprises locate in peripheral locations and develop what are, in effect, company towns. They provide a range of services for their labour, from housing to recreational and medical services, private education for children and so on. It is, in fact, the larger industrial enterprises that have moved out of the central areas of Barcelona, while smaller enterprises (fewer than 50 employees) have been more likely to remain (Banco Urquijo, 1972, p. 415). This movement out of large-scale enterprise has contributed to piecemeal, speculative development in the urban centre. Land speculation has become a major form of profit for capital, both because of the opportunities to sell off unwanted central industrial locations and because of the opportunities to use peripheral land for housing or small-scale industrial development close to the large enterprises.

Under these conditions, state intervention has facilitated a piece-meal economic growth. The state has directly and indirectly supported the massive construction of working-class housing in Barcelona since the 1960s. This housing was built quickly and cheaply by small construction firms which relied on cooperating with other firms or on sub-contracting. This housing was sold to its occupants through loans from private or state banking institutions. The housing was built in the main without adequate infrastructure whether in the shape of green areas, recreational or meeting places, educational or health facilities and adequate streets. Moreover, the fact that residents owned their flats meant that the costs of repairing the cheaply constructed dwellings fell on residents and not on the construction companies or on the state.

The mass provision of housing coincided with the rapid economic expansion of the Barcelona area from the 1960s onwards; the working population had sufficient job opportunities to afford housing loans, especially because several members of the family were able to work if necessary. Given the fragmented and volatile nature of this industrial economy, the ownership of housing by the working class was, it can be suggested, more convenient for capital than rentals, committing families to a relatively fixed pattern of urban consumption, such as television and other household durables, and cars, while avoiding extended responsibility for meeting the social costs of such consumption. One indication of the urban chaos this produced is the large volume of intra-urban movements to work in the Barcelona area. The fixing of workers by the ownership of housing and unstable patterns of employment combined to separate increasingly work from residence. This is even the case for areas, such as S. Adriá, which possess a considerable volume of industrial employment: most workers in S. Adriá live elsewhere and most of S. Adriá residents work elsewhere.

In the Barcelona context, a highly mobile population and an anarchically developed spatial and industrial structure were organised through quite crude forms of control and administration.[13] Administrative style was adjudicative in this context, based on partial interventions by the state to provide the economic infrastructure required by large enterprise, but avoiding comprehensive planning exercises which, it could be suggested, would destroy the basis of this 'fragmented' industrial economy.

The relationships of the state and urban populations in Barcelona have been neither paternalistic nor negotiatory. The class struggle in the urban milieu is thus sharper than in the Manchester case.

Neighbourhood associations in the urban areas are more militant than is the case in England and are more likely to link with labour unions and labour conflict. The weakness of these urban social movements are, however, the lack of a stable base in a settled, industrial population. Economic and urban growth has increased population mobility and individualised consumption. Conflict is endemic in Barcelona's contemporary pattern of growth, but it does not lead, at the moment, to the sustained development of a working-class organisation likely to force change in the pattern of urban development.

Barcelona is similar, I suggest, to some of Latin America's largest metropoli. São Paulo also appears to be a case of an economy based, in part, on the 'permanent' mobility of free labour and on an industrial order dependent on a combination of direct repression and the capacity of private enterprise to manage workers through the controls immanent in the labour process.[14] There also appears to be marked similarities between the urban conflicts, anarchic urban development and state intervention in that city and those described for Barcelona (Kowarick, 1977; Martinez-Alier and Moises, 1977).[15]

The case of the periphery

In this section, I want to explore the case of a more truly peripheral industrial economy, that of Lima. The peripheral type of industrial economy is a common one in Latin America. Its basis is the partial transformation of existing agrarian structures with the integration of Latin America into the world economy as an exporter of primary products. Perhaps the most familiar pattern is that of the plantation or mine which coexisted with a smallholding peasant population, providing seasonal or temporary labour for the large-scale enterprise. The relationship between the peasant population and the mine or plantation was a convenient one for capital because labour costs were effectively cheapened by the continued existence of the sub-sistence sector. Conversely, peasant farming tended to involute as an increasing population was maintained on smaller plots. The peasant sector became organised in terms of combining in the same household different types of economic activity: petty commodity production, trading activities or temporary wage labour in different types of work centre for example. The counterpart to this agrarian structure was the weak development of urban-based industry. Thus, in countries such as Peru, Mexico and Bolivia, mines and plantations often acted as economic enclaves which made little demand on local industrial production. Moreover, the use of labour still tied to the subsistence sector reduced the market for wage goods.

The above characterisation serves to identify the major internal features of the integration of Peru into the world economy of the twentieth century. In this century, Peru's economic growth has been based on export production, mainly in minerals, petroleum, sugar and cotton. Much of this production was either owned or controlled by foreign capital. Also, the large-scale, self-contained nature of much of this production resulted, with the exception of cotton, in few linkages being developed into industrial production (Thorp and Betram, 1978, pp. 39–111). In contrast to the situation of Barcelona, there was little incentive for national capital to invest in industrial production. Thus, despite an impressive spurt of industrialisation in the 1890s, Peru's large export earnings in the early twentieth century did not lead to a sustained industrialisation. Export earnings were remitted abroad, reinvested in the export sectors or spent on conspicuous consumption. The dominant classes in Peru had their major interests in export production or in banking and importing houses.[16]

Most of Peru's population were engaged in peasant farming in the highland zones. They complemented this activity with labour migration to the mines or plantations or with working or sharecropping on the large, mainly pastoral highland estates. In 1950, 59 per cent of the labour force was still working in agriculture. In the first half of the twentieth century, neither agricultural nor industrial production for the internal market was an important source of capital accumulation. There was, then, no basis for either a native industrial bourgeoisie or for powerful landed classes committed to the development of agricultural production in the non-export sector. Export production in agriculture was confined mainly to the narrow coastal strip and in the case of cotton was fragmented amongst peasant-type producers (Thorp and Betram, 1977, pp. 51–62).

When Peru began to industrialise in a more sustained way from the 1950s onwards, it did so as much through export processing industries as through consumer goods industries. Its level of industrialisation was lower than that of Latin American countries of comparable size. By the 1970s, the industrialisation that had occurred was dominated by foreign firms, with native industrialists playing a minor role. This industrialisation has been capital-intensive and concentrated in such industries as automobiles, consumer appliances and pharmaceuticals. Production has been highly dependent on foreign technology and, as a result of the weak development of capital goods industries, on the import of foreign machinery and other inputs. This modern sector industrialisation has increased employment opportunities in recent years. Thus, factory-based manufacturing, most of which is concentrated in Lima, increased its share of the labour force in Peru from 4.5 to 5.4 per cent between 1961 and 1970 (Thorp and Betram, 1977, p. 259). Also, there has been a substantial increase in employment in small-scale manufacturing enterprises of the artisan type. Employment in this sector increased from 8.7 to 9.1 per cent in the same years and, again, most of this employment is concentrated in Lima. Much of this increase in small-scale enterprises, as in employment in such services as commerce and repairs, is closely linked to the development of the large-scale sector through putting-out systems, car and truck repair workshops and small shops.

There is, however, an important distinction to be made between this type of industrialisation and that described for Barcelona. In the Barcelona case, traditions of local industrial capital, including those of capital and intermediate goods manufacture, mean that the small-scale sector represents attractive, if risky, opportunities for investment and entrepreneurship. Thus, small workshops in Barcelona have the technological capacity to manufacture components for the large-scale sector, or to construct relatively sophisticated buildings. In Lima, the high cost or non-availability of certain imported technologies bar locals from entering into many lines of small-scale production, or from providing sophisticated services to large-scale companies. Consequently, opportunities in the small-scale sector in Lima tend to be in areas requiring rudimentary skills or equipment that the large-scale sector finds it convenient to sub-contract, such as assembling operations. Otherwise, opportunities are those linked to the repair sector or to artisan production, both mainly for low-income markets. Small-scale production in Lima is, then, more marginal to the dominant economy and less remunerative than it is in the Barcelona case.

The pattern of rural–urban migration with which this type of industrialisation has been associated includes a considerable amount of pendular migration. Lima has grown at a fast rate since 1940. The urban population was then 10 per cent of the total population; by 1961, it was 18 per cent and by 1972, nearly 25 per cent (Thorp and Betram, p. 353n). This growth relative to that of the national population has been based on migration from all over Peru. However, my own studies and those of others have shown considerable return flows to place of origin or to new areas of the country (Roberts, 1973; Skeldon, 1977). In the 1940s, migration to the capital was mainly from the nearby departments which, like Junin, Ancash and Arequipa, had experienced a considerable though small-scale commercialisation of their agrarian structures. In the 1960s, however, the departments contributing most migrants are the more remote and poorer ones such as Puno and Huancavelica.

The small-scale commercialisation of the provincial economy that resulted from Peru's 'enclave' type incorporation into the world economy created the basis for return migration. Wages for labour migration, the diversification of the household economy to complement the small size of landholdings, trading opportunities with the mines and other work centres meant that little of rural Peru had a truly subsistence economy. For those with some cash to spare, there was a range of opportunities for investing in their area of origin – in buying animals, in setting-up a small store or in buying a truck or bus. This is the basis for the large numbers of return migrants from Lima who can now be found living in departments such as Junin. Though many migrants from Junin, the department of the central highlands in which I carried out my research, were to reside permanently in Lima, others returned back to their village in times of economic recession, in old age or when they had accumulated some capital or saw good investment opportunities at home.

This type of migration pattern depends on the agrarian structure remaining only partially commercialised. Peasant farming is not eliminated by competition from large-scale commercial farming. Small-scale trading or petty commodity production is not, in this situation, superseded by the large enterprise. The relative absence of economically powerful landed interests in the provinces has been an important contributing factor to this situation. There have, in fact, been no strongly organised class interests in the provinces capable of either transforming the productive structure themselves or of obtaining state intervention to do so.

In this situation, Lima's pattern of industrialisation is not sharply differentiated along rural–urban lines. A large part of the foodstuffs for Lima's consumption comes from peasant production. These foodstuffs are transported to the city and sold there by intermediaries who themselves live in peasant villages. If the intermediaries are based in Lima, they often have kinship ties in the villages. Some family enterprises span city, provincial town and village as in the cases reported by Smith (1975). These Lima-based entrepreneurs run market businesses in Lima, exchange products with kinsmen in the province and obtain labour, when needed, from the home village. The trucks and buses that bring down foodstuffs from the highlands take back manufactures, drinks and processed foods.

These rural–urban relationships help us to understand the dynamics of Lima's industrialisation process. The market for the products of Lima's modern industrial sector is a limited one, given the poverty and uneven income distribution of Peru. To expand this market is a riskier venture than it is in the case of the semi-peripheral situation. It is, for example, difficult for firms to cut their distribution or finance costs by selling in bulk or for cash discounts in a situation in which most of the urban population does not have ready cash to buy in large amounts. Consequently, extending the sales of much of Lima's industry depends on the small middlemen who are prepared to invest long hours, much travel and often some of their own cash in selling products throughout the city and provinces.

The market for vehicles is expanded in similar ways: cheap servicing facilities allow consumers to keep cars, trucks and buses running for many years. This both stimulates sales of new vehicles by developing the market for second-hand ones and is one of the bases for the cheap transport which enables middlemen to market goods, or workers to journey to work over long distances.

The provinces contribute to this economy by providing a cheap subsistence base for much of the urban labour force. Some of Lima's labour are single men who have left wives and children at home. Others will return when illness or old age makes subsistence more difficult in the city. Many have received their basic education in the provinces. The continuing social and economic links with the provinces thus makes possible the survival of a large floating labour force in the city, without large demands being made for welfare services. Remittances are made back to the provinces, but these also help the dynamics of the industrial economy, because they are often made in the form of manufactures or consumer items. The close links between city and provinces maximises the market for industrial production in a very poor economy. Little is spent on food or housing. Transport and welfare costs remain relatively low.[17]

This type of industrialisation has been accompanied by a distinctive set of social institutions. Lima's social organisation is marked by the persistence of links with the rural areas. Thus, associations based on village or town of origin proliferate in Lima. They are the basis for *fiestas* and sporting events and have helped organise squatter settlements. Delegations from these associations return to the villages of origin to attend the main *fiesta* of the village and often contribute to some village project. These associations are not agencies for socialising rural migrants into urban life. Rather, they represent the strength of rural–urban linkages. Flourishing associations and active members in these associations are those for whom the rural–urban linkage has remained salient. Villages with good commercial possibilities and migrants with rights to land or with family business in the village are those actively represented in the city associations.

These associations are but one part of the institutional matrix which accompanies Lima's industrialisation. Kinship ties, ties based on place of origin or fictive kinship ties, such as *compadrazgo* are also emphasised and give rise to residential and work groupings. Residence in terms of squatter settlement has been a highly organised movement, including a great deal of mutual aid. Such relationships have become one means of organising the type of small-scale, rural–urban economy which is a mainstay of Lima's industrialisation. Organising a business in Lima or creating income opportunities depends heavily on social relationships. These provide the contacts for obtaining jobs or contracts, for obtaining cheap supplies and for mobilising labour.

Much of this activity is of too small or informal a nature to enable it to seek the protection of legal contract or bear the expense of meeting formal legal obligations such as those of social security. Thus, associational activities, religious celebrations and kinship gatherings provide a cultural context in which relationships needed for economic survival can be consolidated. It is this context which gives to Lima's industrialisation its apparently 'traditional' and marginal overtones in comparison with that of cities such as Barcelona or São Paulo. In Lima, class identities and class-based political organisation are less developed than in the Barcelona case. The centralising forces operating on Lima's industrialisation are also weaker because of the low and uneven pattern of Peru's economic development.

State intervention in Lima's industrialisation has had two major phases. The first phase, which lasted with some interruptions until the late 1960s, was characterised by a weak and vacillating commitment to the development of local industry. In the absence of pressure from a national industrial bourgeoisie, the Peruvian state neither effectively protected native industry nor prevented the massive dominance of industrialisation by foreign capital. Since the late 1960s, the state has begun to intervene more consistently in industrialisation, financing new ventures, often in collaboration with foreign capital, providing economic infrastructure and regulating the labour process.

This state intervention responded to what was seen by many sectors of the Peruvian population as a growing crisis in the economy. This crisis was blamed on monopolistic foreign firms and on the ineffectiveness and self-interest of the Peruvian elite. The measure of the crisis, however, was widespread rural discontent over inadequate land resources, worker militancy in the large-scale enterprises in mining, sugar refining and in textiles, combined with inflation and food shortages in the cities, particularly Lima. The state had, then, to intervene directly in the industrialisation process if capitalist growth were to be salvaged. This intervention was not confined to the urban and industrial sphere and in the policy of the 1968 military government became an attempt at structural reform of the whole economy, including agrarian reform.

For our purposes, it is interesting to note that the structural reforms, despite their radical intent, have on the whole served to maintain the pattern of industrialisation described above, ironing out some of the difficulties created by the imbalance in productivity and income between the large-scale and small-scale sectors. Thus, agrarian reform has not basically altered the agrarian structure. The large landholdings are now controlled by the state, but the position of the smallholding peasant community has been recognised and consolidated (Long and Roberts, 1978; Chapter 11). In the urban sphere, illegal squatter settlements have been given legal recognition and incorporated into urban administration. In the industrial sphere, worker participation in both the running and in the profits of the large enterprise has been instituted. However, this participation has been expressly aimed to diminish the power of the labour unions. Despite the anti-foreign rhetoric of much of the reform period, collaboration with foreign capital has continued and increased in certain sectors. While the state has taken over some of the large foreign enterprises, such as Cerro de Pasco's mining operations, it has left the profitable consumer goods sector in private hands.

State intervention in Peru's industrialisation has thus been more comprehensive in scope than in that of either Manchester or Barcelona. Even in this case, however, the local context has shaped what otherwise would appear to be an autonomous state intervention designed to create the conditions for industrial capitalism. Indeed, much of the idiom of the reform has been in terms of traditional metaphor, such as those of the law of peasant communities and that of industrial communities aimed to implement some worker participation.

Conclusion

The situations that have been explored serve to illustrate tendencies in the pattern of industrialisation. They warn us that issues such as the organisation of production, labour mobility and state intervention should not be treated in isolation either from each other or from the overall organisation of an area's economy. This economy will change over time through the specific outcome of class struggles leading to new differences in the organisation of production and state intervention. Thus, within the same and apparently convergent process – that of industrialisation – there are important differences in the way in which the industrial economy is organised.

My intention is not, however, to stress the particularity of each industrialising situation. There are certain key factors which help us understand the major variations in industrialisation. Thus, structural position within the world economy, the social characteristics and mobility of labour and the labour process are the ones that I have stressed in this paper. I have tended to see state intervention as mainly responsive to the context created by these factors. Though, as the case of Barcelona indicates, traditions of political centralisation can become factors in influencing industrialisation. The important point, however, is to use these perspectives in research if we are to explore further the relative importance that such factors acquire in industrialisation.

11 Urbanism and the Rural Class Structure*
Howard Newby

Introduction

Since 1970 I have been involved in investigating social change in rural England, first through a study of farm workers (Newby, 1977), then later by way of research into the changing situation of farmers and landowners (Newby et al., 1978). In this chapter I want to reflect upon some of the results of this research, thereby allowing myself to draw together a number of issues which have hitherto been considered separately. The thematic focus of this chapter will be the impact of 'urbanisation' on the rural social structure. By 'urbanisation' I do not, of course, mean the physical development of towns and factories where only farms and fields once stood, but the movement into the countryside of an urban population – commuters, second-home owners, retired couples – whose present or past employment is located in towns and cities rather than locally in rural areas. Their arrival in the countryside, particularly since World War II, has ensured that English rural society is no longer entirely, nor even predominantly, an agrarian society. Indeed it is arguable that the single most important social change to have occurred in the countryside in recent years has concerned this changing social and occupational composition of its population. This change has not been entirely ignored by sociologists (Crichton, 1964; Pahl, 1965; Thorns, 1968; Ambrose, 1974; Harris, 1974: an excellent survey of

* Previous versions of this chapter were presented to the Centre for Environmental Studies conference on 'Urban Conflict and Change', Nottingham University, January 1979, the Association of County Librarians' conference, Institute of Local Government Studies, Birmingham University, April 1979, and the Countryside Policy course, School of Advanced Urban Studies, Bristol University, June 1979.

This chapter was based upon research financed by the SSRC.

the literature is Connell, 1974). However, there has been no attempt to analyse systematically the consequences of these changes in so far as they affect the life-chances of the local, predominantly agricultural, population.

This chapter represents, in a very schematic and discursive way, a modest beginning to this task. But first it is necessary to enter a word of caution. The account presented here is based upon research in a part of the country, East Anglia, which is in no sense representative of rural England as a whole. How far it is possible to draw generalised conclusions from this analysis is therefore a moot point. Indeed it is possible to argue that the situation in East Anglia exhibits the effects of urbanisation in the most *exaggerated* form, paradoxically because the region remains so predominantly agricultural, but also because East Anglian agriculture is so capital-intensive and prosperous. As we shall see, this may well have contributed to the relative deprivation of the poorer sections of the local rural population – a factor which, it will be argued, is one of the major consequences of urbanisation – to an extent which is not, or not yet, apparent elsewhere. On the other hand it should be realised that no single area or region of rural England can be regarded as 'typical', such is its variability.

In East Anglia rural society has traditionally been a class-divided society. Farmers and landowners formed an easily identifiable rural ruling class which held a near monopoly over employment opportunities, housing, the magistracy and local politics. Against their extensive domination of rural institutions farm workers and other members of the rural working class were relatively powerless. This domination was, and to a large extent still is, reflected in the distribution of wealth and income in the region's agriculture. There is a marked contrast between the prosperity of the region's farmers and the poverty of its farm workers (Newby, 1972). While the capital value of land approached £2000 per acre (by the mid 1970s), few farm workers own even their own home. For a farm worker to purchase and stock a viable farm in the area he would need to find upwards of £1,000,000, so it is not surprising that social mobility between the two classes remains minimal. It is this rigid and hierarchical class structure which appears to have been complicated by the arrival of ex-urban newcomers. Overwhelmingly professional and managerial by occupation they represent a new 'middle-class' (as they are described by both farmers *and* farm workers) which has been inserted into this dichotomous class structures. Their presence, as most farmers have not been slow to realise, threatens the former political domination of the area's ruling class. They have also rendered the rural class structure less coherent and less easily definable. As we shall see, they have therefore created a certain amount of 'status panic' among the agricultural population, and it has been on this aspect of their impact that sociologists, including myself, have fastened. However, while the cleavages between 'locals' and 'newcomers' which have been introduced are real enough, there are other, more material, consequences which require equal consideration. It is the interplay between these objective changes and the perceptions that those affected have of them which forms a major theme of this chapter.

One of the conclusions which I emphasised in *The Deferential Worker* was that there had been a reduction in the social distance between farmers and farm workers, partly brought about by the impact of newcomers on the village. Because of the ways in which the changes wrought by urbanisation have worked their way through the local social system the contrast between the more affluent lifestyles of the newcomers and the poorer living standards of local farm workers had not resulted in greater conflict between farmers and their employees. If anything, farm workers could now identify more with farmers than they had in the past. For example, farmers could find common cause with their workers in complaining about the 'interference' of outsiders in their own farm's and village's affairs. Moreover, farmers, at least, continued to appreciate the skills of farm workers, so that the latter could obtain much higher esteem from their employers than they could expect from many newcomers. This did not mean that the objective differences in wealth and income have been in any way reduced, but relationships have become easier and more informal. This has been aided by two further factors. The continuing mechanisation of agriculture has, together with other labour-saving innovations, brought about a steady decline in the size of the average farm labour force which has attenuated the workplace oppositional sub-culture of farm workers while allowing more frequent and direct contact with employers. In addition, farmers have become dissociated from many of their former authority roles, partly because of the professionalisation and bureaucratisation of local government and partly because of displacement by new-comers. Consequently farmers and landowners no longer have an *automatic* passport to local political dominance (Newby et al., 1978, Chapter 6).

As far as the newcomers are concerned, they have generally wished no harm to anyone, so that any animosity that they have evoked has been entirely unintended and unanticipated. The newcomers have often acted as easily identifiable scapegoats who can be blamed for many of the deprivations which the contemporary rural popula-tion suffers – poor amenities, remoteness from centres of decision-making and so on. This is not to suggest that the basis of local–newcomer conflict is entirely illusory – far from it. However, the social separation of the two groups and the consequent tendency of each to stereotype the other has magnified the conflict involved. The effect of the urban, middle-class exodus to the countryside has not been entirely a detrimental one, even for the locals. A comparison between a 'commuter village' and one which has suffered the ravages of rural depopulation unhindered by the arrival of newcomers soon shows this. Changes in the village have not so much been *caused* by newcomers moving in, as by the fact that the underlying economic base can no longer support the old 'occupational community'. The disruptions caused by newcomers have been merely a tangible symptom of this change.

Nevertheless at the ideological level the impact of the newcomers has been considerable. Over a wide variety of literally parochial conflicts they have created new social cleavages and prompted rural employers *and* employees to unite against a 'common enemy'. They have allowed the vertical ties between farmers and farm workers to become consolidated, drawn much of the class antagonism arising out of poor pay and conditions away from employers and towards themselves, and enabled a pervasive nostalgia for the 'good old days' when the village was a 'real community' to be substituted for a more realistic assessment of the causes of contemporary rural deprivation. (Compare farm workers' and farmers' images of society in Newby et al., 1978, pp. 309–13.) Thus, 92 per cent of the farm workers that I interviewed in Suffolk believed that they had more in common with farmers than with other members of the working class, even though a majority of farm workers were quite willing to identify themselves as 'working class'. The proportion of farmers who reciprocated in this view, though lower, was still a majority, varying between 53 per cent (in the case of the larger farmers only) and 74 per cent (in the case of a broader range of farmers) (Newby et al., 1978, pp. 314–15).

This, then, has been one major effect of the urbanisation of the countryside in East Anglia, and because I was centrally concerned with the problem of ideology it was on this aspect that I concentrated in *The Deferential Worker*. However, to concentrate attention upon the disruptive social effects of the newcomers *alone* does tend to divert attention from other agents of social change which have been responsible for the urbanisation of rural England. In addition it tends to obscure the workings of the various economic and political mechanisms which are responsible for the allocation of life-chances in the countryside and where the participants might be divided along altogether different lines to those of 'locals' and 'newcomers'. It is to these more material factors, where the urbanisation of the country-side might be considered part cause but also part effect, that I want to devote this chapter. This requires an analysis of social change in rural England from a rather different perspective. In order to understand why the urbanisation of the countryside has taken place at all, it is necessary to begin with an examination of the rural, and particularly the agricultural, economy. This is not to argue that the many changes which have occurred in rural life in recent years can only be considered in economic terms, for this is patently not true. The urban middle-class exodus to the countryside would not have occurred without certain culturally induced assumptions about the wholesome authenticity of rural life. But equally the newcomers could not have been accommodated without an exodus of the rural working population in the opposite direction, an exodus provoked by the continuous substitution of capital for labour in the system of agricultural production. Therefore it is still necessary to regard the production of food (together with associated manufacturing, pro-cessing and service activity) as being responsible, either directly or indirectly, for most of the observed changes in English rural society. Consequently it has been possible to discern a unity in the general direction of rural social change, even though there have been considerable variations in timing and extent from locality to locality. It is to a consideration of these underlying economic trends that we can now turn.

The reconstruction of rural England: the role of the state
The economic conditions of the agriculture industry today are in
complete contrast to those that predominated in the 1920s and 1930s
when thousands of acres of productive land lay unfarmed and de-
generated into wasteland, when fences were pulled down to be used
as firewood and when thousands of farm workers were either unemployed or suffering from falling wages. Since World War II,
however, whatever the short-term fluctuations, the state has implemented the urban demand for cheap (by historical standards)
and plentiful food, while simultaneously offering the farmer the
guarantee of stability and, for the 'efficient' (i.e. low cost) producer,
profitability. The state has also acted as midwife for what has become
known as the second agricultural revolution – the transformation
of the technology of food production and the many social changes
that have flowed from this. Farmers have been granted the conditions
under which they would embark upon a programme of increasing
productivity and cost efficiency which has been unmatched virtually
anywhere in the world. The agricultural sector has plummeted to
a mere 2.8 per cent of the population, while farm productivity has
increased fourfold since 1939. Farms have become fewer, larger and
more specialised, and farming has been transformed from a dignified
and arcadian 'way of life' to a highly rationalised business. (For some
excellent descriptions of this process see Self and Storing, 1962;
Donaldson and Donaldson, 1972; Edwards and Rogers, 1974;
Beresford 1975.)

Agricultural policy has been entirely single minded in its aims:
the production of more and cheaper food. It has not concerned itself
with the social implications of the drive towards 'agribusiness', except
as a twinge of concern over the plight of the uplands. In general,
however, there is a quite startling contrast between the undoubted
success of this policy in terms of its stated goals in successive White
Papers (the expansion of home production, the increase in cost
efficiency, the maintenance of a prosperous agriculture) and its
mostly deleterious *social* effects on the countryside either in depopulat-
ing rural areas at an even faster rate than hitherto or in polarising
them socially between the expanding large producers and the
marginalised smaller ones, between both of these and rural workers
suffering inadequate service provision and, indirectly, between the
local poor and affluent newcomers. These social effects have rarely

been monitored, let alone built into the policy calculations of the Ministry of Agriculture, where the assumption that what is good for farmers must be good for the rural population as a whole has been perpetuated by a mixture of 'bureaucratic and commercially vested interest, self-justification and reluctant necessity', as Josling (1974, p. 231) has put it. In the face of a good deal of evidence to the contrary it has taken three decades for this assumption to be questioned – and even now it remains a central tenet of faith. Thus, although the Ministry has recently appointed 'socio-economic advisers' with a remit to consider the wider social implications of agricultural change, it has done so only as an obligation under EEC policy. Perhaps a charitable view of their role would be to regard them as the 'do-gooders' of the Ministry's advisory service ADAS – tolerated, but ignored when the tough decisions have to be made. In the early days, at least, most were ex-ADAS advisers sent out to grass, already steeped in the Ministry's conventional wisdom and at something of a loss over what their function should be. They therefore tend to accept the view that the vitality of English rural society can be measured by the prosperity of English farmers.

Since farmers comprise a varying but significant proportion of the rural population there is, of course, a grain of truth in this proposition. But by no means all sections of the rural population have benefited equally from postwar agricultural policy and some have been *relatively* disadvantaged. The small farmer might therefore beg to differ from the conventional view – and so might the farm worker and his wife, the environmentalist, the unemployed rural school leaver and even the young couple on the waiting list for a rural council house. It is possible to trace a chain of events from the political economy of modern agriculture to the problems encountered by each of these groups, yet the formulation of agricultural policy has mostly ignored the possible external consequences and at best been indifferent to them. To a large extent this has been the result of a division of labour within the civil service which has allowed the Ministry of Agriculture to respond to a clear and unambiguous demand to reduce the cost of food production, while other departments, both nationally and locally, have been left to mop up the social consequences. Moreover, the urban majority of the population has shown little interest in rural change except in its most visual aspects – tractors and combine harvesters replacing horses, the disappearance of hedgerows, etc. – as long as food has remained cheap. They, too, have remained largely indifferent to the social problems of rural areas, particularly as their perception has often been clouded by misplaced sentiment. As long as agricultural policy was, literally, delivering the goods, what was happening to the fabric of life in the countryside could be complacently overlooked.

As far as the formulation of agricultural policy in the immediate postwar period was concerned, it is doubtful whether any serious consideration was ever given to its possible social implications in the countryside, for all its encouragement of rapid technological change. This was because of its essentially retrospective foundations, built upon the contrasting experiences of agricultural depression during the interwar years and the need to maximise food production at almost any cost during World War II. The invocation of one or the other could always be relied upon to silence any critic, whether from within the farming industry or from outside. The affluence of succeeding decades also ensured that the cost of agricultural support never intruded into the consciousness of the taxpayer and was therefore not too closely examined. Even when the result was chronic over-production or the 'feather-bedding' of 'barley barons', the consumer generally benefited from lower prices and the proportion of public expenditure devoted to agriculture was so small that the extra revenue required was hardly noticed. During the 1970s, however, the political climate surrounding agriculture has changed quite dramatically. Entry into the European Community altered the structure of financial support for agriculture and switched the burden from the taxpayer to the consumer and this, together with the general inflation in the British economy during this decade, has ensured that the cost of food production has become once more a hot political issue. Now that the cost of over-production is borne directly by the consumer, resentment has grown over the support of 'inefficient' farmers, whether at home, or, more often, in Europe. The purely defensive aspects of agricultural policy have come under increasing political pressure with the main emphasis of recent debate having concerned the need to protect consumers rather than producers. This has undoubtedly strengthened the political hand of the large-scale producers still further, even though they already benefit disproportionately from state support, for they can point to their greater cost efficiency and potential for expansion which could be provided by further hefty injections of capital investment. Such a political reaction to inflation, however, continues to be discussed with little or no consideration of what the future of English rural society will look like as a result.

Within the rural population it is not too difficult to discern which groups have been the greatest beneficiaries of postwar agricultural policy. The promotion of 'efficiency' has been of enormous benefit to the large-scale producers, who have swallowed the lion's share of agricultural subsidies (Donaldson and Donaldson, 1972). The massive programme of capitalisation has also allowed a 'knock-on' effect to benefit large sections of the agricultural engineering and agro-chemical industries and even the construction industry. Farm workers, on the other hand, have received little *relative* improvement (see Newby, 1977, Chapter 3). It is also now accepted by agricultural economists (e.g. Josling, 1974) that one of the major beneficiaries has been the landowners (who now, of course, include a majority of farmers). In other words, sustained intervention in agriculture has not only guaranteed the incomes of 'efficient' producers, but has enhanced the investment value of agricultural land – precisely the factor which has recently prompted the renewed interest of the City institutions. Certainly the inflation in land prices, which since the war has consistently outstripped the general rate of inflation, has enormously increased the wealth of the agricultural landowner (Newby et al., 1978, Chapter 3). It is apparent that agricultural policy in this country has not been very concerned with distributive justice.

While agricultural policy was helping to transform rural England from within, a quite different set of land use policies were, ironically, derived to protect and preserve it from the external threat of urban encroachment. It was the aim of town and country planning to preserve the quality of rural life in the postwar period, just as agricultural policy was to provide it with a strong economic basis. In theory the system created by the 1947 Town and Country Planning Act involved a radical reform of the *laissez-faire* approach to land use in the countryside. The underlying political aims were liberal and progressive, containing a strong element of planning for the least fortunate, whereas in practice the system created seems to have almost systematically had the reverse effect. (See the assessment by Hall et al., 1973.) There have been a number of reasons for this. The first concerns the essentially negative and protective nature of most rural planning. The traditional English reverence for the rural way of life has ensured that precisely *what* it was that was being preserved has never been examined too closely. There has been a fallacious belief that the 'traditional rural way of life' was beneficial to *all* rural inhabitants, an influential but unexamined assumption which was a product of an unholy alliance between the farmers and landowners who politically controlled rural England and the radical middle-class reformers who formulated the postwar legislation. Consequently agriculture was given a prior claim over both land use and labour in rural areas and was exempted from most aspects of development control. The aim of agricultural policy to promote an *efficient* agriculture became translated in land use planning terms into the desire to promote a *ubiquitous* agriculture, irrespective of the ensuing distribution of costs and benefits. But restriction of the location of industry in rural areas in the wake of such policies would depress rural wage levels, increase the outward migration of the agricultural population and hinder the viability of rural services.

Some attempt was made to remedy this situation in the Town and Country Planning Act of 1968. This Act introduced a system of structure plans which covered not only land use but population change, employment, transport and housing. In rural areas they were to aim at implementing positive resource development rather than reflect the former predominantly negative planning policies. There was also less emphasis on the production of maps and a move towards surveys of relevant social and economic inputs (until curtailed by public expenditure cuts in 1974). The structure plan system also offered a means of transcending the divide between urban and rural areas, although this did not become a possibility until after the reorganisation of local government in 1973/74. However, there has been a considerable gap between the evidence uncovered by the structure plan surveys and the actual policies which have eventually emerged. In 1976, for example, the Countryside Commission was moved to comment in its *Annual Report* that

> the content of structure plans in general does not convince us that the potential of the new development plans system for tackling rural problems has been realised. (1977)

The reasons for this, as we shall see, have lain not so much in the outlook of the rural planners themselves, but in the balance of political forces which underlie the planning process on the county and district councils.

Since 1947, then, the presumption that the countryside should be preserved, almost exclusively, for agriculture has ensured that the major source of employment in rural areas should be the farming industry. Yet the number of employment opportunities in agriculture has, as we have seen, declined rapidly since the war – a factor which has been written in quite explicitly to state agricultural policy. By directing new industrial development away from rural areas, conventional strategic planning policy has had two important consequences: it has restricted the rate of economic growth in the countryside and it has weakened the bargaining power of existing rural workers by reducing the number of competitors for local labour. Strategic planning has therefore contained a strong element of planning for the interests of the better off. Rural employers have clearly gained from the preservation of a low wage rural economy – indeed, in some areas it has been given indirect encouragement. The ex-urban newcomers, who have arrived to fill the gap left by departing rural workers looking for employment and higher wages in the towns, now fight hard to keep the countryside devoid of any taint of industrial development, thus preserving their 'village in the mind' (Pahl, 1965) and as a by-product enjoying the opportunity of calling upon a pool of local cheap labour to perform the standard upper middle-class range of domestic services. On the other hand farm workers have been trapped in a low paying industry with declining employment opportunities and with increasing dependence upon tied housing. A policy of preserving the rural *status quo* has thus turned out to be *redistributive* – and in a highly regressive manner. Occasionally rural planners have become aware of these tendencies, but the political will has been lacking to bring about a change in policy. For example, in 1974 the report of the East Anglian Regional Strategy Planning Team placed considerable emphasis on the need to attract more industry into the area so that local wage levels would be raised:

Away from the major centres, poor job prospects cause considerable local concern. Opportunities are limited to agricultural employment and incomes tend to be low .... There should be opportunities for individuals to increase their incomes and widen their interests through a better choice of jobs and training opportunities.
(1974)

The report met with considerable opposition from the region's county councils and was later quietly shelved by the Department of the Environment, which had publicly disagreed with many of its conclusions.

Agricultural policy and planning policy were intended to provide a framework whereby rural England could be reconstructed from the ravages visited upon it during the Depression. (They were not, of course, the *only* such policies, but the ones which I have chosen to concentrate on in this chapter.) In many respects these policies have been extraordinarily successful, as any comparison between the situation now and that which prevailed in the 1930s will easily demonstrate. However, this highly abbreviated and generalised account has attempted to highlight some of the less obvious and less publicly discussed aspects of these policies. First, it is apparent that agricultural policy and planning policy have not only been institutionally separated, but have worked against each other. While the Ministry has been promoting widespread technological change and the consequent diminution of the agricultural population, rural planning has been overwhelmingly preservationist in sentiment. The inevitable collision between these policies is currently being fought out over landscape and environmental issues. Secondly, both sets of policies have tended to be socially regressive insofar as they have affected the rural population. Thirdly they have enabled the changing social composition of rural society to proceed virtually unhindered and without much thought for the consequences for the rump of the old rural working population. They have become a *residual* population, the flotsam of agricultural change, left stranded in the countryside and finding their needs being consistently overlooked now that they are in a minority. To appreciate fully the extent of these changes it is necessary to see how these policies have been implemented at the local level. The state has provided a framework for guiding rural social change – but only a framework. Many of the consequences of the urbanisation of the countryside are a result of local political pressures and the routine application of local political power.

The local response
The implementation of state agricultural policy has been left, for the most part, in the hands of individual private landowners and

farmers. Planning policy at the local level has, however, been formally under the aegis of elected councillors, advised by their professional officers. Although apparently separated institutionally (as they still remain nationally) these policies often come to coincide as a result of farmers' traditional domination of local government in rural areas (for data, see Moss and Parker, 1967). Although the balance of political forces has varied from place to place and is changing over time, in general the political power in rural areas remains firmly in the hands of the most prosperous residents. In a few counties this has involved the continuation of the old squirarchical rule of farmers and landowners, although their omnipotence has clearly been declining. Elsewhere they have been displaced in local government by professional and managerial middle-class newcomers, who at least *appear* to threaten the old hegemony. However, the evidence from our study of local political power in Suffolk (Newby et al., 1978, Chapter 6) suggests that appearances are deceptive. In terms of *policies* if not personnel, there is a remarkable continuity. The newcomers fully support the preservationist stance of strategic planning policy for the countryside. They have no desire to admit industrial, or even housing, development which in some cases is the very thing from which they have sought to escape by moving to a rural area. Indeed their zealous advocacy of the status quo frequently brings them into conflict with farmers over the environmental effects of modern farming practice. Similarly, as the major ratepayers (agricultural land is exempt) they wholeheartedly endorse the extremely conservative budgetary policies advocated by farmers and landowners which is the main plank of the latter's political policy at the local level. Both groups are therefore profoundly preservationist in their policies and have maintained a strong accord over the desire to exclude as far as possible virtually any significant industrial or residential development from the countryside, whether for agricultural or environmental reasons. This policy has therefore triumphed, despite the changes which have occurred in the personnel of county council planning committees. It is not therefore coincidental that many of the set-piece rural planning conflicts have concerned the impact of nationally-taken decisions upon particular rural localities (Stansted, Cublington, Drumbuie, etc.), for this is often the only occasion on which the routine of rural planning policy is disturbed. On other occasions the alliance of landowners and affluent newcomers on many county councils continues the everyday routine of directing development proposals away from the countryside.

It would be possible to pursue the effects of these policies across the whole range of resources called upon by the rural population – employment, education, health services, welfare and so on. However, because of restrictions on space in a paper of this kind I shall concentrate on only one: housing. As an illustrative case of the impact of newcomers on the local population housing is an apposite example. Not only is it an intrinsically crucial resource, but it is one for which the entire rural population – locals and newcomers, farmers and farm workers, agricultural and non-agricultural families – are competing. (The same cannot be said of, for example, employment.) It therefore vividly exemplifies the effect of the newcomers at the level of the distribution of material resources. In addition the system of housing allocation acts as an intermediary between the economic changes in agriculture and the structure of rural society by its effect on influencing *who* lives *where*. To this extent housing in the countryside has always been used as a form of social control (see Newby, 1977, Chapter 3).

During the nineteenth century housing in rural areas was kept in chronic short supply by the fear that their occupants might become a burden on the poor rate. In the twentieth century this shortage has remained while many of the principles which underlie the problem have merely reasserted themselves within a new institutional framework. Until the newcomers arrived in the countryside, for example, the domination of rural areas by farmers and landowners, both as employers and as local councillors, ensured that they were effectively the landlords of the housing stock within reach of most farm workers: council housing, privately rented houses and tied cottages. Their desire to keep the rates down made them reluctant to build council houses. Farm workers could instead be housed in tied cottages, which had other advantages in addition to providing suitable accommodation, not least of which concerned the reinforcement of ties of dependency. Tied cottages also depressed farm wages, making farm workers unable to afford council house rents. Thus, the rents could not be lowered without raising the rates, while farmers were not going to raise wages voluntarily just so their workers could afford to live in council houses. Consequently, whether as ratepayers or as employers, the farmers who ran the majority of rural councils found it expedient to construct as few council houses as possible. These tendencies have remained unaltered by the arrival of the newcomers – in fact, in other ways their impact upon rural housing has been little short of calamitous. By 1974, on the eve of local government reorganisation (and the disappearance of separate housing statistics for rural areas), rural district councils provided only 20 per cent of the rural housing stock, compared with 31 per cent provided by local authorities elsewhere. Farm workers were thus becoming increasingly dependent upon tied cottages (up from 32 per cent to 54 per cent since the war) while they and other rural workers were faced by a declining pool of privately rented houses in rural areas, following the effects of successive Rent Acts and their lucrative sales to affluent newcomers. In view of the history of rural housing it was therefore somewhat ironic to find in 1976 that changes in tied cottage legisaltion increasing local authority responsibility for rehousing those who had to leave such accommodation and restricting farmers' reposession were being opposed by the farmers' lobby on the grounds that there were insufficient safeguards against local authorities refusing to meet these housing responsibilities.

Since World War II, however, the political control of rural councils has not been the only factor influencing the rate of rural house building. A salient feature of this period has also been the incorporation of a specifically *rural* housing problem into the general problem of the nation's housing, coupled with increasing central government intervention in, and control of, rural housing provision (Rawson and Rogers, 1976). Rural councils have obviously found themselves hamstrung by expenditure cuts and the imposition of cost yardsticks which rarely take account of the peculiar difficulties of remote rural districts. This has also been accompanied by a change in emphasis in housing policy. Between the wars the aim of housing legislation was to stimulate the construction of as many houses as possible in rural areas; but since 1947 the aim has been to control the number of houses in rural areas as part of overall planning policies designed to contain the growth of urban sprawl, prevent the loss of good agricultural land and protect the visual quality of the countryside. Far from encouraging local authorities and private developers to build more rural houses, as in the 1930s, there has been active discouragement, involving the imposition of strict planning controls, particularly over housing in open countryside and in other sensitive areas such as Green Belts and Areas of Outstanding Natural Beauty. The increasing affluence of the rural population wrought by the urban middle class exodus has tended to mask the continuing and severe pockets of poverty which exist in the countryside and have led the 'problem' of rural housing to be regarded less as a problem of social welfare and more as an issue concerning land use planning and countryside preservation.

Thus since the 1947 Act, the granting of planning permission for rural housing has arguably been concerned more with the visual quality of the countryside than with alleviating problems of housing need among the rural population. By placing strict control on rural housing development these policies have also brought about a planned scarcity of housing, which, in the face of increasing demand from newcomers, has made a rural house a desirable good with a premium price. Until the early 1960s the effects of rural depopulation, the dilapidation of much rural property and the cost of travel to urban centres all contributed to the lower price of rural housing compared with urban areas. But as the surplus rural housing was gradually soaked up by commuters and second-home owners, and as housing which had once been a damning indictment of years of neglect and deprivation was restored and renovated, so relative scarcity began to increase prices above those prevailing for comparable suburban and even urban housing. The pressure on rural development has thus become more intense. Between 1961 and 1971 the population Census recorded an increase of 1,700,000 in the rural population, and although some of this was accounted for by contiguous urban development spilling over the boundaries of surrounding rural districts there is little doubt that the population pressures on most of rural England are now those of increasing demand rather than those resulting from rural depopulation. The preferred solution to this has not been to build even more houses to relieve the upward pressure on rents and prices, but to impose even more stringent controls – conservation areas, village 'envelopes' and so on. As prices inexorably rise, so the population that actually achieves its goal of a house in the country becomes more socially selective.

Planning controls on rural housing have therefore become – in effect, if not in intent – instruments of social exclusivity, although this often depends upon implementation as much as on the principles enshrined in the legislation. For example, the insistence upon the use of certain building materials, the standards of design and external finish and the density of housing development reflect the traditional concern of planning authorities with how a house or a village looks rather than who will actually live in it. Housing which is not 'detrimental to the character of the village' frequently means in effect high-cost, low-density architect-designed houses for the upper middle class. As the environmental lobby has emerged as an influential force in the formulation of rural development control policies, so the dilemma between the requirements of maintaining an attractive village landscape and the provision of rural housing for those in need becomes more acute. This dilemma has been sharpened by the fact that many village newcomers are not only in the vanguard of the environmental lobby but are quite explicitly socially exclusive in their preferences: having made it to their rustic redoubt, they wish to pull up the drawbridge behind them to keep out the madding crowd on the council house waiting lists. They often oppose *any* new housing development, private or public, and, given that snobbery is rarely far from the surface of their judgements, are particularly opposed to the construction of new local authority estates in the countryside. In this case the rhetoric of environmentalism and the pursuit of social exclusivity coincide.

Although there has been some awareness on the part of rural planners that these policies are exaggerating the scarcity of rural housing and achieving comparatively little for those in greatest need, there is not the political will in most areas to remedy the situation. Here the role of the newcomers has been decisive. As the main representatives of the environmental lobby in the countryside, they have pushed the implementation of development control more in the direction of increased restriction rather than greater flexibility. Housing policies thus continue to be concerned with visual quality rather than with the needs of the people who inhabit rural areas. As Rawson and Rogers conclude in their review of recent policies:

> The general restriction of planning methods for rural housing to development control and a concern with the fabric of the built countryside pervades the whole attitude of structure planning to rural housing, not just policies. Only rarely do plans consider more than the simple spatial attributes of the housing stock. Housing

quality is examined usually by area rather than by social group and there is little information on different income groups in the countryside and their needs and demands for housing. This is surprising when one remembers the importance frequently given to local housing need which can only be satisfactorily defined in relation to an understanding of social groups and information on incomes.

It follows that policies for rural housing do not consider the social implications which might result from their implementation. There is, for example, little or no discussion on the possible distributional effects on different social groups of conservation policies regarding rural housing nor of the economic and social implications for rural housing of key settlement strategies.

(Rawson and Rogers, 1976, p. 17)

Current housing policies seem to be producing a polarisation of the rural population. While the *demands* of the rich and the affluent can be met within the framework of current housing policies, the *needs* of the poor increasingly cannot. During the 1970s the provision of rural housing for those who cannot partake in the inflated market sector has been pitiful. Between 1967 and 1973, the number of council houses built annually in rural areas was almost cut in half, from 35,000 to 18,000, while private-sector housing held steady at just over 70,000. Since 1973, with the switch of housing resources – and, equally significantly, rate-support grants – to the inner city areas, conditions have hardly improved. The result is that once those who are unable to purchase, or eschew the tied cottage, have negotiated their way through the labyrinthine and highly variable eligibility rules to achieve a place on a council housing waiting list, they join a queue which is currently growing at a faster rate than additions to the council housing stock and which in some cases even exceeds the total number of families housed by the district council. (For East Anglian evidence, see Newby et al., 1978, Chapter 6.)

The case of housing illustrates well one of the major processes that has accompanied the urbanisation of the countryside – its social polarisation. Hitherto this polarisation has been portrayed in terms of 'locals' and 'newcomers' and at the level of ideology this is undoubtedly accurate. However, at the level of access to material resources and the distribution of life-chances the polarisation occurs between an affluent majority (comprised of both newcomers *and* local farmers and landowners) and a poorer and *relatively* deprived minority. The nature of these cleavages draws the resentment of the deprived minority towards the newcomers. While the newcomers have provoked a gut reaction to the sense of having been taken over by affluent and alien strangers, focusing attention on them alone diverts attention from the fact that rural housing is a matter not only of (increasing) demand, but also of supply and need. Here the antagonism towards newcomers as a tangible manifestation of the rural housing problem (for example, over second-home ownership) allows the role of local farmers and landowners in implementing these policies to go almost unnoticed.

Polarisation and democratic dilemmas

The social polarisation of the countryside has been a slow but inexorable process since the end of World War II. Within agriculture the large-scale landowner and farmer has generally benefited at the expense of the small marginal producer and the farm worker. At the same time a stark contrast has arisen in most villages between a comparatively affluent, immigrant, ex-urban middle class and the remnants of the former agricultural population tied to the locality by their (low paid) employment, by old age and by lack of resources to undertake a move. The former group lives in the countryside mostly by conscious choice (and this includes the majority of farmers and landowners) and has the resources to overcome the problems of distance and access to essential services. The latter group, by contrast, has become increasingly trapped by lack of access to alternative employment, housing and the full range of amenities which the remainder of the population takes for granted. While there can be little doubt that the material conditions of the rural poor, the elderly, the disabled and other deprived groups have undergone a considerable improvement in absolute terms since the war (in the sense that they are better fed, better housed, better clothed and better educated), in relative terms they have encountered little improvement and in many cases in recent years an alarming deterioration. Their poverty is often submerged – socially, and even literally, invisible – and there is a danger that, as rural England increasingly becomes middle-class England, their plight will be ignored and their needs overlooked.

This polarisation process can be observed not only in areas such as housing and employment, but across the whole range of social services, especially health services, and even the provision of apparently mundane amenities from shop to sewerage. The affluent sections of the rural population can, of course, overcome any problems which may arise by stepping into their cars and driving to the nearest town, whereas the poor, the elderly and the disabled are particularly vulnerable to any decrease in the level of local public and private services in rural areas, and especially public transport. It therefore makes little sense any longer (if it ever did) to contrast the backwardness of rural amenities compared with those in the towns, for the major divisions lie *within* the rural population between those in need and suffering multiple social deprivation and those who have benefited from living in the countryside in recent years and for whom access to a full range of services and amenities does not present a problem.

Numerically it is the latter group which has consistently been in the ascendancy over the last thirty years and who has achieved a firm grasp on the levers of local political power. As a result the deprived section has found it increasingly difficult to obtain recognition of its requirements, let alone feel capable of diverting a larger proportion of resources in its direction. The economics of public service provision have suffered from the self-reliance of the newcomers, who, as ratepayers, have demonstrated an understandable reluctance to foot the rapidly rising bill on behalf of their less fortunate neighbours. All too often this is the political reality (and it seems unlikely to change) which underlies the neglect of housing, public transport and the whole range of social, health and welfare services in rural areas.

During a period of general stringency in public expenditure the pressure to preserve only those services which 'pay' – that is, are self-supporting – has become increasingly strong. Ayton has examined the implications of these policies for the rural population in Norfolk:

The opportunities for change in the rural situation are constrained and influenced by the existing physical infrastructure, in terms of settlement pattern, systems of public utilities and communications networks, and the resources available for modifying it. While it is difficult to anticipate the level of financial resources that will be available, it is clear that they will, for some time, be limited, and planning policies must be framed within the content of what is feasible, or reasonably likely. Those services which are financed from the rates (e.g. education, highways, sewerage, water) will be much more of a constraint than those which are 'self-supporting' and budgeted nationally (e.g. electricity, gas, telephones). Investment choices must be made in those sectors which can influence policy-making in a more restrictive and specific way than the general aim of minimising public expenditure.

(Ayton, 1976, p. 62)

This is an interesting comment, albeit presented with a public servant's tact, on local decision-making in a county which is by no means atypical (in its political complexion) for a rural area. What, one wonders, would have happened to rural electrification had it been left in the hands of local ratepayers? Be that as it may, Ayton goes on to discuss the policy options within these constraints and their effects upon individuals and local communities. For the relatively deprived section of the rural population it provides a depressing, though instructive, glimpse of what occurs when their needs are discounted in favour of lower rates. In order to place Ayton's data in some perspective it is important to realise that 66 per cent of Norfolk villages are below 500 in population and 44 per cent below 300, while at the other extreme only 11 per cent are over 1000. As Ayton points out:

It is the small size of average village that is critical in terms of the services and facilities that can be expected in each one. Studies carried out by the Planning Department of Norfolk County Council have identified critical thresholds related to various services. For example, at the 300–500 population level, it is estimated that the village can support a shop, a pub and a school with between 30 and 50 pupils. But a primary school with 100 pupils, a fairly economic level, requires a support population of 1000, while a 'middle' school of 240 pupils requires a population of 4000. Each doctor has to have at least 2000 patients and so a practice of three doctors needs a support population of about 6000. A regular surgery seems viable only where a village population exceeds 1800. A district nurse is provided for 3000 population and chemists are provided on the basis of a 4000 to 4500 population catchment.

(Ayton, 1976, p. 65)

In a rural county such as Norfolk this places the location of many of these services at some considerable distance, and therefore cost, from many of those who need them. Although Ayton is simply bowing to economic realities here, it is worth pointing out that, in the case of public services, these 'realities' are in principle (though, one suspects, increasingly rarely in practice) politically negotiable. Within the context of existing rural politics, however, Ayton's conclusions are inevitable: to concentrate service provision in the largest villages, 'backed by programmes to maintain reasonable social services in settlements not selected (e.g. mobile libraries, health visitors, meals-on-wheels, and public transport). . . . [The individual must make an informed choice between] 'a small village [and] direct access to services – he cannot get both together.' (Ayton, 1976, p. 67).

To the affluent rural ratepayer, whose opinions carry considerable weight in county hall, this seems an entirely rational solution. Not only is the cost of service provision held down or even reduced, but by taking advantage of economies of scale it may even be possible to avoid needless under-utilisation and improve the range of services offered. The reality for the deprived is, however, rather different – the two-mile trudge down the muddy lane for the farm worker's wife to catch the Monday and Thursdays only (except Bank Holidays) under-threat-of-closure bus; the elderly trapped in their isolated cottages; the post office two miles away; the hospital twenty miles distant. The poor and the elderly have not 'chosen' to live in their villages in any meaningful sense: they have been stranded there by three decades of rural social change and by growing public indifference to their plight. They lack the resources to convert their needs into demands, yet it is to demand rather than to need which most rural public services respond. While the level of rates remains sacrosanct the rural poor have no voice in the decision-making process, form no lobbies or pressure groups but quietly grumble or complain and somehow struggle on. Meanwhile the level of rural services has slowly but irreversibly declined.

It is easy to overlook these problems amidst the restored cottages and the two-car homes which now pervade the English village. The other face of rural England is more difficult to seek out since it is now less openly admitted. At least in the past when rural poverty was the norm, the experience of deprivation was one which could be shared by the majority of the village population. But now poverty brings with it a sense of exclusion rather than mutuality. The urbanisation of the countryside has enabled a life-style that was once only distantly and fleetingly observed to be encountered at first hand among the new inhabitants. The rural poor find, somewhat disconcertingly, that they and their needs are increasingly regarded as residual – or even unacknowledged. Publicly debated issues have moved on to problems in which they are denied the luxury of participating. They find that more attention seems to be given to the visual appearance of the countryside than to the standard of living of those who are employed in maintaining it; that greater concern is expressed over the effects of pesticides on butterflies than on farm workers. Their new minority status hardly lends itself to making a fuss, however, nor to the expectation that they can achieve any tangible change if they attempted to do so. Consequently their inclination is to 'make do', while the general public is given little reason to alter its image of a cosy and contented countryside.

Conclusion

The major effect of urbanisation in the countryside has therefore been to transform rural England into a predominantly middle-class territory. The policies which systematically disadvantage the rural poor can now, therefore, be assured of local democratic support. This suggests that any striking improvement in the relative living standard of the rural poor will in the future – as in the past – be brought about by changes initiated nationally rather than locally, through the trickling down into rural areas of reforms and innovations introduced on a universalistic basis. While there is a paradox in the growing polarisation of rural society being accompanied by the increasing identification between farmers and farm workers, in many respects the newcomers have provided the wherewithal for *both* of these processes. Estranged from the alien newcomers farm workers have increasingly recognised a common identity with farmers as fellow 'locals'. However, the farm workers, together with others among the deprived rural population, are often entirely unaware that, miles away in the council chamber, representatives of both the farmers' and the newcomers' interests are busy agreeing upon political policies which are to their detriment, *plus ça change* . . . .

Notes

Introduction

1. Some of the first steps in the revision of his approach are to be found in material added to the English edition of *The Urban Question* (Castells, 1977a), see also Castells, 1978, pp. 174–82.
2. For a critique of Castells on both these grounds see Harloe, 1979.
3. For an account of these developments see Harloe, 1981.
4. For a critique of Lojkine see Harloe, 1979.
5. See the papers by Lojkine and Bleitrach/Chenu in Harloe and Lebas, 1981.
6. It is interesting to compare, by reference to Lambert and Rees's paper, the very different relationship of nationalist ideologies to the state in South Wales.
7. See the remarks of Lebas (1981) for an expansion of this point.
8. Castells has discussed some of this background recently (1978, pp. 1–14).
9. The changes centred on the establishment of a new set of 'customer–contractor' relationships between the state and the researchers modelled on the way in which governments and others commissioned applied scientific research, a model which clearly presumed that social problems could be dealt with in a technocratic framework.
10. Some flavour of the disfavour with which research that queried the *status quo* was viewed may be gained by the reference to the suggestion by the last Labour Secretary of State for the Environment that quite modest (and wholly un-Marxist) proposals for a gradual reform in the regressive nature of housing subsidies was no more than a 'theoretical or academic dogma' (Department of the Environment, 1977b, p. iv).
11. The attitude, for example, of the current (late 1980) Secretary of State for the Environment is that attempts to assess the future effects of policies are not worthwhile; nor is it worthwhile to attempt to project housing needs. With such views it is not surprising that most of the social scientific research carried out by his Department appears to be being terminated. (For his views noted above see House of Commons Environment Committee, 1980.)

Chapter 4

1. The same is true of the debate on 'inner city' policy in the House of Commons on 6 April 1977. In his opening speech, Peter Shore (then Secretary of State for the Environment) stated that:

   the extent and the changed character of the inner city is only now becoming fully understood . . . . During the past decade inner cities have suffered a massive and disproportionate loss of jobs and a major exodus of population. Substantial ethnic minorities in some cities have added an extra dimension.

   Exactly what it is that constitutes the 'extra dimension' was not made clear in Peter Shore's speech, nor in the subsequent debate.
2. A more detailed account of capitalist development and decline in Willesden can be found in Phizacklea and Miles (1981). It should be noted that the borough of Willesden became part of the borough of Brent in 1965. Where the data base

refers to Brent rather than to the area that was previously the borough of Willesden, we have to refer to Brent.

3. In any case, we are not convinced that the injection of a few hundred million pounds into the 'inner cities' will, in the absence of more fundamental changes to the process of capitalist production, have any dramatic, overall effect on their material decline: the precedent of 'special assistance' to those regions experiencing industrial decline is relevant here (Holland, 1976a; 1976b).

Chapter 5

1. Most of the local Community Development Projects eventually rejected the official Home Office framework, but there were differences in their various final analyses based on the local political situation and the project personnel themselves. See the survey done by the National CDP (1975) for an idea of the diversity of ideas and activities within CDP.

2. The North Tyneside CDP was, by the end of its lifetime, very active in working with local unions. After the initial difficulty of convincing the unions that community workers had something to offer them, the CDP was involved in such activities as the establishment of a local trades union research unit, the Tynes Conference of Shop Stewards, various joint efforts with the North Tyneside Trades Council, as well as its efforts to form an unemployed workers group. In addition, it tried to help in several specific local issues such as two large-scale redundancy operations.

   In spite of this, however, it was never able to overcome the ideological and organisational constraints that divided the point of production from the reproductive process. So it was rarely possible to get the labour movement involved in issues traditionally considered outside the 'mainstream' of union concern (North Tyneside CDP, 1978a, pp. 157–86).

Chapter 8

1. For convenience we define the North of Scotland as comprising the Grampian and Highland regions and the Northern and Western Isles.

2. These figures are drawn from a variety of sources including Department of Employment data and the work of the North Sea study team in the Department of Political Economy, Aberdeen University. I am grateful to the latter – and especially to Tony MacKay, now at the Institute for the Study of Sparsely Populated Areas, Aberdeen University – for permission to use them.

3. See Bettelheim (Emmanuel, 1972, p. 301), quoted and discussed in Wolpe (1975).

4. 'Capital created underdevelopment, not because it exploited the underdeveloped world, but because it did not exploit it enough.' (Kay, 1975, discussed in Foster–Carter, 1978; on this see also Rosenberg, 1976).

5. The status of which is discussed by Judith Ennew (1977; 1978).

6. Not, at least, in anything like the same sense – but see, *inter alia*, Mandel (1978) on revising the time-scale of periods of transition.

7. For an introduction to this debate see Foster–Carter (1978).

8. '"Industrial relations", the consecrated euphemism for the permanent conflict, now acute, now subdued, between capital and labour' (Miliband, 1973, p. 73).

9. From a recent survey conducted by the North Sea study team (see note 2 above). More recent figures from a survey of my own will be available soon.

10. Comprising, essentially, the East Ross and Cromarty areas and excluding Inverness.

11. I do not suggest that it is the only significant factor: housing policy and corresponding availability is another and is described in detail for East Ross by Isobel Grigor (1978).

12. This is, of course, just one small corner of the topic of labour market segmentation. This is considered further in a forthcoming paper, 'Conceptualising Migrant Labour'.

13. I should make it clear that the full force of these remarks does not apply to the very few rigs owned and operated by the British and part-British oil companies, BP and Shell Expro, where conditions were much better, most workers were on contracts and labour turnover has been much lower. Both have, however, tacitly participated in resistance to unionisation offshore.

14. I am grateful to Gordon Philip of the Department of Sociology, Aberdeen University, who has been centrally involved in the observation at Nigg, for this information.

15. This aspect of work offshore has also been researched by Kit Carson and Hilary Idzikowski of the Department of Criminology, University of Edinburgh.

Chapter 9

1. For the analysis of urbanisation as a purely private-capitalist enterprise, see Sola Moralies, 1977.

2. Several authors, such as Capel (1974, p. 45), stress the 'minifundist' character of the construction industry while Sala (1974) deals with the opposite tendency, the concentration of capital in large firms which dominate the construction industry, through vertical integration.

3. See Pradas (1974) for details of some of the social and cultural features of the spontaneously created slums (*barriadas*).

4. It has been argued (Capel, 1974, p. 49) that there is a link between political stability in the urban domain and the development of petty bourgeois enterprises.

5. This urban component of inflation is not simply that created by the demand for urban land, but includes the increase in costs of transport and assembly caused by the fragmentation of workshops, factories, offices and commercial agencies.

6. Indeed, the Catalan government of the Generalitat before the Civil War had considerable influence on local affairs. The changes the Generalitat introduced in schooling, health services, public culture and political participation were felt more deeply than the changes introduced by the Francoist regime which were more restrictive than encouraging.

Chapter 10

1. The choice of examples has been dictated, in part, by the data available from a British Social Science Research Council financed project comparing Barcelona and Manchester. However, this comparison has the advantage of providing us with not only the first industrialising situation, but with Barcelona which while

similar to some of the Latin American situations, has a longer history of industrialisation. The type of analysis is similar to that of Balan (1978). I would like to thank
Harley Browning for his comments on an earlier draft of this paper.

2. Such an analysis of migration is provided, for example, in Balan et al., (1973).
The kind of analysis suggested here is aimed to complement these other analyses,
identifying possible reasons for the diversity of migration patterns that are
reported and trying to see what is significant about different types of migration
pattern.

3. My point of reference is Wallerstein's types of incorporation into the modern
world system. I have thus chosen examples of industrialisation affected by the
structural position of the particular country in the world economy. Manchester,
Barcelona and Lima are the first major examples of industrialisation in their
respective countries. The argument is more difficult to extend to comparing
regions within the same country. Where existing agrarian and urban conditions
are highly uneven, however, such an extension may be possible.

4. By social flexibility I refer to several related issues, such as the nature of family
responsibilities that tie individuals to localities, or to the extent that ownership of
property or of the means of production are diffused among a population. Flexible
labour is, in this sense, totally free labour that is available to be readily traded as
a commodity in the market.

5. The influence of labour supply on technology is the theme of Habakkuk (1967).
An example of labour influencing the growth of a particular sector of industry
is that of Barcelona. As we will see later, the construction industry in Barcelona
grew rapidly on the basis of the large supply of unskilled migrant labour.

6. The transformation of the agrarian structure is, to a great extent, linked to structural position within the world economy. Thus, Britain had a thoroughly commercialised agrarian structure which was the basis for industrialisation and for its
dominant economic positions in the eighteenth century. However, there are
variations that are independent of structural position. Thus, São Paulo's economic
growth had to be based on international migration because of the absence of
available rural populations. Likewise, Peru's available rural population lived in
the highlands, while most economic growth has occurred on the coast. Also, in
comparison with a country such as Guatemala, Peru's rural population has been
highly differentiated economically before industrialisation.

7. I have taken this contrast between horizontal relationships and vertical relationships from a paper by Ian Procter (1979). In this paper, Procter argues, with
reference to British material, for the need both to identify systematically the
distinguishing characteristics of different cities and their patterns of urbanisation
and to retain in the analysis the importance of national forces structuring local
economic and political space.

8. State intervention has two aspects in this context which I do not develop in this
chapter. The first is the national pattern of intervention, brought about by the
general economic and political conditions of a country within the international
economy. The second is that intervention which is specific to the industrialising
situation, as when special regulations, economic assistance or police force are
applied there, but not elsewhere in the country. A full analysis of the effect of
industrialisation on the state would need to differentiate these two aspects, for

example, by comparing state intervention in different regions of the same country.

9. Since by 1901, Manchester's industrial structure was quite mature, it is interesting to note the sectoral distribution of labour (see table). These figures should be taken with some caution, because the Census did not classify occupations in a way that makes them exactly comparable to modern classifications.

10. See Robert Roberts (1971) for a description of this moral order in a Salford 'slum' area.

11. At times, tariff protection was given to industry, but at other times favourable terms were given to foreign imports. The general weakness of the Spanish state meant that contraband was a constant threat to local industry.

12. It is interesting to contrast the case of the southern English agricultural labourers in the first half of the nineteenth century. These were existing under conditions of extreme poverty and exploitation, but never moved in substantial numbers to the industrial areas of the North, despite attempts by northern manufacturers to sponsor such migration.

13. This analysis applies to the years of the Franco administration in Spain. Changes in administrative style since Franco are results both of internal forces such as trade union and neighbourhood-based struggles and of external factors such as integration into the European economy.

14. Such controls are the skill and reward hierarchies of the factory, the availability of an industrial reserve and so on.

15. I am not clear, however, as to the extent to which São Paulo's industrial expansion is based on small as well as large-scale establishments, or as to the extent of labour mobility there.

16. A full analysis of the growth of the Peruvian economy in the twentieth century is given in Thorp and Betram (1977). They detail the position of both foreign and national capital, looking at each sector of production in turn. My own account is taken from theirs, though in a simplified form.

17. Mangin (1959) and Doughty (1970) provide accounts of this provincial presence in Lima. An important factor differentiating Lima from other peripheral Latin American situations, however, is the vitality of the provincial economy. Thus, in Guatemala City, there is less evidence of a provincial presence. See Roberts (1974).

Male (over aged 10) Employment by Industrial Sector 1901

	Services			Transport	Personal	Manufacture*		Construction	Extractive	Other
	Collective (administration, teaching, local government)	Professions	Commerce			Large	Small			
Manchester city	2.1	3.1	17.5	16.3	3.1	27.1	13.1	9.9	1.3	6.3
Oldham	1.2	1.9	10.3	6.2	2.1	56.9	7.1	7.6	1.8	4.9

† In Oldham female employment was seemingly concentrated in large-scale manufacture (69 per cent) with only 7 per cent of females working in small-scale manufacturing. In the city of Manchester 18.1 per cent of females were employed in large-scale manufacturing establishments, compared with 28.6 per cent for small establishments.

* This is a crude distinction made by myself on the basis of what I take to be the overall organisation of a particular branch of manufacturing. Thus, textiles and metal trades I classed as large; woodwork, tailoring and printing as small.

Source: *Census of England and Wales*, 1901, Lancashire.

References

Abrams, P. (1978), 'Towns and Economic Growth', in P. Abrams and E. A. Wrigley (eds.), *Towns in Societies* (London: Cambridge University Press).

Althusser, L. (1969), 'On the Materialist Dialectic', in L. Althusser (ed.), *For Marx* (Harmondsworth: Penguin).

Ambrose, P. (1974), *The Quiet Revolution* (London: Chatto and Windus for Sussex University Press).

Ambrose, P. and Colenutt, R. (1975), *The Property Machine* (Harmondsworth: Penguin).

Ayton, J. (1976), 'Rural Settlement Policy: Problems and Conflict', in P. J. Drudy (ed.), *Regional and Rural Development: Essays in Theory and Practice* (Chalfont St. Giles: Alpha Academic), pp. 59–68.

Balan, J. (1978), *Estructure Agraria, Desarollo Capitalista y Mercados de Trabajo en America Latina: La migración rural–urbana en una perspectiva historica*, Estudio Sociales no. 10 (Buenos Aires: CEDES).

Balan, J., Browning, H. and Jeling, E. (1973), *The Lives of Men* (Austin and London: The University of Texas Press).

Banco Urquijo (1972), *El Área Metropolitana de Barcelona: génesis y problemática* (Madrid: Moeda y Crédito).

Bedale, C. (1978), *Property Relations and Housing Policy in Oldham: an historical perspective*, M.A. thesis, Manchester University.

Bell, C. and Newby, H. (1971), *Community Studies* (London: George Allen and Unwin).

Bell, C. and Newby, H. (1977), 'Community, Communion, Class and Community Action', in D. Herbert and R. Johnson (eds.), *Social Geography and the Study of Urban Areas* (London: Wiley).

Bell, D. (1973), *The Coming of Post-industrial Society* (New York: Basic Books).

Bell, D. (1979), 'The New Class: a Muddled Concept', *Transaction*, vol. 16, no. 2.

Benwell Community Development Project (1979), *The Making of a Ruling Class*, Final Report Series, no. 6, Newcastle-upon-Tyne, Benwell CDP Publications.

Beresford, T. (1975), *We Plough the Fields* (Harmondsworth: Penguin).

Bertaux, D. (1977), *Destins Personnels et Structure de Classe* (Paris: Presse Universitaire de France).

Birch, A. (1964), *Representative and Responsible Government* (London: George Allen and Unwin).

Birmingham Inner Area Study (1974), *Small Heath Birmingham: a social survey* (London: Department of the Environment).

Birmingham Inner Area Study (1977a), *Circumstances of Families* (London: Department of the Environment).

Birmingham Inner Area Study (1977b), *Unequal City* (London: HMSO).

Blau, P. (1973), *The Dynamics of Bureaucracy*, 2nd edn. (Chicago: University of Chicago Press).

Borough of Brent (1977), *Brent: a statement of forward planning policies* (London: Borough of Brent).

Brant, V. (1977), 'Do Colono ao boia-fria; transformacoes na agriculture e constituicao do mercado de trabalho na alta sorocabana de Assis', *Estudos CEBRAP*, no. 19, pp. 37–92.

Briggs, A. (1968), *Victorian Cities* (Harmondsworth: Penguin).

Bulmer (1977), 'Tammany Hall beside the Wear', *New Society*, 24 November.

Bulmer, M. (ed.) (1978), *Mining anh Social Change* (London: Croom Helm).

Burgess, K. (1977), *The Family Economy of the Lancashire Cotton Manufacture under Capital: a discussion paper*, Department of Economic History, University of Glasgow.

Butt Philip, A. (1975), *The Welsh Question: Nationalism in Welsh Politics 1945–70* (Cardiff: University of Wales Press).

Cambridge Political Economy Group (1974), *Britain's Economic Crisis*, Spokesman Pamphlet no. 44 (Nottingham: Spokesman Books).

Canning Town CDP (1974), *Information Centre and Neighbourhood Work Report* (London: Home Office).

Capel, H. (1974), 'Agentes y Estrategias en la Producción del Espacio Urbano Español', Revista de Geografía.

Carney, J., Hudson, R., Ive, C. and Lewis, J. (1975), 'Regional Underdevelopment in Late Capitalism: a study of the Northeast of England', in I. Masser (ed.), *Theory and Practice in Regional Science* (London: Pion), pp. 11–29.

Carney, J. and Lewis, J. (eds.) (1978), 'Accumulation, the Regional Problem and Nationalism', in P. Batey (ed.), *Theory and Method in Urban and Regional Analysis* (London: Pion), pp. 67–81.

Carney, J., Lewis, J. and Hudson, R. (1977), 'Coal Combines and Interregional Uneven Development in the UK', in D. Massey and P. Batey (eds.), *Alternative Frameworks for Analysis* (London: Pion), pp. 52–67.

Carter, I. R. (1971), 'Economic Models and the recent history of the Highlands', *Scottish Studies*, no. XV.

Carter, I. R. (1972), *In the Beginning was the Board: thoughts on the ideology of regional planning*, mimeo, Department of Sociology, University of Aberdeen.

Carter, I. R. (1974), 'The Highlands of Scotland as an Undeveloped Region', in E. deKadt and G. Williams (eds.), *Sociology of Development* (London: Tavistock).

Carter, I. R. (1978), *Farm Life in the Northeast of Scotland: the poor man's country* (Edinburgh: John Donald).

Castells, M. (1976), 'Theoretical Propositions for an Experimental Study of Urban Social Movements', in C. G. Pickvance (ed.), *Urban Sociology: critical essays* (London: Tavistock), pp. 147–73.

Castells, M. (1977a), *The Urban Question*, rev. Eng. edn. (London: Edward Arnold).

Castells, M. (1977b), 'Towards a Political Urban Sociology', in M. H. Harloe (ed.), *Captive Cities* (London: Wiley), pp. 61–78.

Castells, M. (1978), *City, Class and Power* (London: Macmillan).

Chapman, S. J. and Abbott, W. (1912/13), 'The Tendency of Children to Enter their Fathers' Trades', *Journal of the Royal Statistical Society*, no. LXXVI.

Circulo de Economia (1973), *Gestión o Caos: el área metropolitana de Barcelona* (Barcelona: Ariel).

Cockburn, C. (1977), *The Local State: Management of Cities and People* (London: Pluto Press).

Community Development Project (1977), *The Costs of Industrial Change* (London: CDP Inter-Project Editorial Team).

Connell, J. (1974), 'The Metropolitan Village: spatial and social processes in discontinuous suburbs', in J. H. Johnson (ed.), *The Geography of Suburban Growth*

(London: Wiley).

Cooke, P. (1980), 'Capital Relation and State Dependency: an analysis of urban development policy', in G. Rees and T. Rees (eds.), *Poverty and Social Inequality in Wales* (London: Croom Helm).

Corrigan, P. (1977), 'Feudal Relics on Capitalist Monuments? Notes on the Sociology of Unfree Labour', *Sociology*, vol. XI, no. 3.

Counter Information Services (1973), *The Recurrent Crisis of London* (London: CIS).

Countryside Commission (1977), *Annual Report 1976* (London: HMSO).

Crichton, R. (1964), *Commuter Village* (Newton Abbot: David and Charles).

Crozier, M. (1964), The Bureaucratic Phenomenon (Chicago: University of Chicago Press).

Dahl, R. (1956), *Preface to Democratic Theory* (Chicago: University of Chicago Press).

Dahl, R. (1961), *Who Governs?* (New Haven: Yale University Press).

Dahl, R. (1963), *Modern Political Analysis* (Englewood Cliffs, New Jersey: Prentice-Hall).

Davies, G. and Thomas, I. (1976), *Overseas Investment in Wales* (Llandybie: Christopher Davies).

Dearlove, J. (1974), 'The Control of Change and the Regulation of Community Action', in D. Jones and M. Mayo (eds.), *Community Work One* (London: Routledge and Kegan Paul).

Dearlove, J. (1979), *The Reorganisation of British Local Government* (London: Cambridge University Press).

Department of the Environment (1977a), *Inner Area Studies: summaries of consultants' final reports* (London: HMSO).

Department of the Environment (1977b), *Housing Policy. A Consultative Document* (London: HMSO).

Department of the Environment (1977c), *Policy for the Inner Cities*, Cmnd 6845 (London: HMSO).

Donaldson, J. G. S. and Donaldson, F. (1972), *Farming in Britain Today* (Harmondsworth: Penguin).

Donnison, D. (1973), 'The Micro-politics of the City', in D. Donnison and D. Eversley (eds.), *London: Urban Patterns, Problems and Policies* (London: Heinemann Educational Books).

Dos Santos, A. (1973), 'The Crisis of Development Theory and the Problem of Dependence in Latin America', in H. Bernstein (ed.), *Underdevelopment and Development* (Harmondsworth: Penguin).

Doughty, P. L. (1970), 'Behind the Back of the City: provincial life in Lima, Peru', in W. Mangin (ed.), *Peasants in Cities* (Boston: Houghton Mifflin), pp. 30–46.

Downs, A. (1967), *Inside Bureaucracy* (Boston: Little, Brown and Company).

Drake, M., McLoughlin, B., Thompson, R. and Thornley, J. (1975), *Aspects of Structure Planning in Britain* (London: Centre for Environmental Studies).

Dunleavy, P. (1979), 'The Urban Basis of Political Alignment', *British Journal of Political Science*, vol. 9, part 4.

East Anglian Regional Strategy Team (1974), *Strategic Choice for East Anglia* (London: HMSO).

Edwards, A. and Rogers, A. (eds.) (1974), *Agricultural Resources* (London: Faber and Faber).

Edwards, J. and Thomas, W. (eds.) (1974), *Llantrisant New Town: the case against* (Merthyr: Heads of the Valleys Authorities Standing Conference).

Eldridge, J. E. T. and Cameron, G. C. (1968), 'Unofficial Strikes', in J. E. T. Eldridge (ed.), *Industrial Disputes* (London: Routledge and Kegan Paul).

Elliott, B., McCrone, D. and Skelton, J. (1978), 'Property and Politics: Edinburgh 1875–1975', in J. Garrard et al. (eds.), *The Middle Class in Politics* (Farnborough: Saxon House).

Emmanuel, A. (1972), *Unequal Exchange: A Study of the Imperalism of Trade* (London: New Left Books).

Ennew, J. (1977), 'The Changing Croft', *New Society*, 17 June.

Ennew, J. (1978), 'Gaelic as the Language of Industrial Relations', *Scottish Journal of Sociology*, vol. 2, no. 3.

Esteva Fabregat, C. (1973), 'Immigración a Barcelona', *Ethnica*, no. 5.

Fernandez-Cavada, F. (1975), 'La Plantificación Territorial Como Instrumento de Integración de la Acción Regional y la Ordenación Urbanística', *CERCHA*, no. 16.

Ferras, R. (1976), 'Barcelona. Creixement d'una Metropoli', *Revista de Geografía*.

Flynn, R. (1978), 'The State and Planning', *Public Administration Bulletin*, no. 28, December.

Flynn, R. (1979), 'Urban Managers in Local Government Planning', *Sociological Review*, vol. 27, no. 4, November.

Fong, H. D. (1930), *Triumph of Factory System in England* (Tientsin: Chihli Press).

Foster, J. (1974), *Class Struggle and the Industrial Revolution* (London: Methuen).

Foster-Carter, A. (1978), 'The Mode of Production Debate', *New Left Review*, no. 107.

Frank, A. G. (1967), *Capitalism and Underdevelopment in Latin America* (New York: Monthly Review Press).

Francis, J. (1974), *Scotland's Pipedream* (Edinburgh: Church of Scotland Home Board).

Fraser of Allender Institute (1978), *Quarterly Economic Commentary*, vol. 4, no. 2, October.

Fraser, D. (1976), *Urban Politics in Victorian England* (Leicester: Leicester University Press).

Friedland, R., Piven, F. F. and Alford, R. (1977), 'Political Conflict, Urban Structure and the Fiscal Crisis', *International Journal of Urban and Regional Research*, vol. 1, no. 3, pp. 447–71.

Frigole, J. (1975), 'Creación y Evolución de una Cooperativa Agricola en le Vega Alta del Segura desde 1962 a 1974', *Revista de Estudio Sociales*, no. 14–15, pp. 167–200.

Frigole, J. (1977), '"Ser Cacique" y "Ser Hombre" o la negación de las Relaciones de Patronazgo en un Pueblo de la Vega Alta del Segura', *Agricultura y Sociedad*, October–December.

Galtung, J. (1971), 'The European Community and the Developing Countries', mimeo, Makerere University.

Garcia, M. S. (1978), *Desarrollo Industrial y Formación Social en un Area de Barcelona*, Tesis de Dicenciatura, Faculty of Geography and History, University of Barcelona.

Gardiner, J. (1977), 'Women in the Labour Process and Class Structure', in A. Hunt (ed.), *Class and Class Structure* (London: Lawrence and Wishart).

Gaskin, M. and MacKay, D. I. (1978), *The Economic Impact of North Sea Oil on Scotland* (London: HMSO).

Gill, O. (1977), *Luke Street* (London: Macmillan).

Gold, D., Lo, C. and Wright, E. (1976), 'Recent Developments in Marxist Theories of the Capitalist State', *Monthly Review*, vol. 27, pp. 37–51.

Goldthorpe, J. (1978), 'Comment' on F. Bechhofer, B. Elliott and D. McCrone, 'Structure, Consciousness and Action', *British Journal of Sociology*, vol. XXIV, no. 4.

Gorz, A. (1968), *Strategy for Labor: a radical proposal* (Boston: Beacon Press).

Gough, I. (1975), 'State Expenditure in Advanced Capitalism', *New Left Review*, no. 92, pp. 53–92.

Grigor, I. (1978), 'Local Authority Accommodation of Oil-Related Developments in East Ross', *Scottish Journal of Sociology*, vol. 2, no. 3.

Habbakkuk, H. J. (1967), *American and British Technology in the Nineteenth Century* (Cambridge: Cambridge University Press).

Habermas, J. (1976), *Legitimation Crisis* (London: Heinemann Educational Books).

Hall, P., Thomas, R., Gracey, H. and Drewett, R. (1973), *The Containment of Urban England* (London: George Allen and Unwin).

Harloe, M. H. (ed.) (1975), *Proceedings of the Urban Change and Conflict Conference, 1975* (London: Centre for Environmental Studies).

Harloe, M. H. (1979), 'Marxism, the State and the Urban Question: Critical Notes on two recent French Theories', in C. Crouch (ed.), *State and Economy in Contemporary Capitalism* (London: Croom Helm).

Harloe, M. H. (1981), 'The Recommodification of Housing', in M. H. Harloe and E. Lebas (eds.), *City, Class and Capital. New Developments in the Political Economy of Cities and Regions* (London: Edward Arnold).

Harloe, M. H. and Lebas, E. (eds.), *City, Class and Capital. New Developments in the Political Economy of Cities and Regions* (London: Edward Arnold).

Harrington, M. (1979), 'The New Class and the Left', *Transaction*, vol. 16, no. 2.

Harris, C. (1974), *Hennage: a social structure in miniature* (New York: Holt, Rinehart and Winston).

Hartmann, P. and Husbands, C. (1974), *Racism and the Mass Media* (London: Davis-Poynter).

Harvey, D. (1978), 'The urban process under capitalism: a framework for analysis', *International Journal of Urban and Regional Research*, vol. 2, no. 1, pp. 101–31.

Haymen, K. (1977), 'Links with the Labour Movement – an example from North Tyneside', *Community Action*, no. 32, pp. 23–7.

Heller, F. (1977), 'Infrastructures or Organised Power: a process model', in M. Warner (ed.), *Organisational Choice and Constraint* (Farnborough: Saxon House).

Hennock, E. P. (1973), *Fit and Proper Persons* (London: Edward Arnold).

Hill, M. (1972), *The Sociology of Public Administration* (London: Weidenfeld and Nicolson).

Hindess, B. (1977), *Philosophy and Methodology in the Social Sciences* (Hassocks: Harvester).

Hindess, B. (1978), 'Classes and Politics in Marxist Theory', in G. Littlejohn, B. Smart, J. Wakeford and N. Yuval-Davis (eds.), *Power and the State* (London: Croom Helm).

Hirsch, J. (1978), 'The State Apparatus and Social Reproduction: elements of a theory of the bourgeois state', in J. Holloway and S. Picciotto (eds.), *State and Capital: a Marxist debate* (London: Edward Arnold), pp. 57–107.

Hirst, P. (1977), 'Economic Classes and Politics', in A. Hunt (ed.), *Class and Class Structure* (London: Lawrence and Wishart).

Hobsbawm, E. J. (1968), *Industry and Empire: an economic history of Britain since 1750*

(London: Weidenfeld and Nicolson).

Holland, S. (1976a), *Capital versus the Regions* (London: Macmillan).

Holland, S. (1976b), *The Regional Problem* (London: Macmillan).

Holloway, J. and Picciotto, S. (eds.) (1978), *State and Capital: a Marxist debate* (London: Edward Arnold).

House of Commons Environment Committee (1980), *Inquiry into Implications of Government's Expenditure Plans 1980/81 to 1983/84 for the Housing Policies of the Department of the Environment. Minutes of Evidence. Thursday 24 April 1980* (London: HMSO).

Huertas-Claveria, J. (1973), 'Los Nueve Barrios (que pronto seran diez)', *Construction, Arquitecture, Urbanismo*, no. 20.

Humphrys, G. (1972), *South Wales* (Newton Abbot: David and Charles).

Hunt, D. (1978), *The Engineering Industry in the Grampian Region* (Aberdeen: North East Scotland Development Association).

Hunter, J. (1976), *The Making of the Crofting Community* (Edinburgh: John Donald).

Husbands, C. T. (1979), 'The "Threat" Hypothesis and Racist Voting in England and the United States', in R. Miles and A. Phizacklea (eds.), *Racism and Political Action in Britain* (London: Routledge and Kegan Paul).

Jessop, B. (1978), 'Capitalism and Democracy: the best political shell?', in G. Littlejohn, B. Smart, J. Wakeford and N. Yuval-Davis (eds.), *Power and the State* (London: Croom Helm).

Johnson, R. W. (1973), 'The British Political Elite, 1955–1972', *Archives Européen de Sociologie*, vol. XIV.

Jones, J. and Wilford, R. A. (1979), *The Welsh Veto: the politics of the devolution campaign in Wales*, Studies in Public Policy no. 39, Glasgow, Centre for the Study of Public Policy, University of Strathclyde.

Josling, T. E. (1974), 'Agricultural Policies in Developed Countries: an overview', *Journal of Agricultural Economics*, vol. 25, no. 1, pp. 229–63.

Kay, G. (1975), *Development and Underdevelopment: a Marxist analysis* (London: Macmillan).

Kirkpatrick, J. (1979), 'Politics and the New Class', *Transaction*, vol. 16, no. 2.

Kolakowski, L. (1972), *Positivist Philosophy* (Harmondsworth: Penguin).

Kowarick, L. (1977), *The Logic of Disorder: capitalist expansion in the metropolitan area of greater São Paulo*, Discussion Paper, Institute of Development Studies, University of Sussex.

Kraushaar, R. (1979), 'Pragmatic Radicalism', *International Journal of Urban and Regional Research*, vol. 3, no. 1, pp. 61–80.

Laclau, E. (1971), 'Feudalism and Capitalism in Latin America', *New Left Review*, no. 67.

Lambert, J., Paris, C. and Blackaby, B. (1978), *Housing Policy and the State. Allocation, Access and Control* (London: Macmillan).

Lambeth Inner Area Study (1974), *People, Housing and District* (London: Department of the Environment).

Landes, D. (1970), *The Unbound Prometheus* (Cambridge: Cambridge University Press).

Lawton, R. (1962), 'Population Trends in Lancashire and Cheshire from 1801', *Transactions of the Historical Society of Lancashire and Cheshire*, no. CXIV, pp. 189–213.

Lebas, E. (1981), 'The New School of Urban and Regional Research: Into the Second Decade', in M. H. Harloe and E. Lebas (eds.), *City, Class and Capital. New Develop-*

ments in the *Political Economy of Cities and Regions* (London: Edward Arnold).

Leff, V. and Blunden, G. H. (n.d.) *The Willesden Story* (London: Research Writers).

Leonard, P. (ed.) (1975), 'The Sociology of Community Action', *Sociological Review Monograph*, no. 21.

Lindberg, L., Alford, R. Crouch, C. and Offe, C. (eds.) (1975), *Stress and Contradiction in Modern Capitalism* (Mass.: Lexington).

Lindblom, C. (1959), 'The Science of "Muddling Through"', *Public Administration Review*, vol. 19, pp. 79-99.

Localización de Actividades en el Área Metropolitana de Barcelona (n.d.), mimeo, Barcelona.

Lojkine, J. (1977), 'Big Firm's Strategies, Urban Policy and Urban Social Movements', in M. H. Harloe (ed.) *Captive Cities* (London: Wiley), pp. 141-56.

Lomas, G. (1975), *The Inner City* (London: London Council of Social Service).

Long, N. and Roberts, B. (eds.) (1978), *Peasant Cooperation and Capitalist Expansion in Central Peru* (Austin and London: Institute of Latin American Studies, The University of Texas at Austin).

López, C. (1978), 'Un Barrio en Busca de Redención', *La Vanguardia*, June, 1st week.

Lorimer, J. (1972), *A Citizen's Guide to City Politics* (Toronto: James Lewis R. Samuel).

Lorimer, J. (1978), *The Developers* (Toronto: Lorimer).

Lovering, J. (1978), *Dependence and the Welsh Economy?* Economic research papers reg 22, Bangor, University College of North Wales.

Lukes, S. (1977), 'The New Democracy', in S. Lukes, *Essays in Social Theory* (London: Macmillan), pp. 30-51.

McKenzie, R. T. and Silver, A. (1968), *Angels in Marble* (London: Heinemann).

McNabb, R. (1980), 'Segmented Labour Markets, Female Employment and Poverty in Wales', in G. Rees and T. Rees (eds.) *Poverty and Social Inequality in Wales* (London: Croom Helm).

MacPherson, C. (1973), *Democratic Theory: essays in retrieval* (Oxford: Clarendon Press).

Mandel, E. (1978), 'The Nature of the Soviet State', *New Left Review*, vol. 108, March–April.

Mangin, W. (1959), 'The Role of Regional Associations in the Adaptation of Rural Migrants to Cities in Peru', in D. B. Heath and R. N. Adams (eds.), *Contemporary Customs and Socities of Latin America* (New York: Random House), pp. 311-23.

Manners, G. (ed.) (1964), *South Wales in the Sixties* (London: Macmillan).

Marsh, A. (1977), *Protest and Political Consciousness* (Beverly Hills, California: Sage).

Marshall, J. D. (1968), 'Colonisation as a factor in the Planning of Towns in northwest England', in H. J. Dyos (ed.), *The Study of Urban History* (London: Edward Arnold).

Marti, M. (1974), *Barcelona – a dónde vas?* (Barcelona: Ed. Dirosa).

Martinez-Alier, V. and Moises, J. (1977), 'A Revolta dos suburbanos ou 'patrao, o trem astrasou', in Centro de Estudos de Cultura Contemperânea, *Contradicoes urbanas e movimentos sociasis* (Rio de Janeiro: Paz e terra), pp. 13-64.

Mason, T. (1978), 'Community Action and the Local Authority: a study in the Incorporation of Protest', in *1977 Urban Change and Conflict Conference: Proceedings* (London: Centre for Environmental Studies), pp. 89-116.

Massey, D. (1978), 'Regionalism: some Current Issues', *Capital and Class*, no. 6, pp. 233-44.

Massey, D. (1979), 'In What Sense a Regional Problem?', *Regional Studies*, no. 13, pp. 233–44.

Mayo, M. (1975), 'The History and Early Development of CDP', in R. Lees and G. Smith (eds.), *Action-research in Community Development* (London: Routledge and Kegan Paul), pp. 6–18.

Miles, R. and Phizacklea, A. (1977), 'Class, Race, Ethnicity and Political Action', *Political Studies*, vol. XXV, no. 4, pp. 491–507.

Miles, R. and Phizacklea. A. (1978), 'Some Introductory Observations on Race and Politics in Britain', in R. Miles and A. Phizacklea (eds.), *Racism and Political Action in Britain* (London: Routledge and Kegan Paul).

Miles, R. (1978), *Between Two Cultures? the Case of Rastafarianism* SSRC Research Unit on Ethnic Relations Working Paper no. 10.

Miliband, R. (1969), *The State in Capitalist Society* (London: Weidenfeld and Nicolson).

Miliband, R. (1972), *Parliamentary Socialism*, 2nd edn. (London: Merlin Press).

Miliband, R. (1973), *The State in Capitalist Society* (London: Quartet).

Miliband. R. (1977), *Marxism and Politics* (London: Oxford University Press).

Miliband, R. (1978), 'A State of De-Subordination', *British Journal of Sociology*, vol. XXIX, no. 4.

Moore, R. (1975), *Racism and Black Resistance* (London: Pluto Press).

Moore, R. (1978), 'Northern Notes Towards a Sociology of Oil', *Scottish Journal of Sociology*, vol. 2, no. 3 (September).

Moore, R. (1981), *A Study of the Social Impact of Oil on Peterhead* (London: Routledge and Kegan Paul).

Morgan. K. (1979), 'State Regional Interventions and Industrial Reconstruction in Postwar Britain: the case of Wales', Working Paper 16, Urban and Regional Studies, University of Sussex.

Morgan, K. O. (1970), *Wales in British Politics 1868–1922*, 2nd edn. (Cardiff: University of Wales Press).

Moss, L. and Parker, S. (1967), *The Local Government Councillor* (London: HMSO).

Nairn, T. (1977). *The Break-up of Britain* (London: New Left Books).

National CDP (1975), *Forward Plan, 1975/76* (London: Home Office).

National CDP (1977a), *The Costs of Industrial Change* (London: Home Office).

National CDP (1977b), *Gilding the Ghetto: the state and the poverty experiments* (London: Home Office).

Newby, H. (1972), 'The Low Earnings of Agricultural Workers: a sociological approach', *Journal of Agricultural Economics*, vol. 23, no. 1, pp. 15–24.

Newby, H. (1977), *The Deferential Worker* (London: Allen Lane).

Newby, H., Bell, C. Rose, D. and Saunders, P. (1978), *Property, Paternalism and Power* (London: Hutchinson).

Newcastle CDP (1978), *Slums on the Drawing Board* (London: Home Office).

Nichols, T. and Armstrong, P. (1976), *Workers Divided* (London: Fontana).

Norman, P. (1975), 'Urban Managerialism: a review of recent work', in M. H. Harloe (ed.), *Proceedings of the Conference on Urban Change and Conflict* (London: Centre for Environmental Studies) pp. 62–86.

North Tyneside CDP (1975a), *A Report on the Project's Work during 1974* (unpublished).

North Tyneside CDP (1975b), *Welfare Rights: the North Shields Campaign* (unpublished).

North Tyneside CDP (1975c), Position Paper (unpublished).

North Tyneside CDP (1978a), *North Shields: living with industrial Change*, Final Report, vol. 2 (London: Home Office).

North Tyneside CDP (1978b), *North Shields: organising for change in a working ctass area*, Final Report, vol. 3 (London: Home Office).

North Tyneside CDP (1978c), *North Shields: organising for change in a working class area – the action groups*, Final Report, vol. 4 (London: Home Office).

O'Brien, P. J. (1975), 'A Critique of Latin American Theories of Dependency', in I. Oxaal, T. Barnett and D. Booth (eds.), *Beyond the Sociology of Development* (London: Routledge and Kegan Paul).

O'Connor, J. (1973), *The Fiscal Crisis of the State* (New York: St. Martin's Press).

Offe, C. (1975a), 'The Theory of the Capitalist State and the Problem of Policy Formation', in L. Lindberg, R. Alford, C. Crouch and C. Offe (eds.), *Stress and Contradiction in Modern Capitalism* (Mass.: Lexington).

Offe, C. (1975b), 'Introduction to Part II: Legitimacy versus Efficiency', in L. Lindberg, R. Alford, C. Crouch and C. Offe (eds.), *Stress and Contradiction in Modern Capitalism* (Mass.: Lexington).

Offe, C. (1975c), 'Further Comments on Muller and Neususs', *Telos*, no. 25, pp. 99–111.

Offe, C. (1976), 'Political Authority and Class Structures', in P. Connerton (ed.), *Critical Sociology* (Harmondsworth: Penguin) pp. 388–421.

O'Malley, J. (1975), *The Politics of Community Action* (Nottingham: Spokesman Books).

Organización sindical (1976), *Servicio de Estadística* (Barcelona: Pva. de Barcelona).

Oxaal, I., Barnett, T. and Booth, D. (1975), *Beyond the Sociology of Development* (London: Routledge and Kegan Paul).

Pahl, R. E. (1965), *Urbs in Rure* (London: Weidenfeld and Nicolson).

Pahl, R. E. (1970), *Whose City?*, 1st edn. (London: Longmans).

Pahl, R. E. (1975), *Whose City?*, 2nd edn. (Harmondsworth: Penguin).

Panitch, L. (1978), *Recent Theorisation of Corporatism: reflections on a growth industry*, paper read at the 9th World Congress of Sociology at Uppsala, Sweden.

Paris, C. (1978), '"The parallels are striking" ... crisis in the inner city? G.B. 1977', *International Journal of Urban and Regional Research*, vol. 2, no. 1, pp. 160–70.

Parsons, T. (1967), 'On the Concept of Political Power', in T. Parsons, *Sociological Theory and Modern Society* (Glencoe, Illinois: Free Press).

Perman, D. (1972), *Cublington: Blueprint for Resistance* (Oxford: Bodley Head).

Pettigrew, A. M. (1973), *The Politics of Organisational Decision-making* (London: Tavistock).

Phizacklea, A. and Miles, R. (1979), 'Working-class Racist Beliefs in the Inner City', in R. Miles and A. Phizacklea (eds.), *Racism and Political Action in Britain* (London: Routledge and Kegan Paul).

Phizacklea, A. and Miles, R. (1981), *Labour and Racism* (London: Routledge and Kegan Paul).

Parker, R. and Shapiro, D. (eds.) (1980), *The Social Impact of Scottish Oil* (Farnborough: Saxon House).

Pickvance, C. G. (1976a), 'On the Study of Urban Social Movements', in C. G. Pickvance (ed.), *Urban Sociology: Critical Essays* (London: Methuen), pp. 198–218.

Pickvance, C. G. (ed.) (1976b), *Urban Sociology: Critical Essays* (London: Methuen).

Pickvance, C. G. (1979), 'Policies as Chameleons: an interpretation of regional policy and office policy in Britain', in M. J. Dear and A. Scott (eds.), *Urbanisation and Urban*

Planning in Capitalist Societies (Chicago: Maharoufa).

Piven, F. and Cloward, R. (1979a), *Poor People's Movements: Why They Succeed, How They Fail* (New York: Vintage Books).

Piven, F. and Cloward, R. (1979b), 'State Structures and Political Protest: Notes Towards a Theory', unpublished paper given at Centre for Environmental Studies Conference on Urban Change and Conflict, 1979.

Plaid Cymru (1970), *An Economic Plan for Wales* (Cardiff: Plaid Cymru).

Popper, K. (1959), *The Logic of Scientific Discovery* (London: Hutchinson).

Popplestone, G. (1976), *Action Strategies in CDP* (unpublished).

Poulantzas, N. (1973), *Political Power and Social Classes* (London: New Left Books).

Poulantzas, N. (1975), *Classes in Contemporary Capitalism* (London: New Left Books).

Poulantzas, N. (1978), *Classes in Contemporary Capitalism* (London: Verso).

Pradas, R. (1974), 'Ocupaciones Populares de Terrenos', *Construcción, Arquitectura, Urbanismo*, no. 27.

Procter, I. (1979), 'Urbanisation within the framework of the Spatial Structuring of Social Institutions: a conceptual discussion with reference to British material', mimeo, Department of Sociology, University of Warwick.

Rawkins, P. M. (1979), 'An Approach to the Political Sociology of the Welsh Nationalist Movement', *Political Studies*, vol. xxvii, no. 3, pp. 440–57.

Rawson, M. and Rogers, A. (1976), *Rural Housing and Structure Plans*, Countryside Planning Unit Occasional Paper, London, Wye College.

Recolons, L. (1976), *La Població de Catalunga: Distribució Territorial i Evolució Demogràfica (1900–1970)* (Barcelona: Ed. Laia).

Redford, A. and Russell, I. S. (1940), *The History of Local Government in Manchester*, II (London: New York and Toronto: Longmans, Green and Company).

Rees, G. (1980), 'Uneven Development, State Intervention and the Generation of Inequality: the case of industrial South Wales', in G. Rees and T. Rees (eds.), *Poverty and Social Inequality in Wales* (London: Croom Helm).

Rex, J. (1978), 'Race and the Inner City', in Commission for Racial Equality, *Five Views of Multi-racial Britain* (London: Commission for Racial Equality).

Rex, J. (1979), 'Black Militancy and Class Conflict', in R. Miles and A. Phizacklea (eds.), *Racism and Political Action in Britain* (London: Routledge and Kegan Paul).

Rex, J. and Moore, R. (1967), *Race, Community and Conflict* (London: Oxford University Press).

Roberts, B. R. (1973), 'Migración Urbana y Cambio en la organización Provincial en la Sierra Central de Peru', *Ethnica* (Barcelona), no. 6, pp. 237–61.

Roberts, B. R. (1974), 'The Interrelationships of City and Provinces in Peru and Guatemala', in *Latin American Urban Research*, vol. 4 (Beverly Hills, California: Sage Publications), pp. 207–36.

Roberts, B. R. (1978), 'Agrarian Organisation and Urban Development', in J. Wirth (ed.), *Manchester and São Paulo. Problems of Urban Growth* (Stanford: Stanford University Press).

Roberts, K., Cook, F., Clark, S. and Semeonoff, V. (1977), *The Fragmentary Class Structure* (London: Heinemann).

Roberts, R. (1971), *The Classic Slum* (Manchester: Manchester University Press).

Rose, A. (1967), *The Power Structure* (London: Oxford University Press).

Rose, R. (1974), *Politics in England Today* (London: Faber and Faber).

Rosenberg, D. (1976), 'Underdeveloped Sociology', *Sociology*, vol. X, no. 2.

Rosie, G. (1974), *Cromarty: the scramble for oil* (Edinburgh: Canongate).

Sala, M. (1974), 'Crisis y Concentración Capitalista en la Construción', *Construción, Arquitectura, Urbanisme*, no. 28.

Saunders, P. (1978), 'Domestic Property and Social Class', *International Journal of Urban and Regional Research*, vol. 2, no. 2.

Saunders, P. (1979a), *Urban Politics: a sociological interpretation* (London: Hutchinson).

Saunders, P. (1979b), *On the Specificity of the Urban*, unpublished paper, University of Sussex, School of Cultural and Community Studies.

Sayer, A. (1979), *Theory and Empirical Research in Urban and Regional Political Economy: a sympathetic critique*, Urban and Regional Studies Working Paper, no. 14, University of Sussex.

Scharpf, F. W., Reissert, B. and Schnabel, F. (1978), 'Policy Effectiveness and Conflict Avoidance in Intergovernmental Policy Formation', in K. Hanf and F. W. Scharpf (eds.), *Inter-organisational Policy-making* (London: Sage).

Schoen, D. S. (1977), *Enoch Powell and the Powellites* (London: Macmillan).

Schumpeter, J. (1954), *Capitalism, Socialism and Democracy* (London: George Allen and Unwin).

Secretary of State for Wales (1967), *Wales: the way ahead*, Cmnd 3334 (Cardiff: HMSO).

Self, P. and Storing, H. (1962), *The State and the Farmer* (London: George Allen and Unwin).

Serra Ramoneda, A. (1968), *La Ifraestructure e Iniciativa Privada: comentarios a una tendencia* (Barcelona: Banca Catalana).

Shapiro, D. (1981), *A Study of Labour Relations at Nigg and Kishorn* (Harmondsworth: Penguin).

Shirley, R. (1978), 'Legal Institutions and Early Industrial Growth', in J. Wirth (ed.), *Manchester and São Paulo. Problems of Urban Growth* (Stanford: Stanford University Press).

Sivanandan, A. (1976), 'Race, Class and the State: the Black Experience in Britain', *Race and Class*, vol. XVII, no. 4, pp. 347–68.

Skeldon, R. (1977), 'The evolution of Migration Patterns during Urbanisation in Peru', *Geographical Review*, vol. 67, no. 4, pp. 394–411.

Smith, G. A. (1975), *Internal Migration and Economic Activity*, Centre for Developing Area Studies Working Papers, no. 14, Montreal, McGill University.

Sola Morales, M. (1977), 'Crecimiento Urbano como Inversión de Capital Fijo. El caso de Barcelona. 1840–1975', *Cuidad y Territorio*, no. 2.

Tarragó, S. (1975), *La Barcelona de Porcioles* (Barcelona: Laia).

Taylor, S. (1978), 'Racism and Youth', *New Society*, 3 August, pp. 249–50.

Taylor, S. (1979), 'The National Front: anatomy of a political movement', in R. Miles and A. Phizacklea (eds.), *Racism and Political Action in Britain* (London: Routledge and Kegan Paul).

Terrades, I. (1978), *The Making of a Catalan Industrial Colony: a comparative study in the fiscal development of the Spanish state*, Ph.D. thesis, Manchester University.

Thompson, E. (1978), 'The Poverty of Theory', in E. Thompson, *The Poverty of Theory and Other Essays* (London: Merlin Press), pp. 193–397.

Thorns, D. (1968), 'The Changing System of Rural Stratification', *Sociologica Ruralis*, vol. VIII, no. 2, pp. 161–78.

Thorp, R. and Betram, G. (1977), *Peru, 1890–1977* (London: Macmillan).

Touraine, A. (1971), *Post-industrial Society* (New York: Random House).

Verba, S. (1965), *The Civic Culture* (Boston: Little, Brown and Company).

Walton, P. and Gamble, A. (1972), *From Alienation to Surplus Value* (London: Sheed and Ward).

Wates, N. (1976), *The Battle for Tolmers Square* (London: Routledge and Kegan Paul).

Weber, M. (1958), *The City* (London: Free Press).

Weber, M. (1968), *Economy and Society* (New York: Bedminster Press).

Westergaard, J. and Resler, H. (1976), *Class in a Capitalist Society: a study of contemporary Britain* (Harmondsworth: Penguin).

Williams, G. (1971), *Economic Planning Machinery in Wales 1965–1968*, Occasional papers series A, London, Regional Studies Association.

Winkler, J. (1976), 'Corporatism', *European Journal of Sociology*, vol. 17, no. 1, pp. 100–36.

Wolpe, H. (1975), 'The Theory of Internal Colonialism', in I. Oxaal, T. Barnett and D. Booth (eds.), *Beyond the Sociology of Development* (London: Routledge and Kegan Paul).

Wright, E. O. (1976), 'Class Boundaries in Advanced Capitalist Societies', *New Left Review*, no. 98, pp. 3–41.

Wybrow, P. (1978), *Marxist Theories of the State: North Sea Oil – a case study*, B.Sc. thesis, Bath University.

Young, K. and Kramer, J. (1978) *Strategy and Conflict in Metropolitan Housing* (London: Heinemann Educational Books).

Index